THEN & NOW

DOBBS FERRY

OPPOSITE: Dr. James H. Pooley occupied the mansion at right at 19 Livingston Avenue from 1855 to 1881. The street was paved in 1915–1916. In the 20th century, the mansion was a country inn, a roadhouse, a supper club, a restaurant, and finally a catering hall, under a succession of names—most recently Rudy's Beau Rivage. Rudy's was sold in 2000 for renovation but the project failed, leaving behind a ravaged hulk that was demolished on April 5, 2012. (Courtesy of the Dobbs Ferry Historical Society.)

THEN & NOW

DOBBS FERRY

Judith Doolin Spikes
and Anne Marie Leone

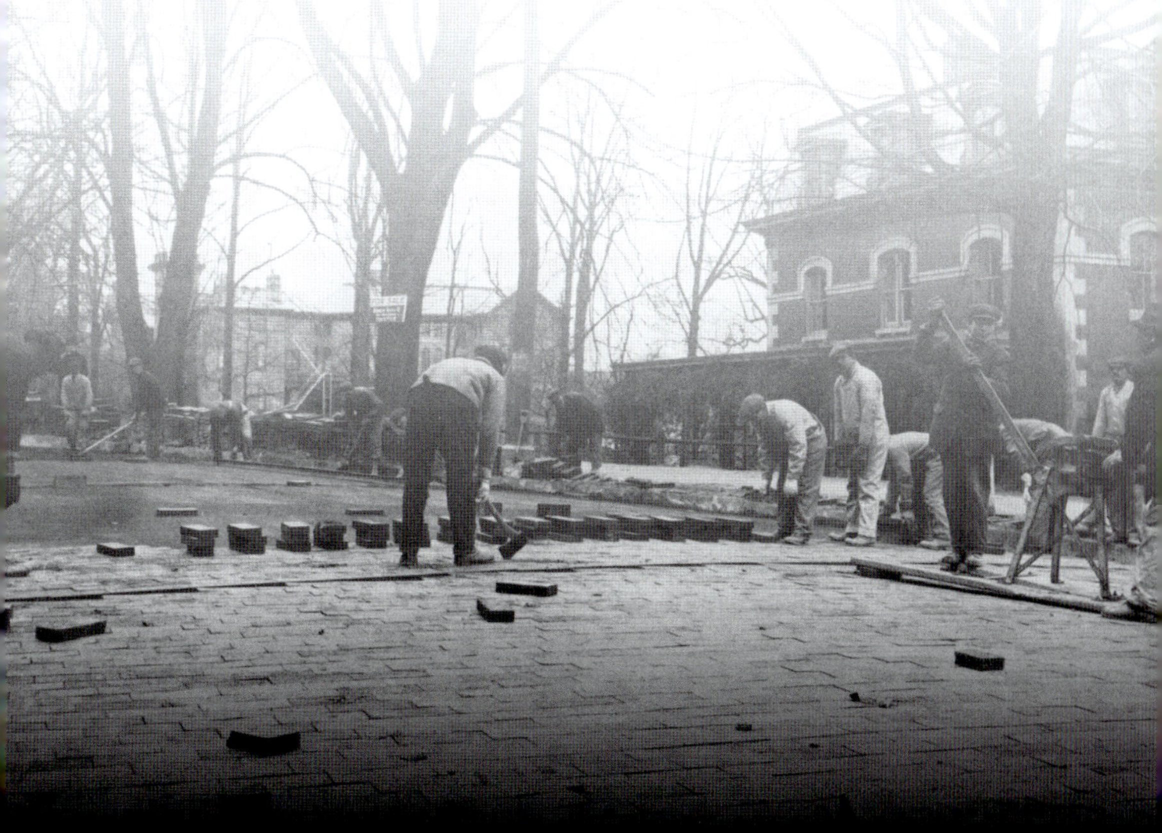

ISBN 978-0-7385-9296-1

Library of Congress Control Number: 2012935534

Published by Arcadia Publishing
Charleston, South Carolina

Printed in the United States of America

For all general information, please contact Arcadia Publishing:
Telephone 843-853-2070
Fax 843-853-0044
E-mail sales@arcadiapublishing.com
For customer service and orders:
Toll-Free 1-888-313-2665

Visit us on the Internet at www.arcadiapublishing.com

On the Front Cover: This view is from the north end of Main Street, looking south toward the eastward bend in the Hudson River. Seen in the far background are the Palisades, a steep cliff formation on the west side of the river. (Then image courtesy of the Dobbs Ferry Historical Society; now image by Anne Marie Leone.)

On the Back Cover: This vintage view—held by the Library of Congress— shows the iconic Dobbs Ferry waterfront in the early 1900s, including the 1890 railroad station, the beach, the willow grove, the Hudson River, and the Palisades. (Now image courtesy of Anne Marie Leone.)

Contents

Acknowledgments vii

Introduction ix

1. Downtown: Commercial and Residential 11

2. West End: Between Broadway and the Hudson River 35

3. North and East Ends: Belden Park and Ardsley Park, Ashford Avenue, and Chauncey 59

4. The Hilltop: Villard Hill and Riverview Manor 81

Acknowledgments

This book exists at the instigation of the Dobbs Ferry Historical Society, whose collections, members, and friends contributed most of the graphic and verbal sources on which the book is based.

We are grateful to Peggy and Larry Blizard, Linda and Richard Borkow, Madeline Byrne, Mary S. Donovan, and Jean and Ernie Howell—talented and passionate local historians all—for giving our manuscript a critical reading. It was much improved by their efforts, and all remaining errors of fact or judgment are solely our own.

All contemporary images are by Anne Marie Leone, and all vintage images are courtesy of the Dobbs Ferry Historical Society, except where otherwise noted. Alan Steinfeld contributed genealogical research. The Westchester County Historical Society and the Westchester County Archives generously extended access to their collections and expertise. We thank Caitrin Cunningham, our editor at Arcadia Publishing, for her good humor and support.

To all those who were stopped on the street and asked, "Do you know anything about . . . " whatever we were looking for, we thank you for your courtesy, whether you could answer our questions or not. Jack and Peggy Coffey, Jock Thornton, Brian Monahan, Ernie Howell, and Robert Casino either sat for formal oral history interviews or cheerfully answered many questions over the course of our research. And to the multitude who had no information to offer but were just as interested in the answers to our questions as we were, our everlasting gratitude for giving us the encouragement we needed to keep searching.

Our understanding of Dobbs Ferry is based on *The Ferryman*, the periodical of the Dobbs Ferry Historical Society; *Life of a River Village: Dobbs Ferry, a Centennial Publication* (1974); *Profiles of Dobbs Ferry* (1976) by Mary Agnes Parrell; *Greenburgh: A Glimpse of Our Past, Town of Greenburgh Bicentennial 1788–1988*; and "Our Village of Dobbs Ferry in Westchester County, NY: A History Compiled by the Local History Group of the Library Council of the Dobbs Ferry Public Library," edited by Rebecca B. Rankin, village historian, in 1959 and subsequently published in part in the *Dobbs Ferry Register*. We are also indebted to the standard 19th-century histories of Westchester County by Robert Bolton, Alvah P. French, Thomas Scharf, Frederic Shonnard, and W.W. Spooner, as well as to such modern works as Frank Sanchis's *American Architecture: Westchester County, New York* (1977). Where secondary accounts differ, we have favored the version best supported by our primary sources—local and regional newspapers of earlier days together with village, town, and county maps and land records.

What one knows of the past depends on what survives into the present. We apologize to the historically and architecturally significant sites excluded for lack of a high-quality vintage image.

Introduction

Dobbs Ferry is an incorporated village 21 miles north of New York City, on the Hudson River Line of the Metro North Railroad—one of dozens of stops on this and two other commuter lines leading north through Westchester County from Grand Central Terminal.

Dobbs Ferry has much in common with the other villages on those lines, especially those with their western borders on the Hudson River. It is distinguished, however, by bearing a closer resemblance to a small-town hometown than to a commuter suburb. In a population of about 11,000 on 2.5 square miles of land, hundreds of residents bear surnames found on headstones in the 18th-century burial ground, and enough men and women in the prime of their lives work within the village to fill the rosters of three volunteer fire companies and a volunteer ambulance corps. A majority of the shopkeepers, tradespeople, and professionals live locally. Dobbs Ferry may not be a "place where everybody knows your name," but it may be as close as one can come in the New York metropolitan area.

At the time of European discovery, Broadway was the Native American footpath connecting Manhattan Island to what became Albany. Today's Ashford Avenue led from the Hudson River through a gap in the Westchester Hills to interior hunting grounds and farther eastward to Long Island Sound. Human settlement has always revolved around the intersection of those thoroughfares, which today includes, like spokes in a wheel, Cedar, Estherwood, and Walgrove Avenues—the entire complex constituting "The Gateway" into which traffic flows from the north, south, east, and west.

Proximity to the Hudson River has been the major influence on Dobbs Ferry history. The Weckquaesgeek (anglicized as "Wickers Creek") tribe of the Algonquin confederation made their home on the riverbank at the mouth of a powerful stream from 4000 BC into the 17th century. By means of the river, Henry Hudson explored the region for the Dutch East India Company in 1609, and the river was the primary means of transportation until the railroad came through in 1849. This major waterway attracted trade, settlement, and, beginning in the early 19th century, tourists who christened the area "the heart of the American Rhine" for the spectacular river views and the Rhenish-style castles clinging to the hillsides.

In the colonial period, Dobbs Ferry was part of Philipsburg Manor, belonging first to the Dutch patroon Frederick Philipse and subsequently to two of his heirs of the same name. Philipsburg Manor, composed of large tenant farms supporting transatlantic triangle and domestic trade, lay along the southwest side of Westchester County up to and during the American Revolution. Sitting along a strategic stretch of the Hudson River, Dobbs Ferry played an important role in the Revolutionary War, especially during the summer encampment of Washington and Rochambeau's armies in 1781.

At that time, the third Frederick Philipse joined the British cause. After the Americans prevailed, the manor was confiscated by the new government and sold in 1785 at auction, mostly to its tenants. In Dobbs Ferry, the first postwar owners bore the surnames Storm/Storms, Dusenbury, Stymets, LaForge, Wilsea, Odell, and the sole non-tenant, Livingston, who bought the Hyatt farm. Throughout this period, there were other, smaller landowners and renters, such as William Dobbs, the ferryman whose name became identified with the settlement around 1700.

The boundaries of these large farms remained on the landscape to shape land development in the early Federal period and beyond. Philip Livingston, a city gentleman with Tory ties, bought the Thomas

Hyatt farm along the Hudson and managed it as a country estate as the old farms grew into a village with Livingston's dock as its focus. Later, the railroad depot attracted development. In 1825, the Erie Canal moved the center of agriculture westward and farming declined precipitously on the alternately rocky and marshy soil of Westchester County.

For five years, from 1837 to 1842, the Croton Aqueduct slashed its way across fields and pastures paralleling the King's Highway (now Broadway), cutting the remaining farms into smaller and smaller parcels. At the same time, gentlemen's country estates multiplied, divided between the postwar class of inherited wealth and position and the rising industrial nouveau riche. When the railroad arrived in 1849, land rose to a price that made farming unprofitable because with daily commuting to the city now a possibility, not only gentry but industrialists and financiers sought year-round dwellings in the fresh air of the nascent suburbs.

By 1873, there were enough permanent residents to justify incorporation as a village, and soon chateaus, villas, and more modest mansions were rising on the ridge of the Westchester Hills 100 feet above the Hudson, while working people both domestic and foreign arrived to service them. The Civil War created a new class of industrialists and merchants who sought country retreats, adding to the population of wealthy part-time residents.

In the 20th century, two world wars, imposition of real estate and income taxes, new technologies, and other innovations brought that way of life to an end. Five of the largest local estates were acquired by tax-exempt educational or social institutions, another by a health-care facility, and some 100 acres here and there were set aside for parks and protected woodlands. The age of the condominium claimed a dozen more estates and the site of the Wisquaqua (Wickers Creek) Native American settlement.

Today, many Dobbs Ferryites commute by rail to New York City and move in and out as their jobs and school taxes take them, but at this writing, commerce is locally owned and operated and there is no chain, franchise, or big-box store other than the supermarket within the boundaries of Dobbs Ferry, which retains its identity as a true community in both its population and its architecture.

CHAPTER 1

Downtown

Commercial and Residential

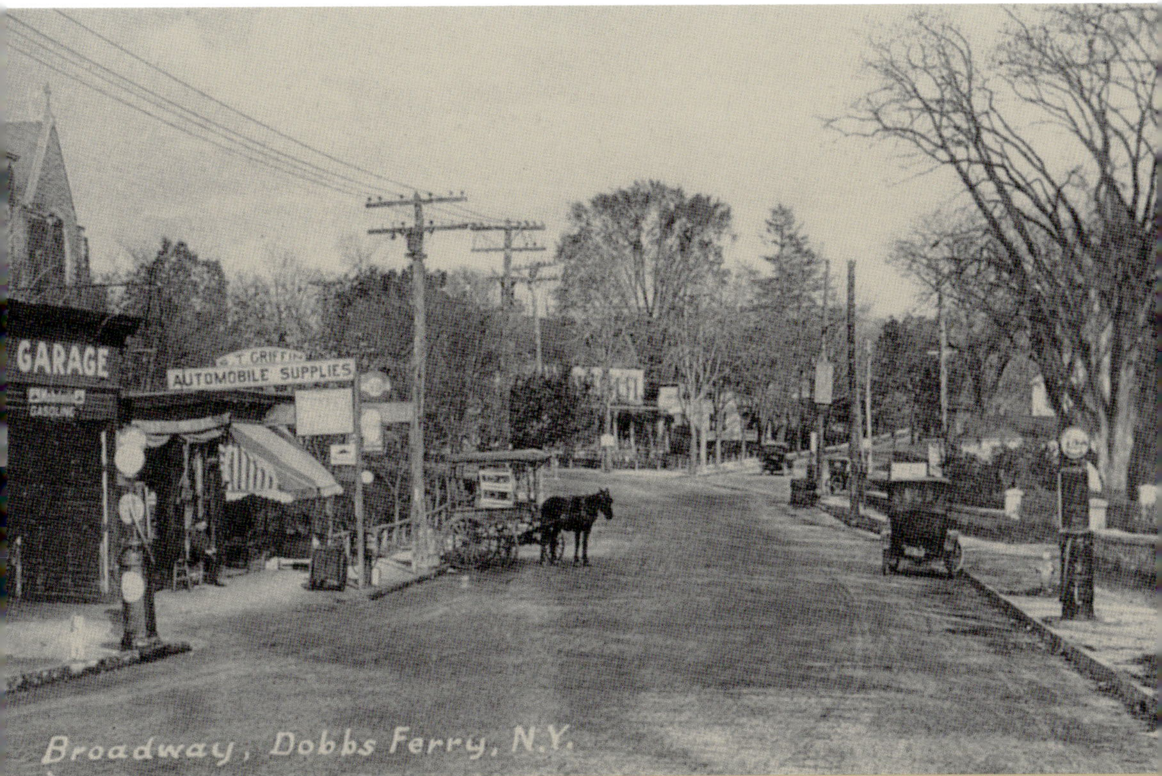

From Broadway looking northeast toward the intersection with Ashford Avenue around 1915, the Charles G. Storms house appears behind the large tree in the middle background. In the left foreground, C.T. Griffin's garage and automotive supply carries on—overlooked by Sacred Heart Church—where just a few years earlier Golden's carriage shop held sway. Gas pumps are seen on both sides of Broadway, with a horse and wagon on the left and a Model T Ford on the right. (Courtesy of Patricia Arone.)

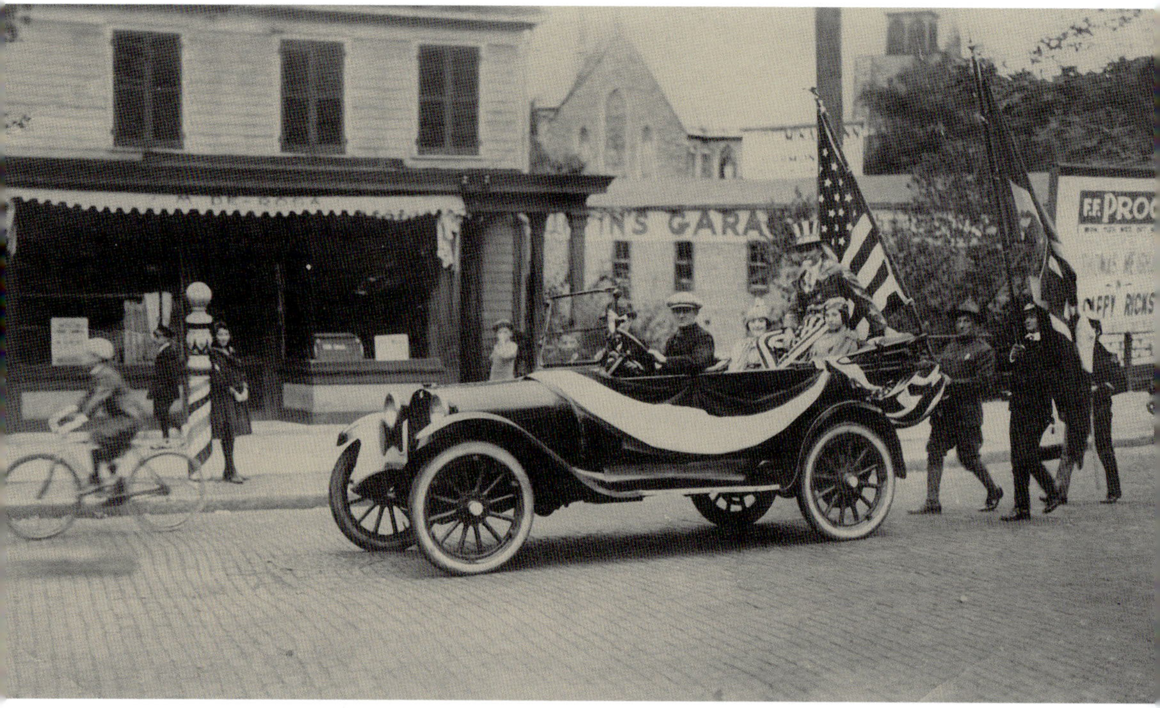

The 1921 Fourth of July parade rounds the northwest corner of Broadway and Cedar Street, led by Uncle Sam in the back of a 1919 Cadillac. Griffin's Garage and Sacred Heart Church are visible behind the billboard at right that advertises *Cappy Ricks*, a 1921 movie starring Thomas Meighan. De Rosa's barbershop stands in the foreground. It was replaced about 1927 by the Prince & Ripley Building, which now houses Rochambeau Wines and Liquors. Performance Motor Cars of Westchester is in the background.

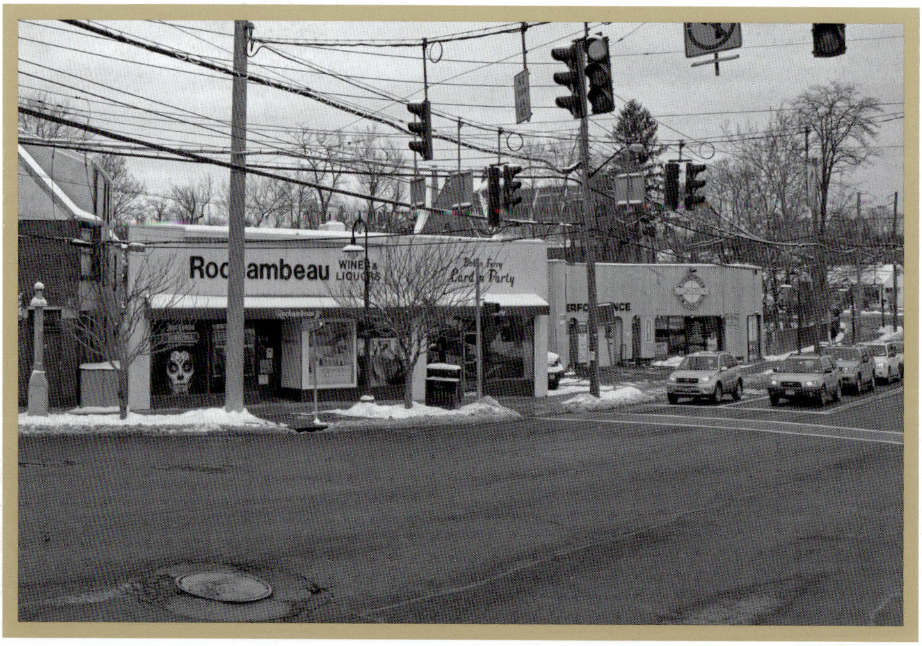

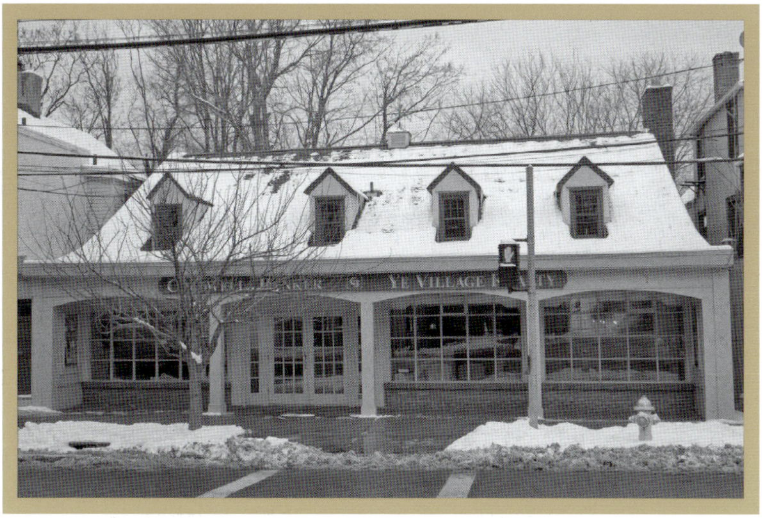

The King House at 6 Cedar Street was built in 1856 for descendants of John King, the husband of Eliza Ann Dobbs and the captain of a Hudson River sloop. King also grew cucumbers for New York pickle factories on his farm at Willow Point, near the dock and railroad. The building was occupied in the 1900s by an antique shop, a tearoom, and a five-and-ten before it was converted into a realty office and altered beyond recognition in 1974. (Then image courtesy of Patricia Arone.)

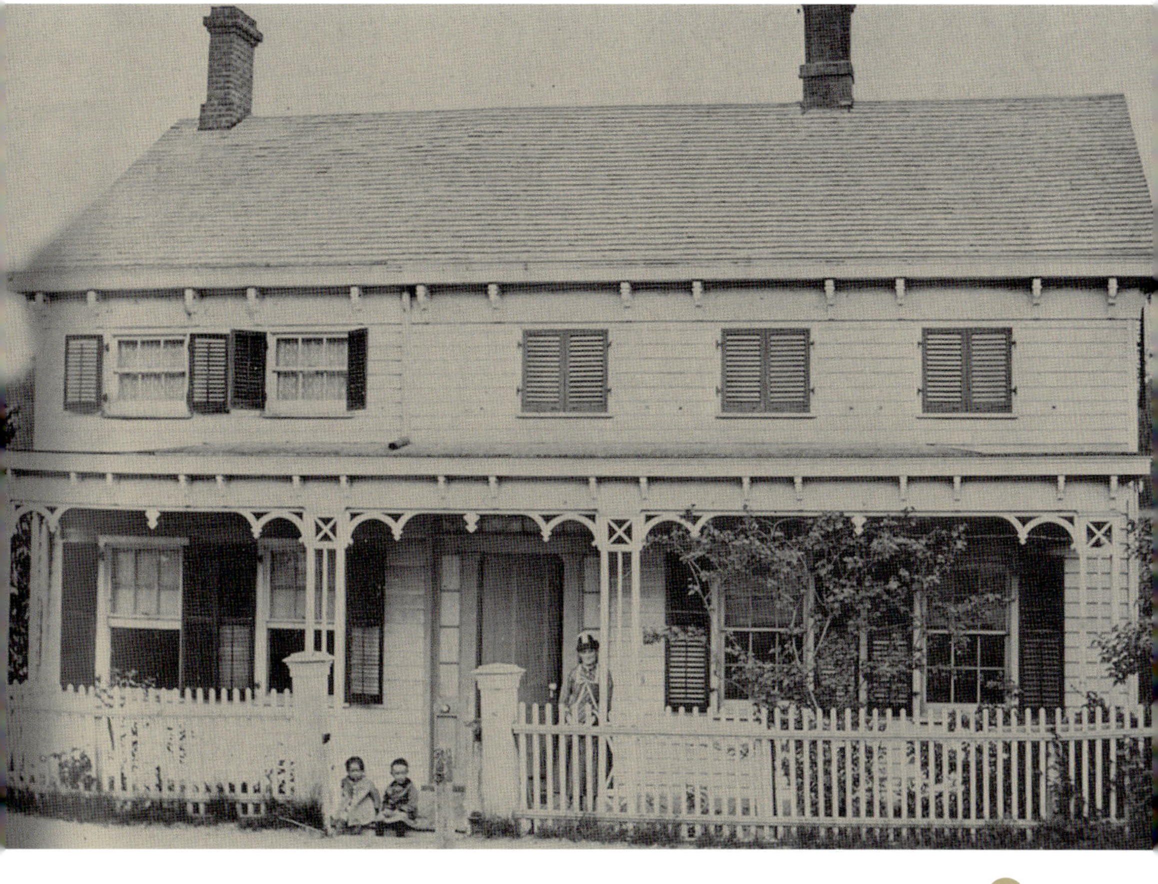

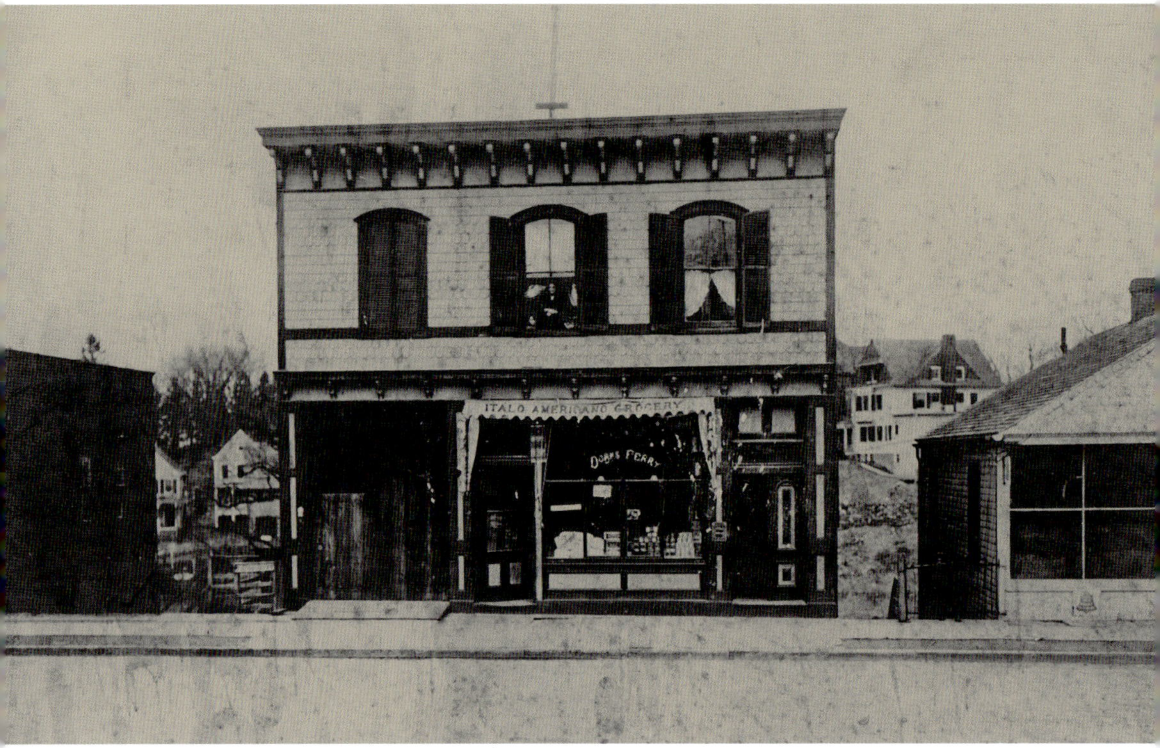

In this 1895 view of 14 Cedar Avenue, the original Resolute Hook and Ladder Company headquarters has been remodeled for use by Francesco Ricciardi's Italo Americano Grocery. Subsequently, the building housed the *Dobbs Ferry Register*, the Building and Loan Cooperative Society from 1901 to 1915, a synagogue, Streb Realty, Allstate Insurance, and since 2010, a restaurant and wine bar.

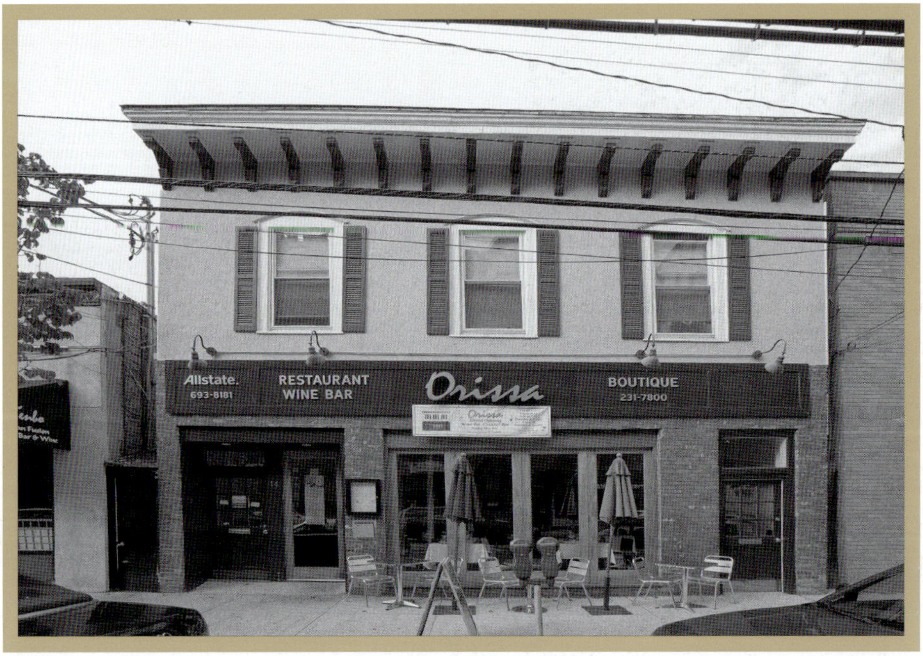

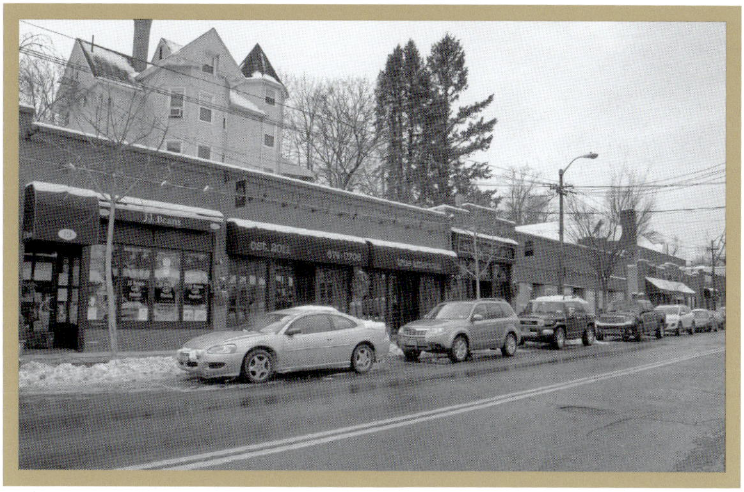

This residence at 25 Cedar Street, which appeared on maps as early as 1888, was the home and office of dentist John Parliman Cole from 1900 to 1920. In 1927, just before this photograph was taken, the sloping front yard was excavated and the line of seven double storefronts was erected. The first commercial tenants included a law office, a travel and insurance office, two auto dealerships, a tavern, a beauty salon, a cleaner's, and a liquor store. The dwelling now houses five families, with four eating establishments and a spa occupying the storefronts.

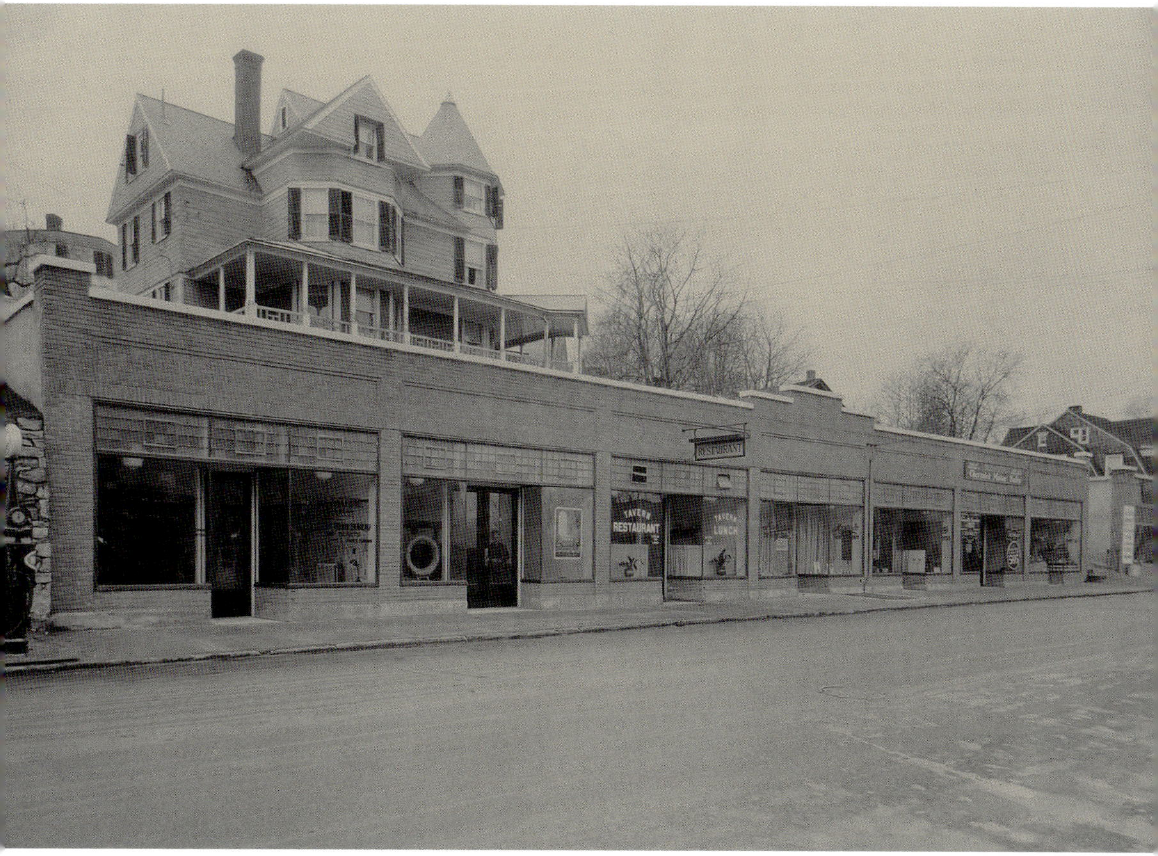

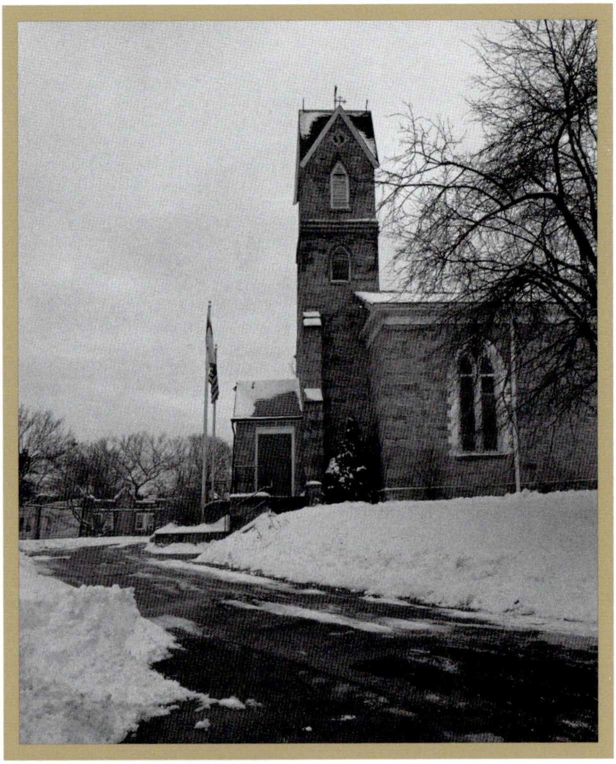

Zion Episcopal Church was founded in 1833 on land donated by Peter Van Brugh Livingston. Washington Irving was a vestryman of the church and a godfather to many infants. Zion's imposing bell tower was added in 1853, and a new bell is being dedicated in this 1920 photograph. Livingston had previously given the Presbyterians land for their church, but when he insisted they foreswear alcohol, they refused and he turned to Zion. But Livingston quarreled with the Episcopalians, too, and eventually died a Catholic.

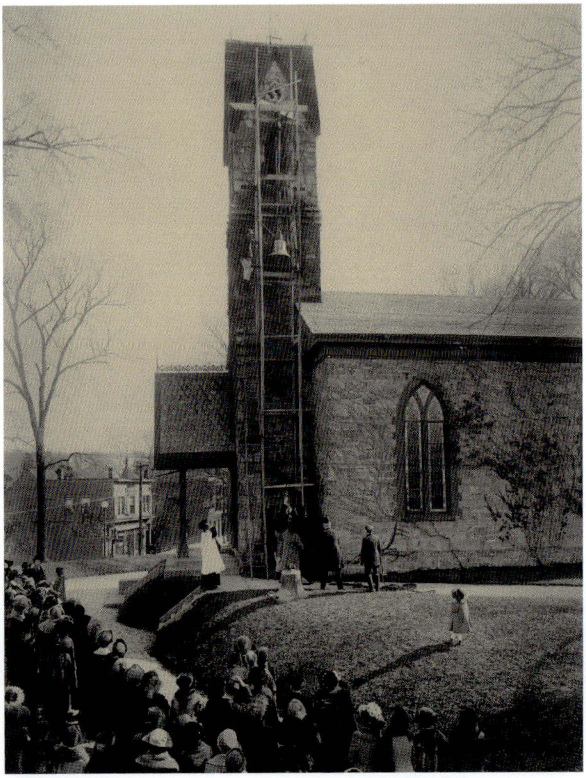

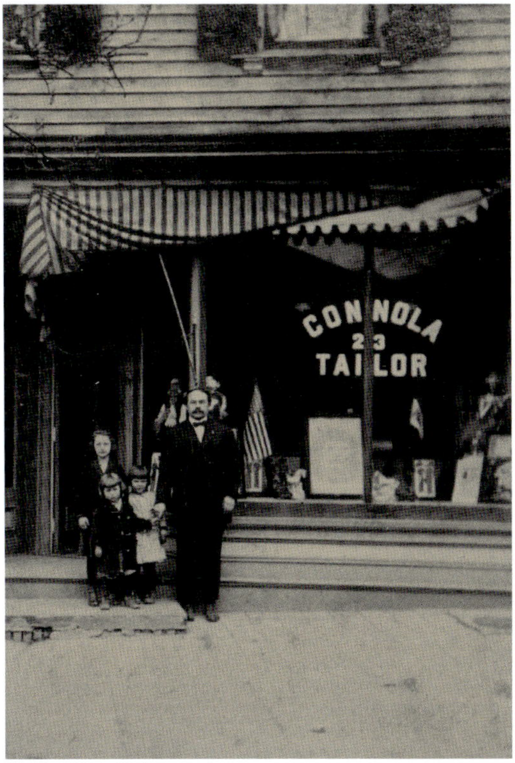

Pasquale Connola stands in front of his tailor shop with his children around 1917. By then, he owned the entire building at 23 (now 60) Cedar Street, and his family lived above the store. The building still stands, with its original clapboard siding covered during the 1934 Cedar Street Beautification project. (Then image courtesy of Allen Anderson.)

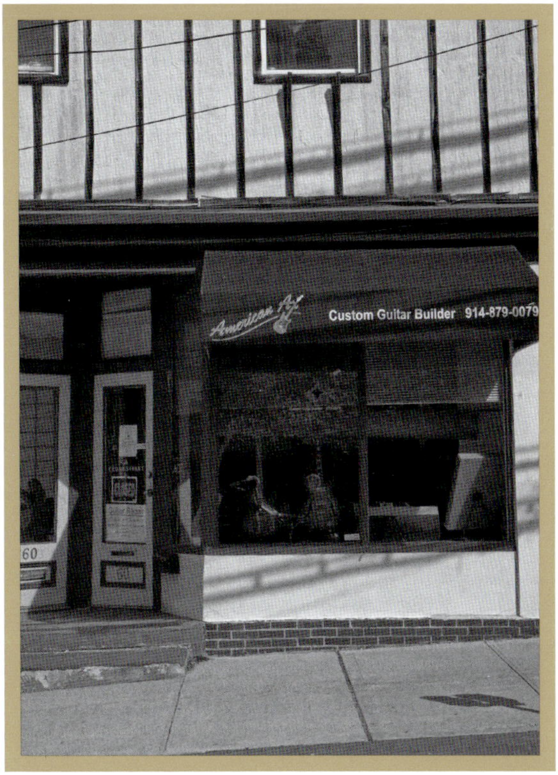

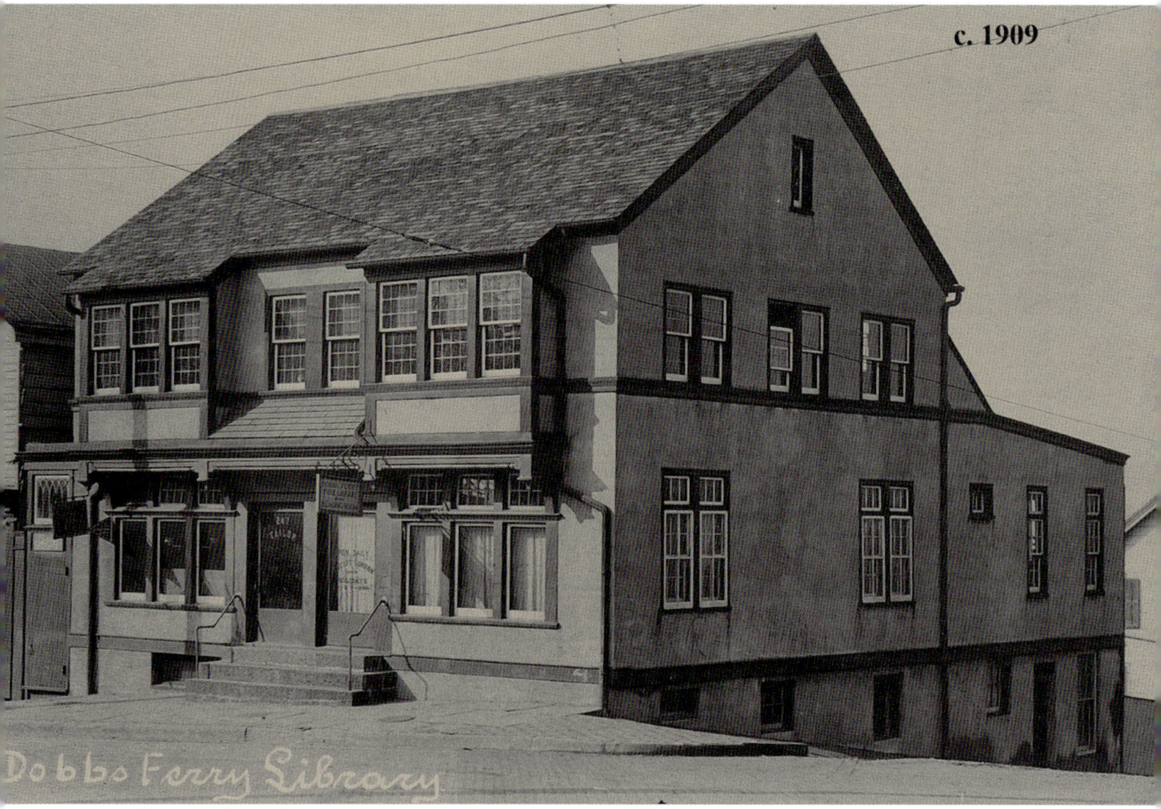

John J. Storm built this structure at 153 Main Street prior to 1842. It became the second home of the Dobbs Ferry Free Library in 1909. Owned by banker and local benefactor Franklin Quimby Brown, whose wife, Ida Eldridge Brown, organized a free kindergarten and mothers' club there, it was remodeled in the Tudor style in 1923. It is now a private home.

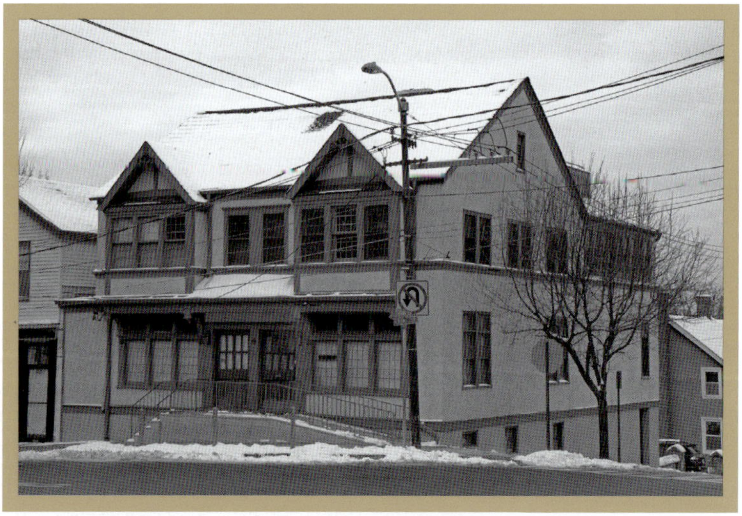

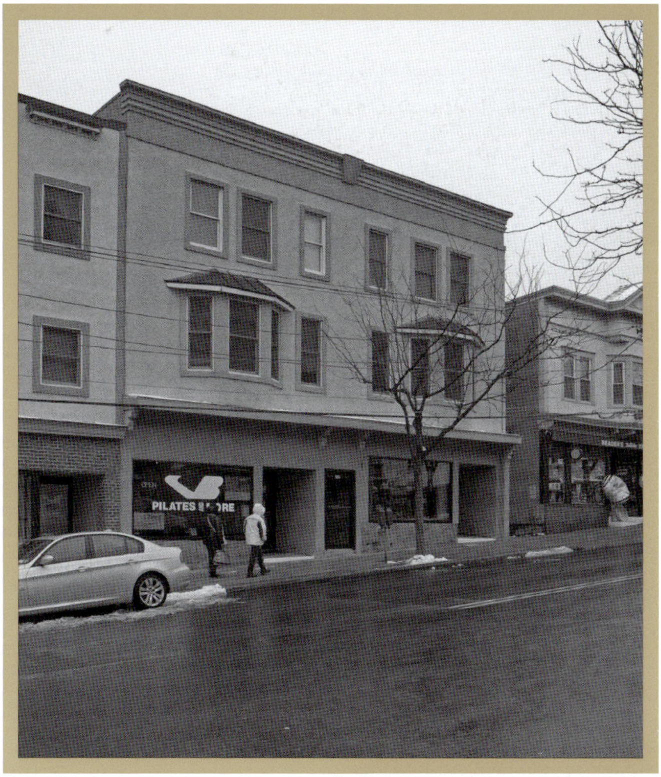

When Isaac N. "He Never Put a Union Man in Jail" Mills ran for state senate in 1900, J.V. Langenberg was operating a hot water, steam heating, plumbing, and gas fitting concern out of the right storefront of 131 Main Street; the post office was at left. The building was erected in 1897 on part of the former site of the Main Street High School and remodeled after a fire in the 1990s. At the far right is Dobbs Ferry's longtime general store, Readers Hardware. (Then image courtesy of William DiVico.)

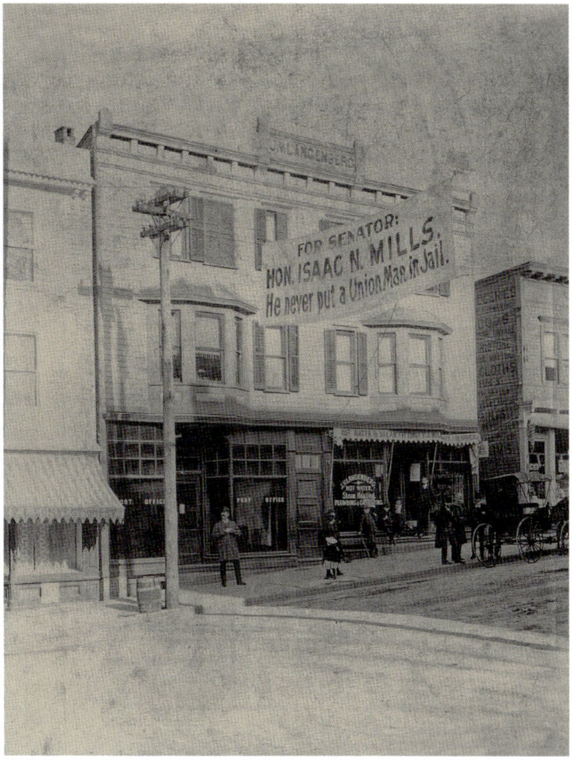

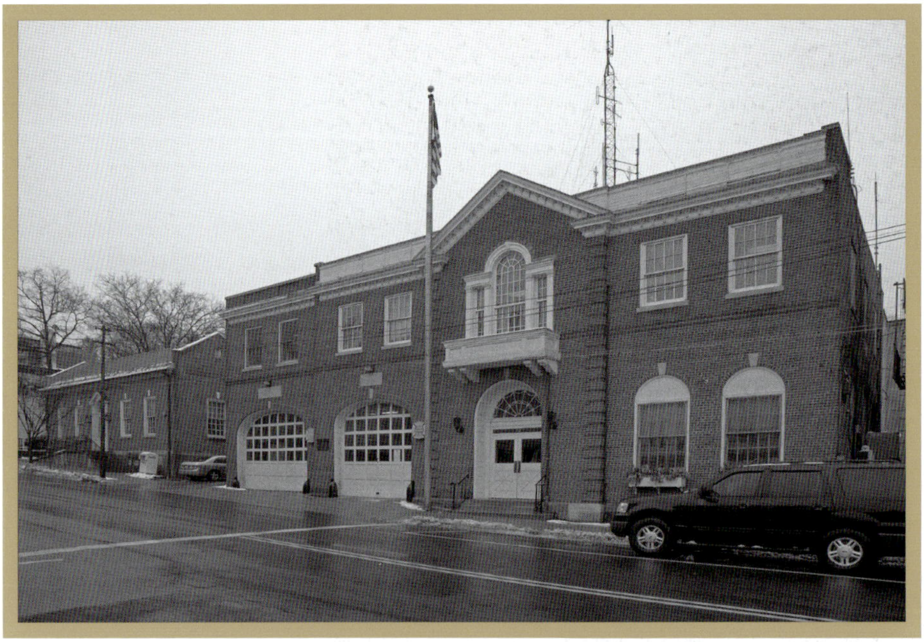

In the early years, municipal affairs were conducted out of a rented storefront at 63 Main Street. Franklin Quimby Brown, a public-spirited citizen and senior partner in the firm that became Merrill Lynch, donated this vacant lot on Main Street for a municipal building to include fire and police headquarters and administrative offices. Donors and village officials participated in this groundbreaking ceremony in 1926. Brown's wife, Ida Eldridge Brown, hoists the first shovelful of dirt.

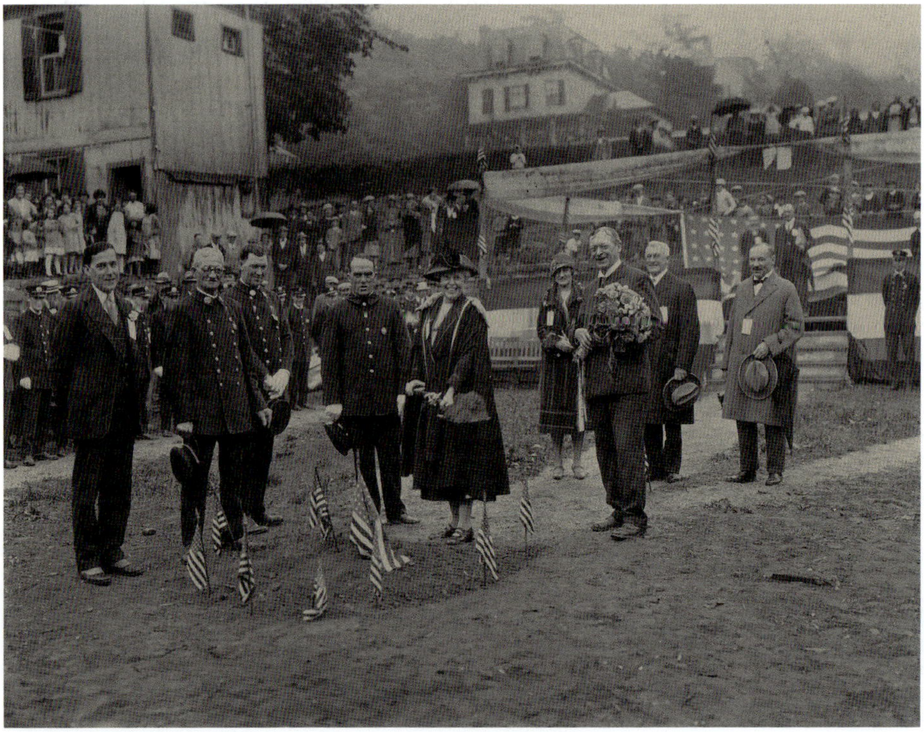

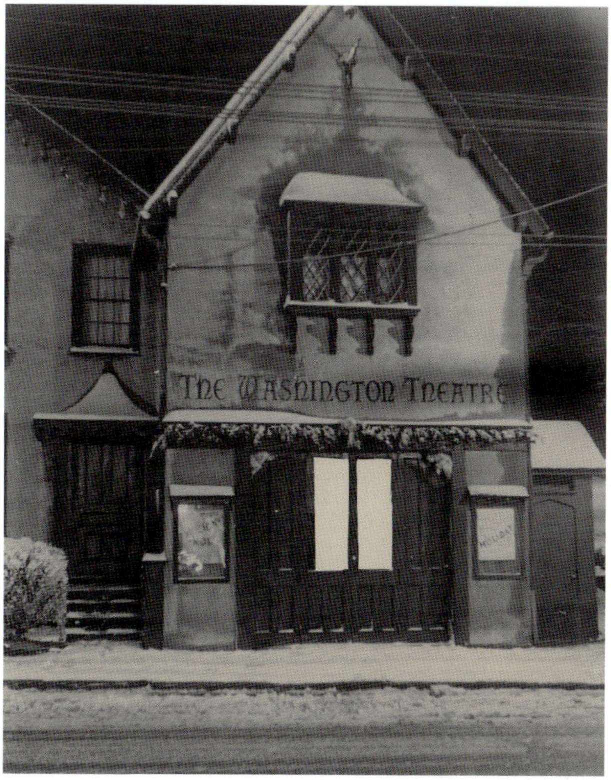

The building addressed 22 Elm Street began as Henry Hill's blacksmith shop. In 1914, Ida Brown remodeled it into the Washington Theatre, a silent movie house designed by architect Bertram Grosvenor Goodhue. In 1934, it became a venue for Broadway tryouts thanks to resident Kathleen Evans. Ethel Barrymore opened the first season. The theater closed in 1958, and Frank Caldara used it as a storage facility for 28 years. Stephen Tilley renovated it in 1987 for his architectural offices.

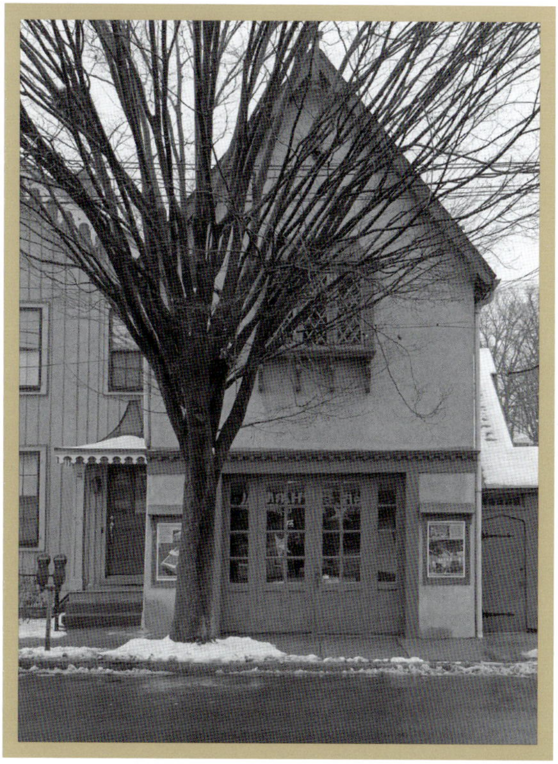

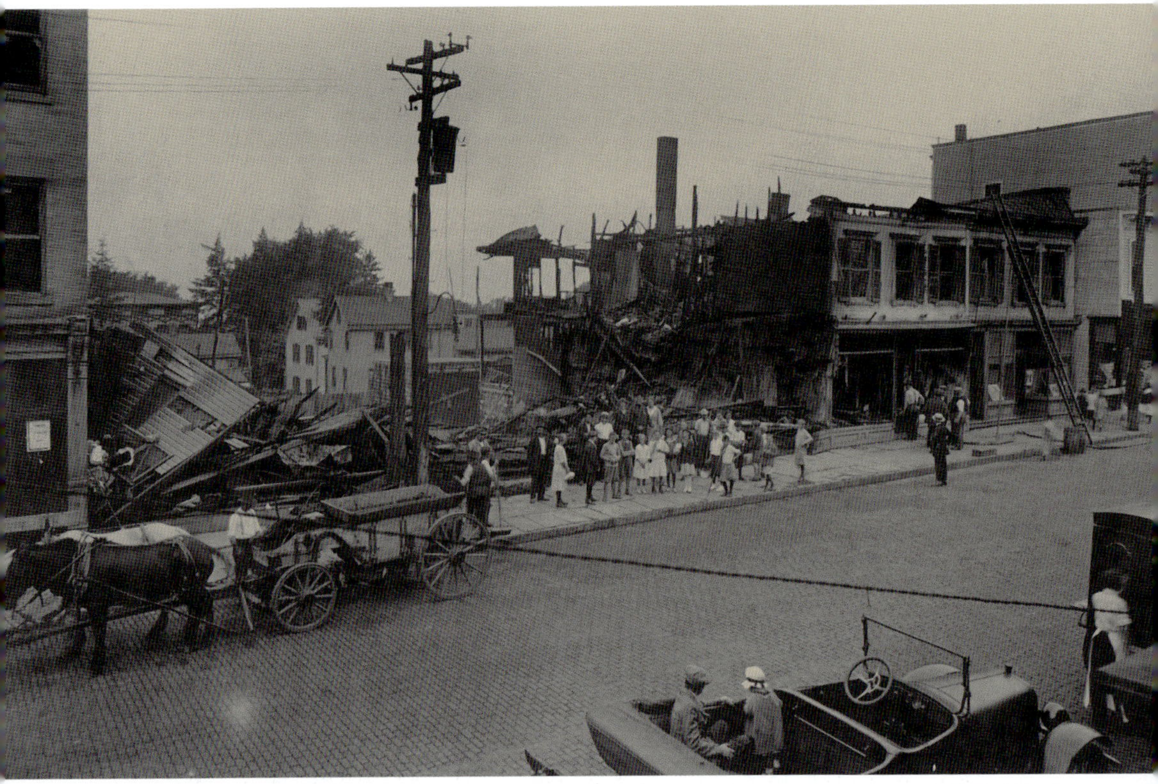

On August 30, 1918, fire destroyed the buildings from 91 to 103 Main Street. The conflagration began in a pile of packing boxes in the basement of the Kiffel Shoe Store and consumed the shops of tailor Frederick Ravekes, dry goods merchant Joseph Israel, barber Louis Pellegrino, and greengrocer L. Bazzini, all of whom had apartments above. This resulted in a local law requiring that commercial buildings be fireproof and authorizing the purchase of an "up-to-date" fire whistle.

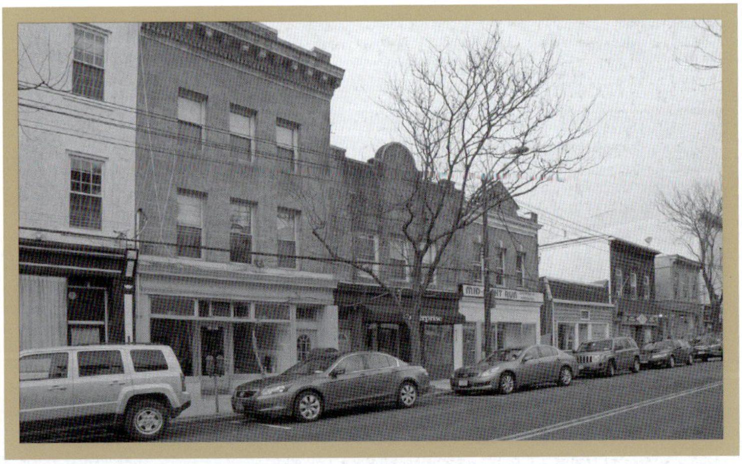

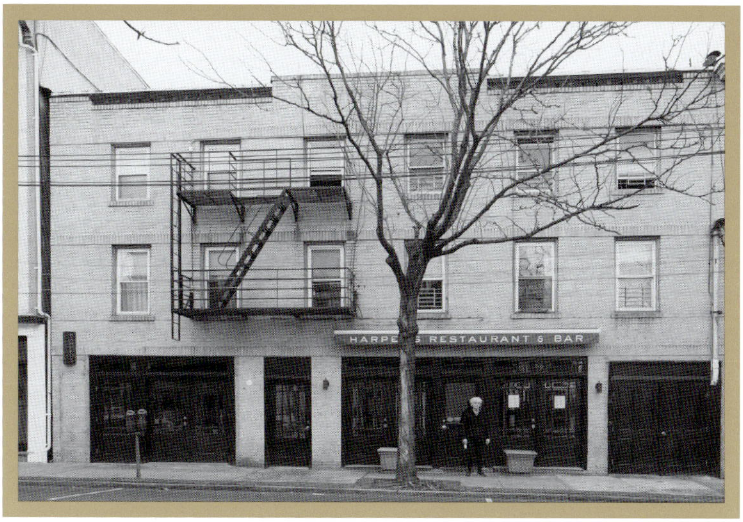

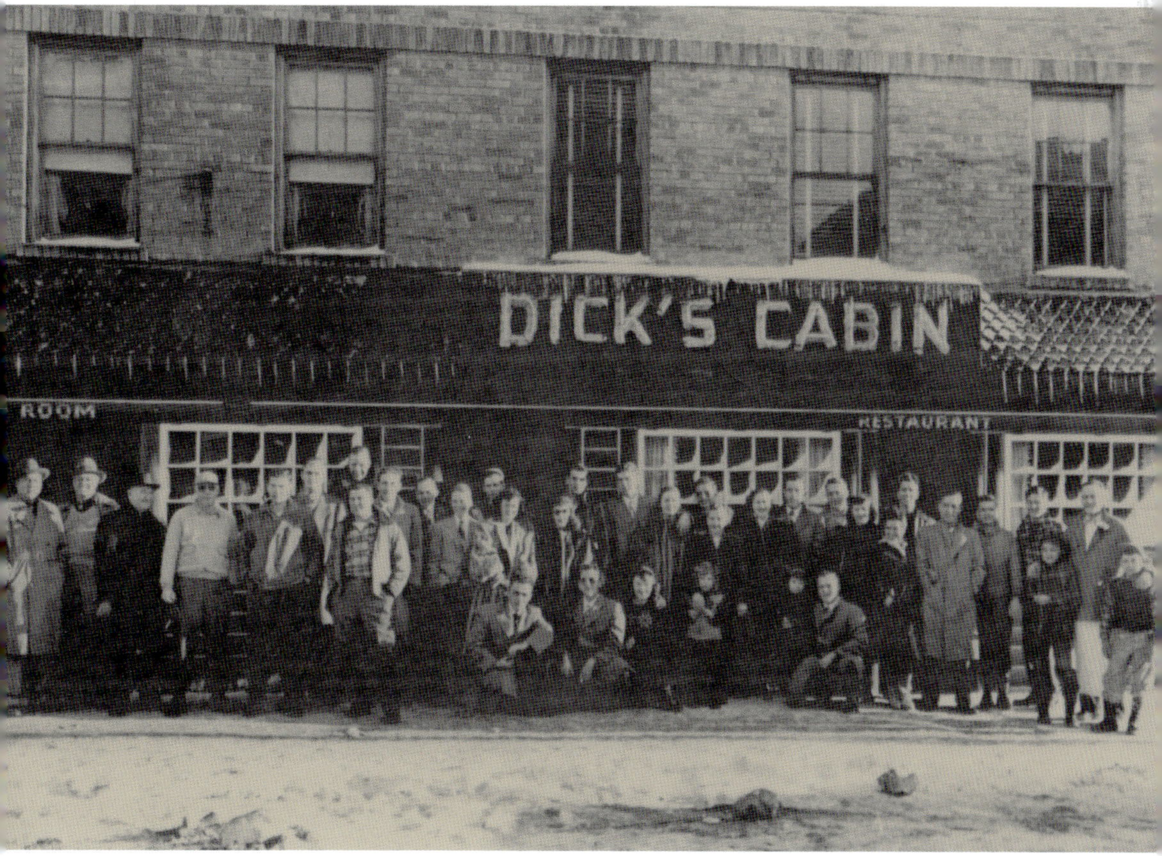

Dick Cavallero opened Dick's Cabin at 92 Main Street in 1932. The people in this photograph were dining inside when the photographer dropped by. The eatery was especially popular with seasonal residents, such as summer stock actors and, in the 1950s, New York Giants baseball players. Dominick Ciancio operated the business from 1980 to 1987 as the Swiss Cabin, and more recently, it has housed Mimosa and now Harper's Restaurant & Bar.

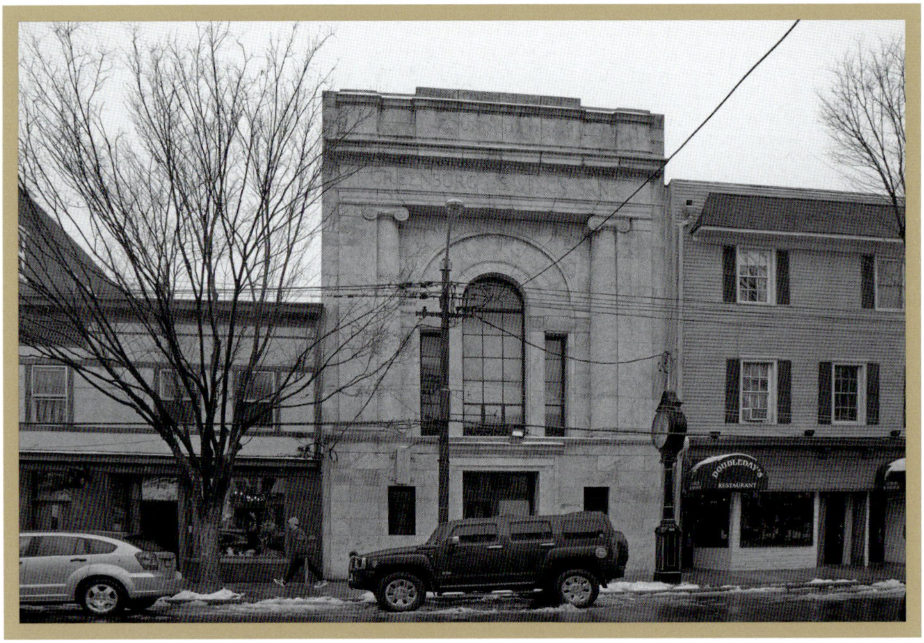

The Greenburgh Savings Bank was incorporated in 1869, four years before the village itself. The bank was housed in what became the Shamrock Liquor Store and is now the southern end of Doubleday's Restaurant. A new home for the bank was erected in 1927 at 81 Main Street, just south of its original building. The last tenant of 81 Main Street, a branch of Wachovia Bank, closed in June 2006.

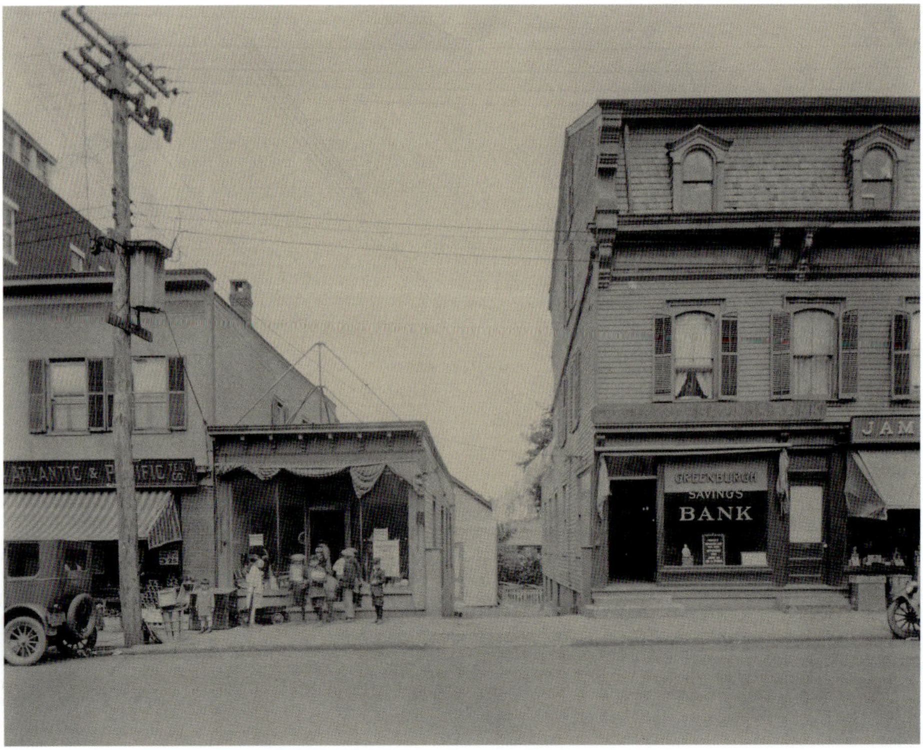

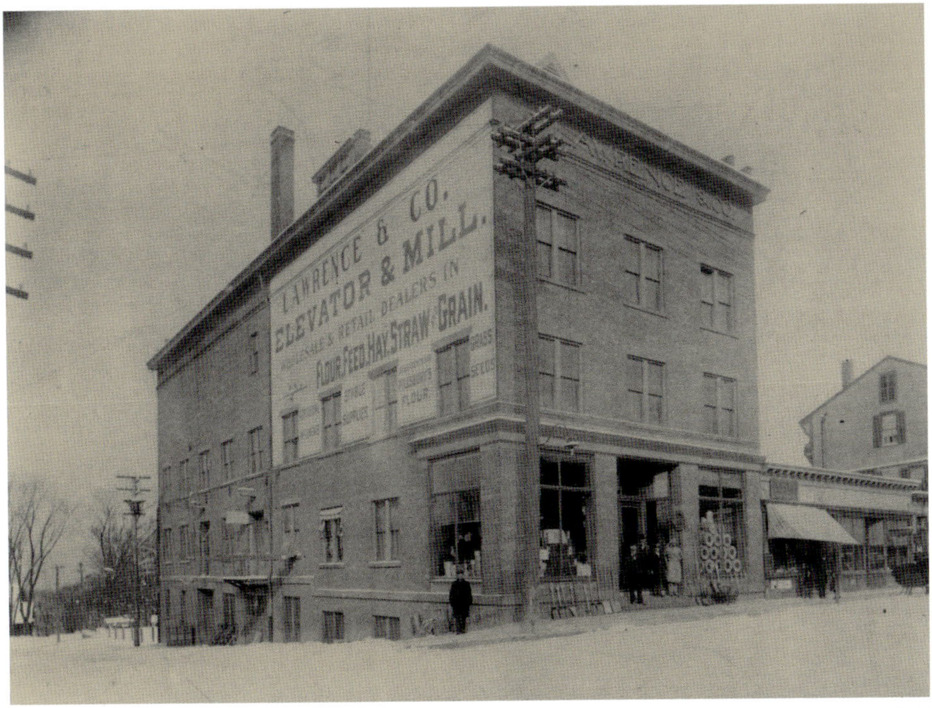

Founded in 1864, Diamond Lodge met in the hay and feed store at 75 Main Street, in rooms provided by owner Charles G. Storms, a member of the lodge and the president of the village. In 1893, that structure was replaced by the Nathaniel and John W. Lawrence grain elevators and mill, seen here. Subsequently the site of a W.D. Hannah Shoe factory, the building was converted in 1948 into headquarters for Oceana Publications, a division of Oxford University Press that published legal reference materials until 2005.

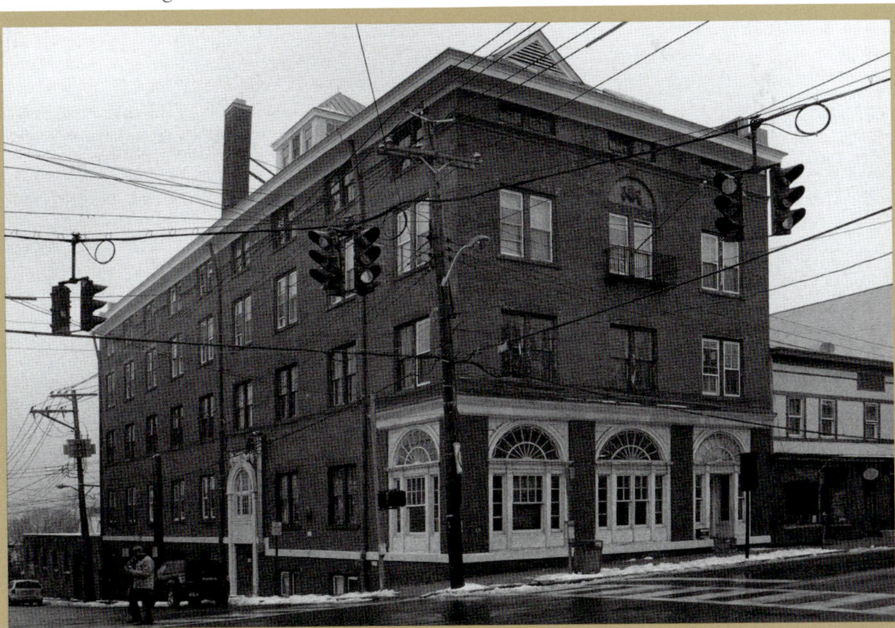

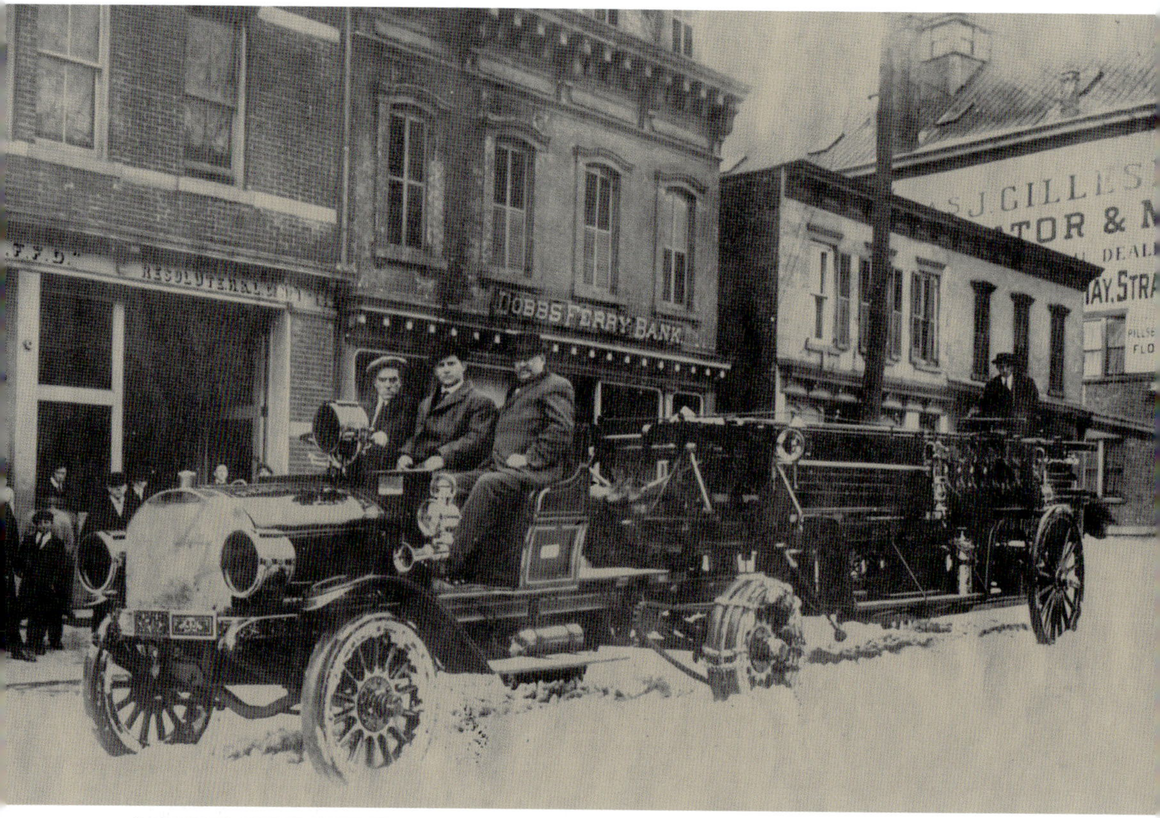

Dobbs Ferry's first power-driven hook and ladder truck is seen in front of the 1917 town headquarters, which housed the village hall, the police station, and Resolute Hook and Ladder Company (63 Main Street, at left). The 1850 building second from left (67 Main Street) was originally a general store and became the Dobbs Ferry Bank around 1890, followed by County Trust, Bank of New York, and in 1959 the corporate offices and machine shop of P.W. Blackburn's Rembar Company, supplying the aerospace and biotech industries with custom-made rare-metals parts. (Then image courtesy of Frank Firor.)

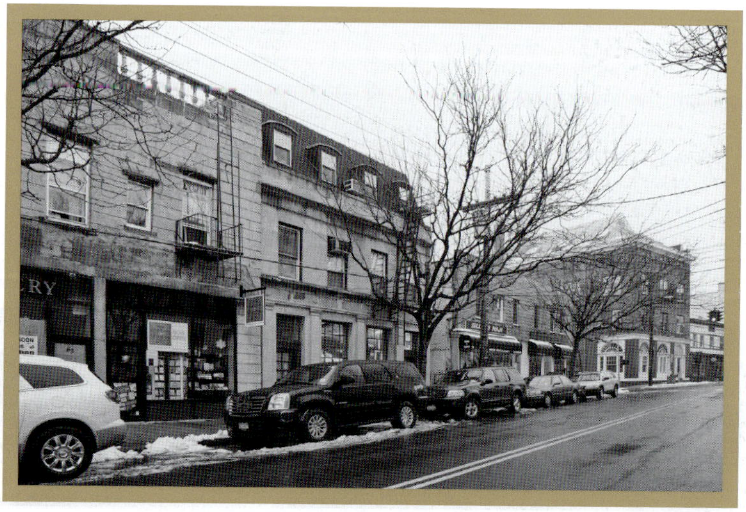

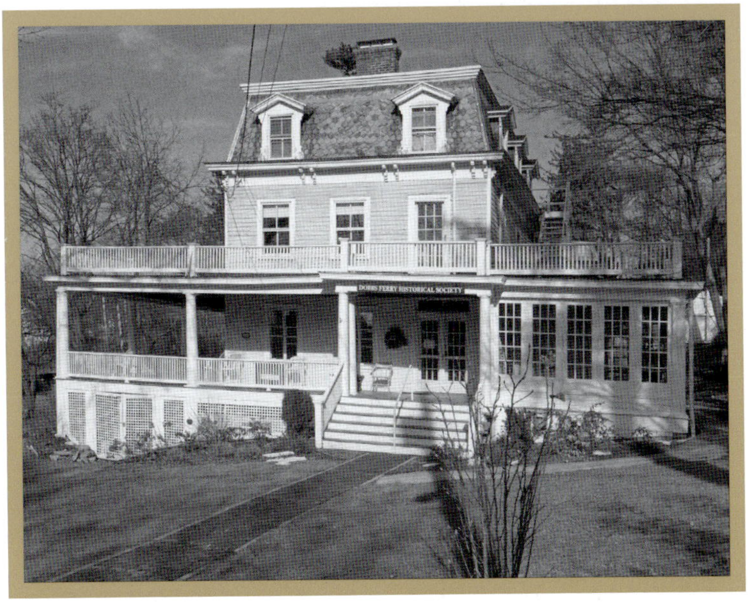

Mead House, now the Dobbs Ferry Historical Society, at 12 Elm Street was built in 1855 by Abram Willsea. By 1920, it was owned by the Herbert Mead family. Upon her death in 1991 at age 85, Clara Mead surprised the Dobbs Ferry Historical Society by leaving them her home. She had attended the Masters School and was a 1926 graduate of Wellesley College. A member of South Presbyterian Church and of the Woman's Club, she had a lively interest in local history.

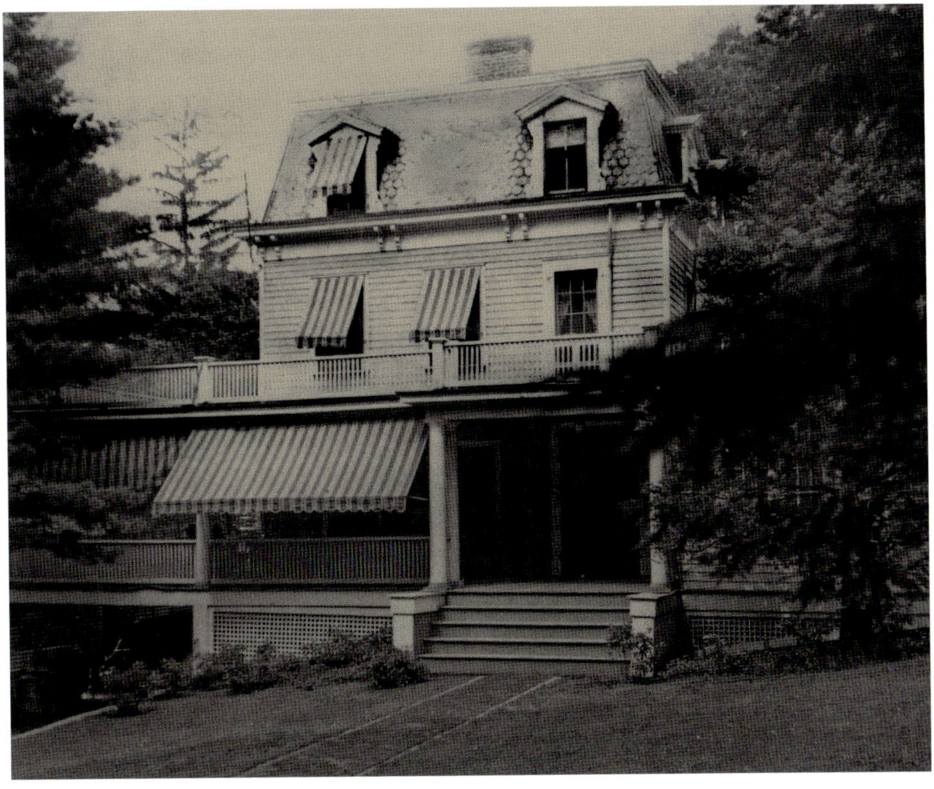

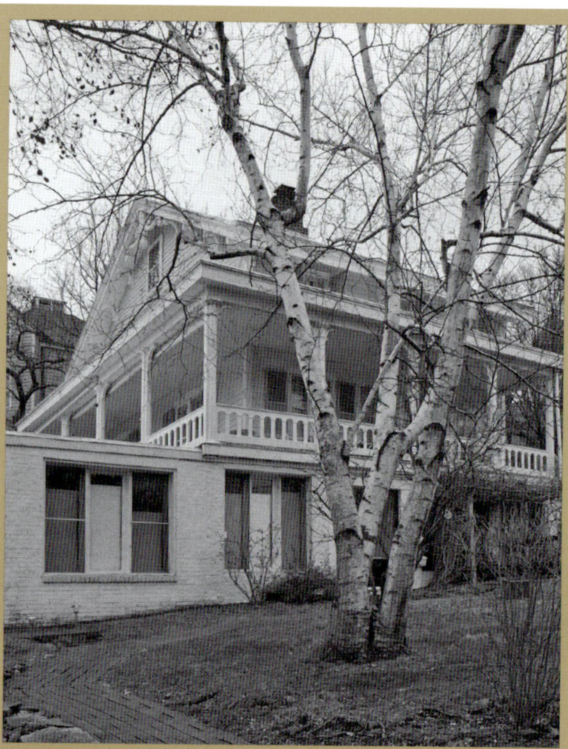

The home at 12 Chestnut Street was built in 1856 by M.K. Couzens, a local engineer and mapmaker. Thomas J. Jewell bought it in 1864. Jewell's son Thomas A. Jewell conducted a grocery business with a member of the Odell family and later purchased Lemuel Lawrence's boot and shoe store at 72 Main Street. Thomas J. Jewell's grandson Thomas A. Jr. was born in the house in 1881 and remained there until his death in 1964, when the house was sold out of the family.

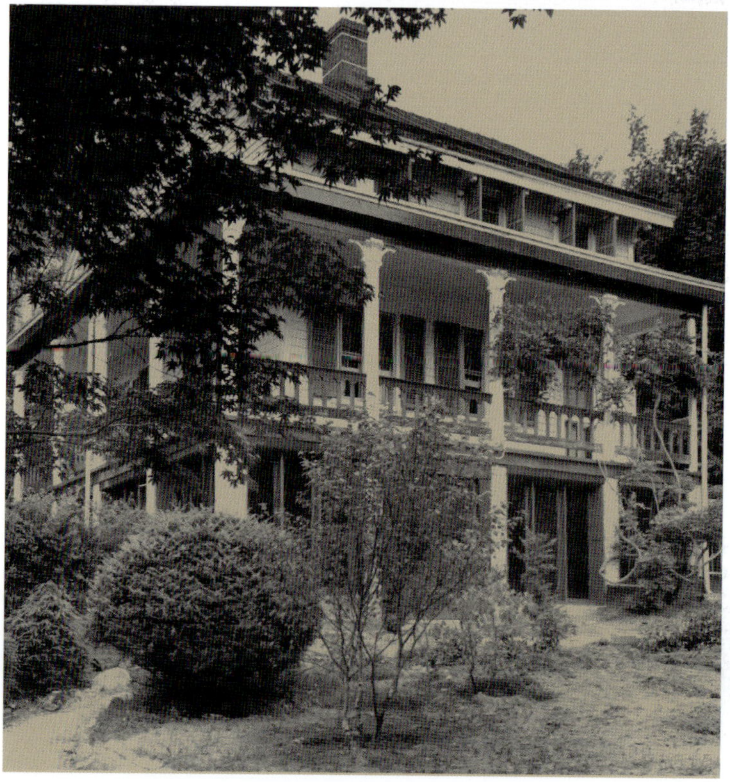

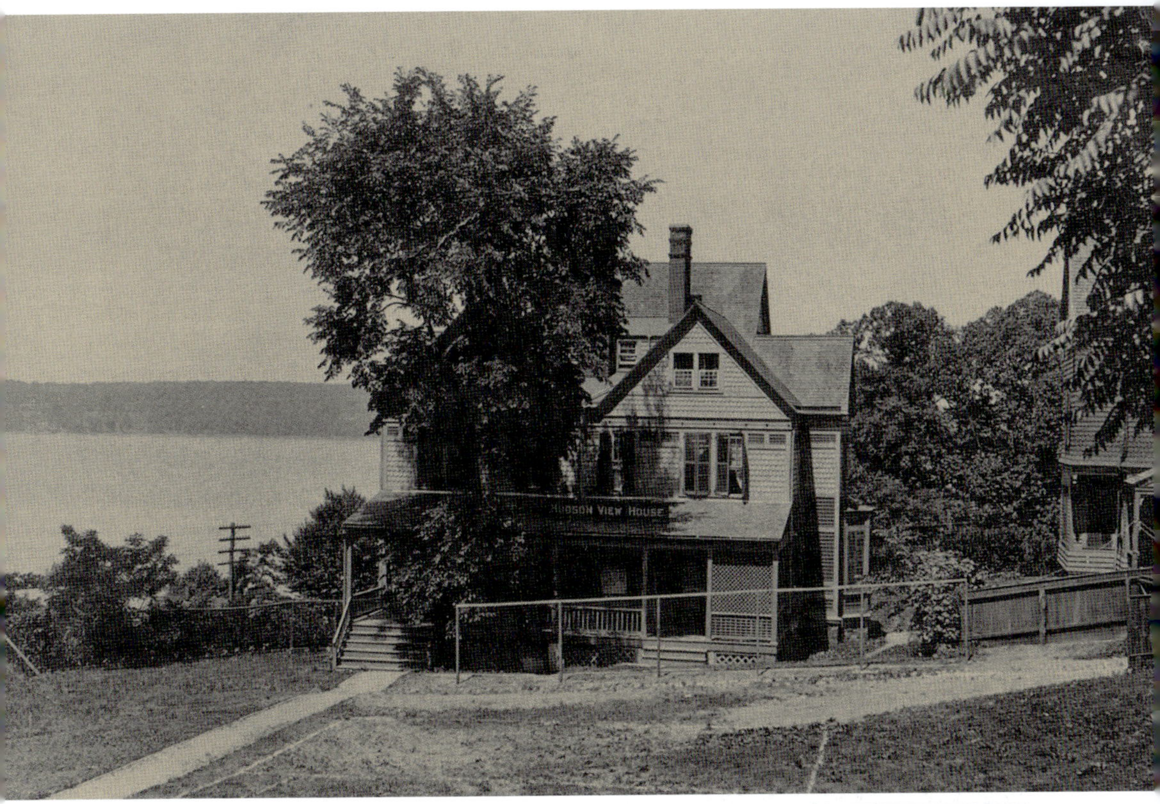

Photographed in 1904, the southernmost of six multifamily dwellings facing the Hudson River is 7–8 Hudson Terrace. The row was designed in the 1880s for investor John J. McComb by George Palliser, one of the best-known architects of the late Victorian period due to his popular pattern books. Palliser owned a summer home in Dobbs Ferry near the Hudson at that time. (Then image courtesy of Patricia Arone.)

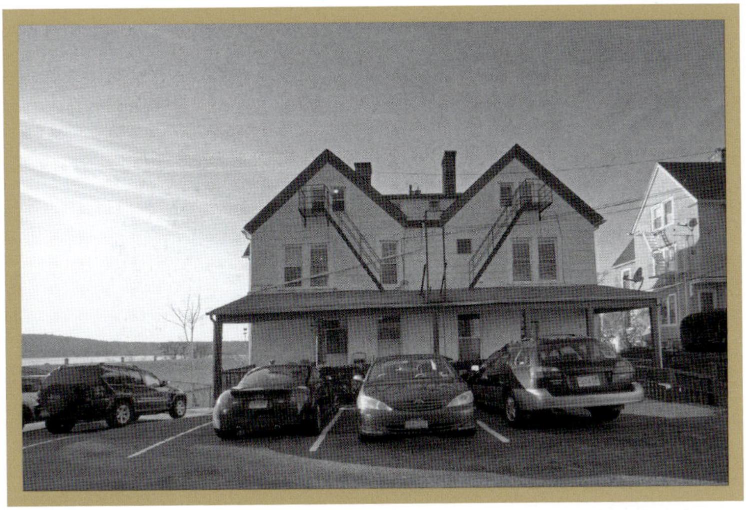

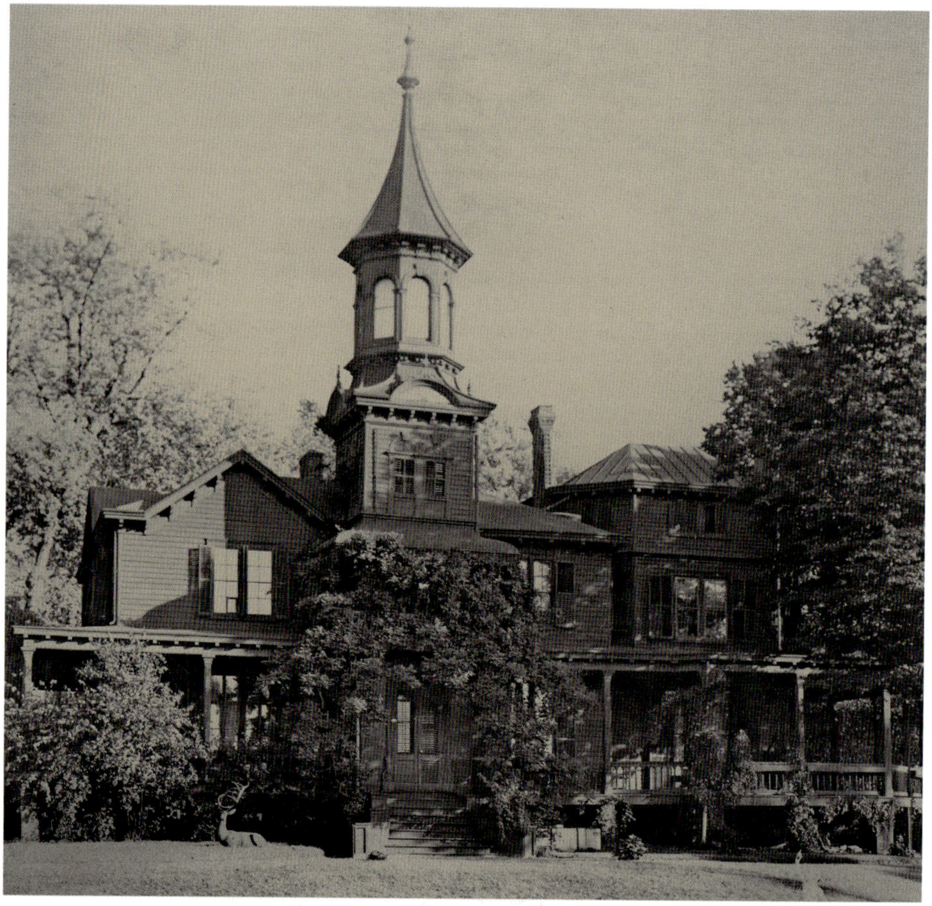

David Ogden Bradley, a prominent attorney, politician, landowner, and long-term president of Dobbs Ferry, built this mansion, Palavista, in 1865 in what is now Memorial Park on Palisade Street. By 1914, it was the property of Marietta Ubert and her third husband, the Main Street tailor John H. Ravekes, who was also the Dobbs Ferry assessor, tax collector, and vice chair of the zoning board, as well as a volunteer fireman. In 1962, part of the Bradley/Ravekes estate was combined with the adjacent Frances Gully—a public dump from 1909 to 1962—to create Memorial Park.

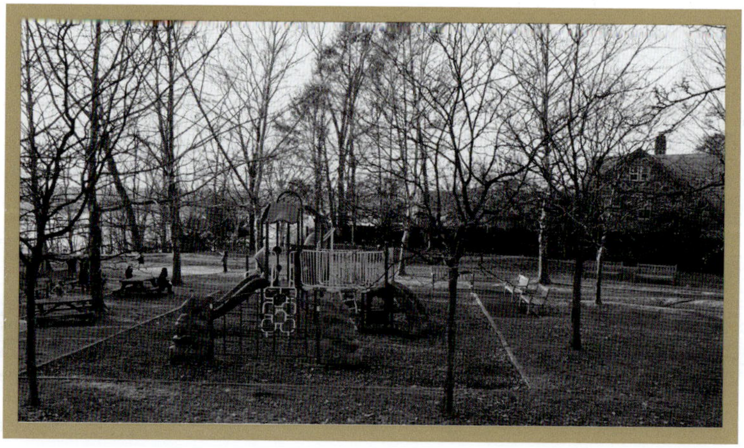

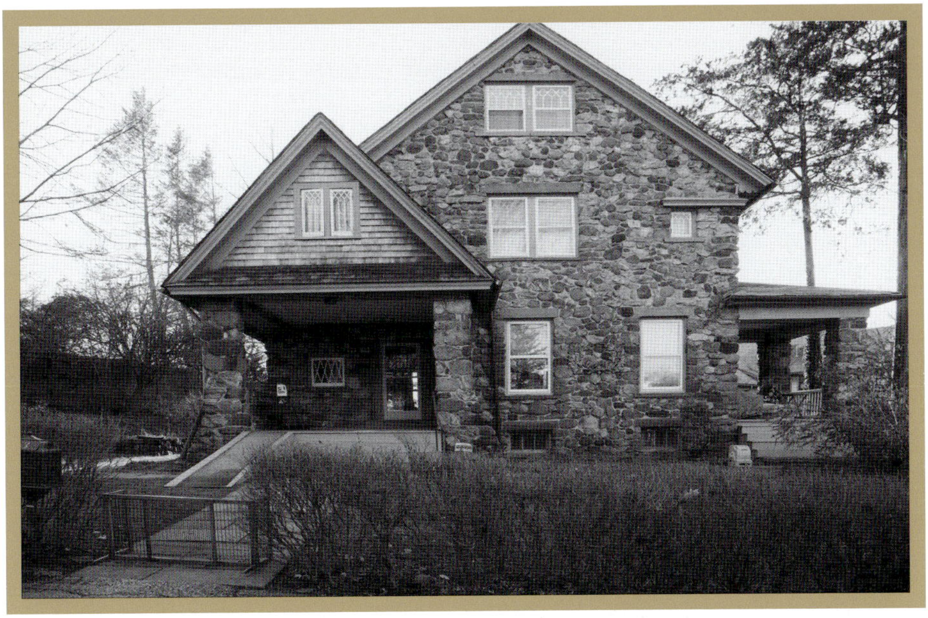

Ogden Park, at the western end of Chestnut Street, is made up of three stone residences designed in 1906 by Elizabeth Ogden Bystrom, MD. A daughter of David Ogden Bradley, Dr. Bystrom resided at 77 Chestnut Street, which has three iron caducei built into its eastern facade. Ionic columns on the three dwellings were salvaged from the 1904 St. Louis World's Fair. Seen here is 63 Chestnut Avenue; the columns are on the rear facade.

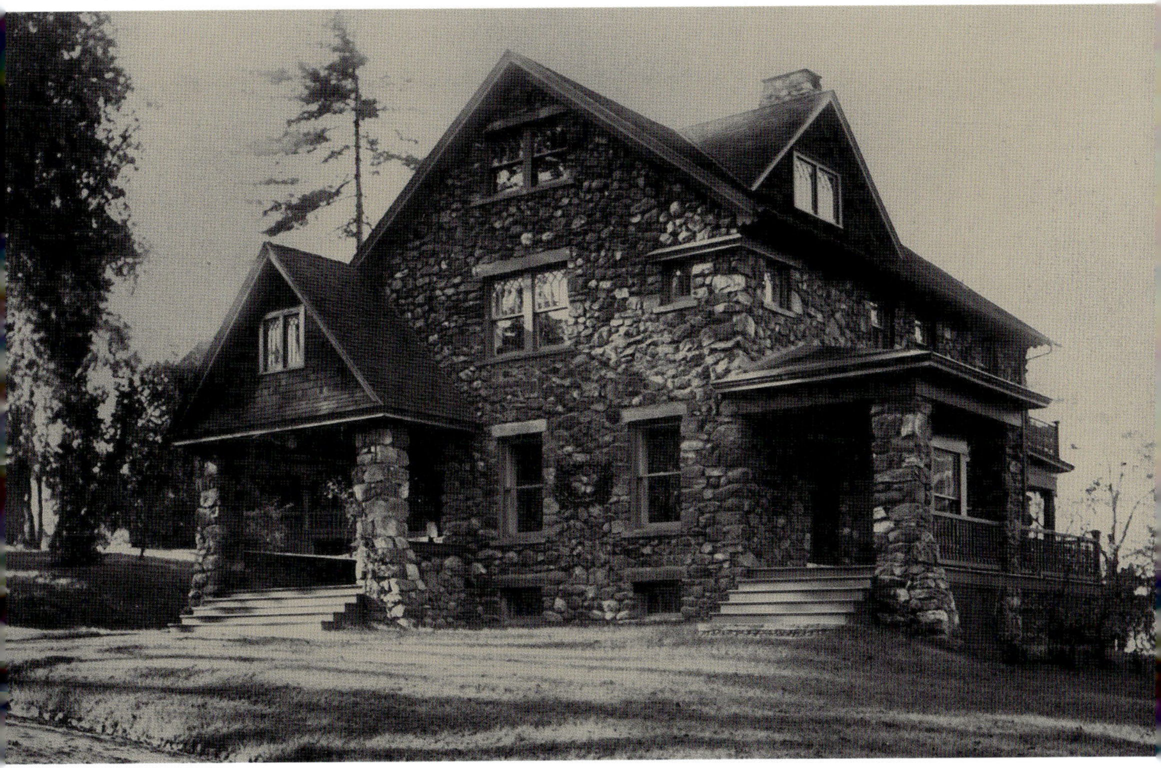

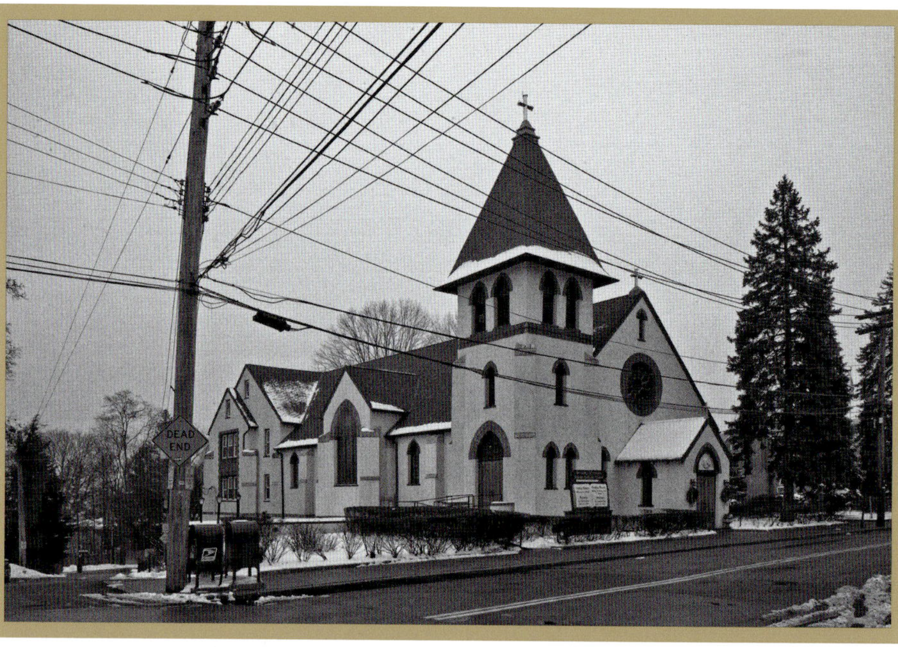

Our Lady of Pompeii Roman Catholic Church at 95 Palisade Street was built in 1925 by a congregation founded in 1922, reflecting the influx of Italian immigrants. The building, seen here in 1940, was constructed by Domenic Altieri, whose family home at 10 Main Street is known as The Palazzo.

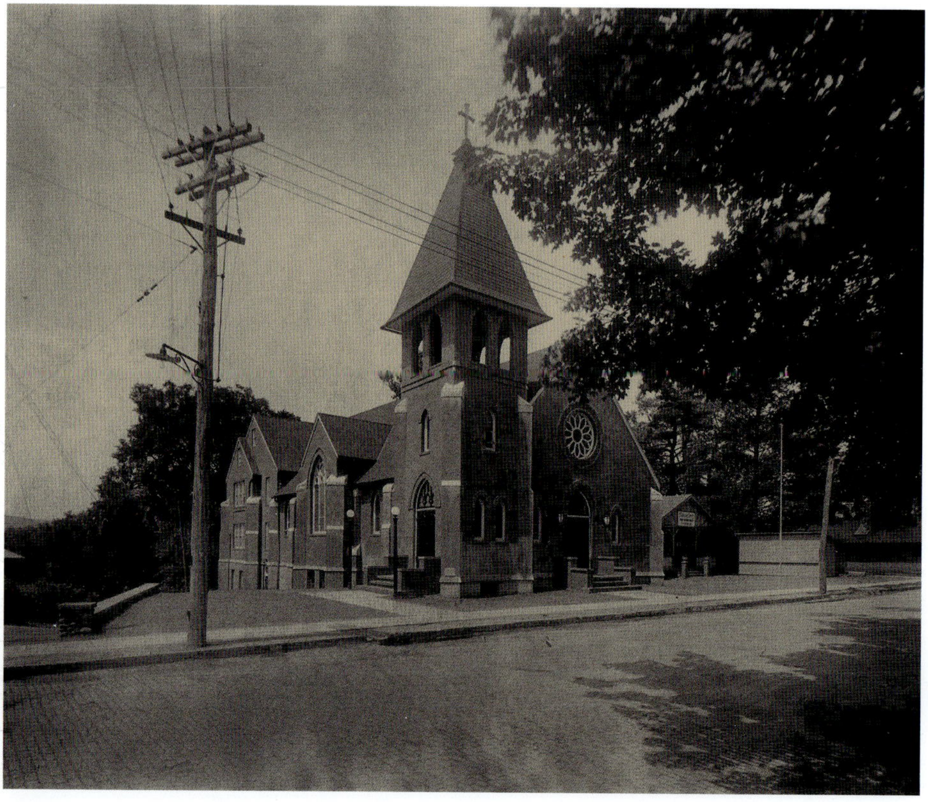

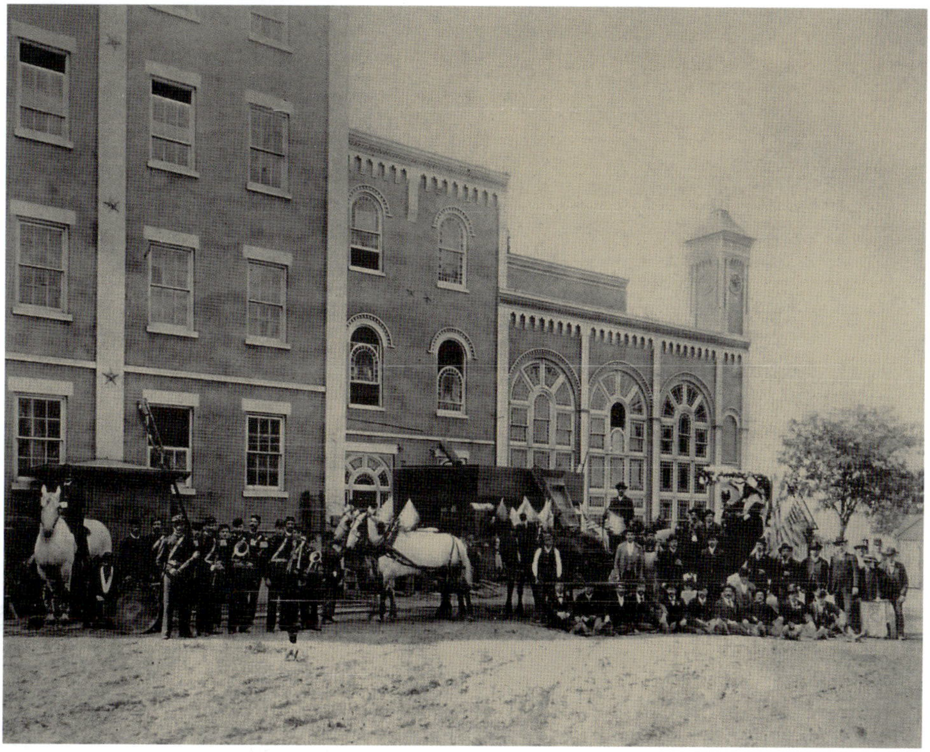

Peter Biegen established a brewery in 1853 at 145 Palisade Street that became the largest employer in Dobbs Ferry, continuing under various names until Prohibition. The building was demolished in July 1925, and the Methodist Book Concern erected a factory on the site. Sold to the North American Philips Company in 1942 for the manufacture of war materials, the facility was leased in 1951 by Columbia University for a physics research laboratory and is now occupied by artists' studios and small businesses.

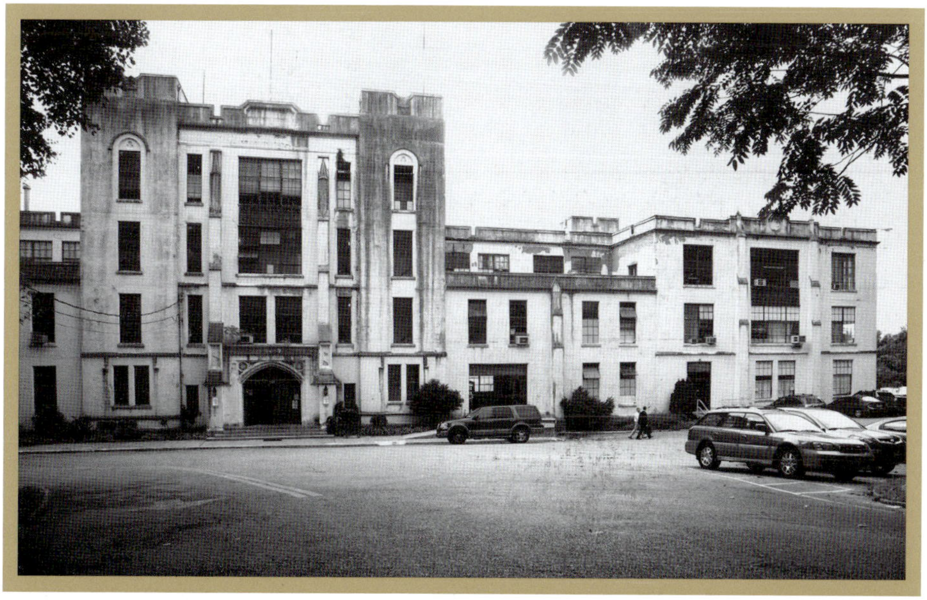

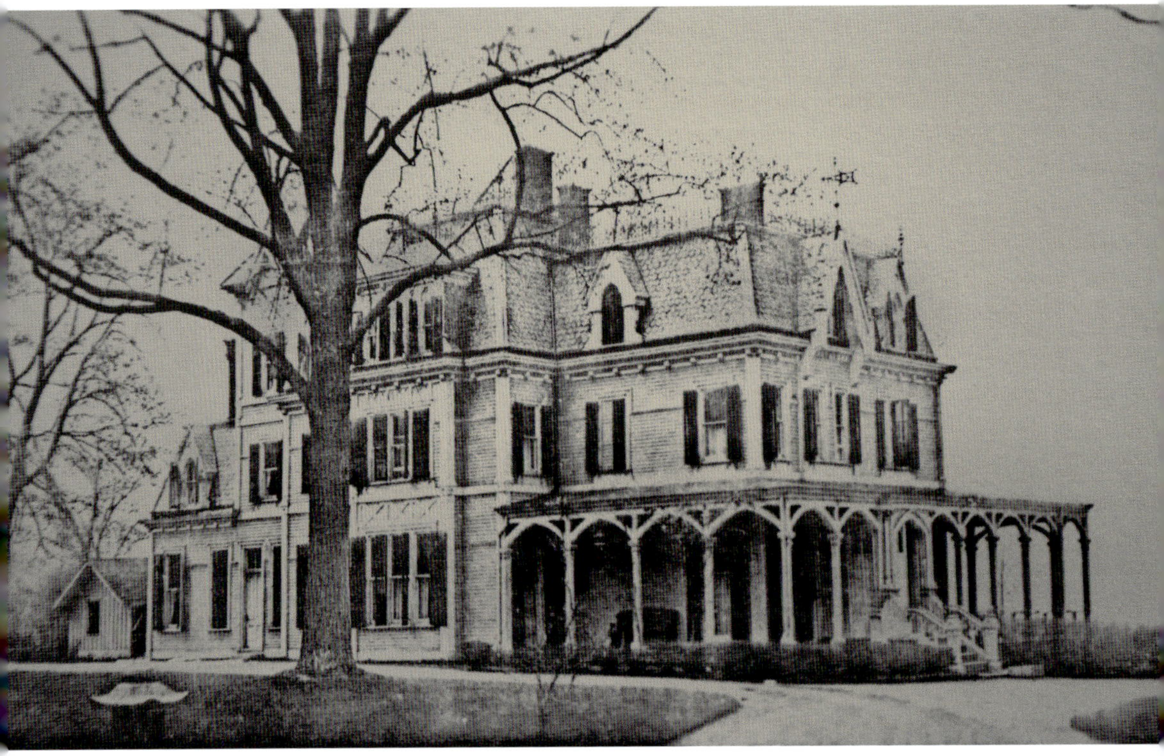

Wykaska, the 1860 estate of Courtlandt Palmer, a prominent Freethinker, lay at the end of Cedar Street on the Hudson River. His daughter married Dr. Henry Draper, the astronomer and celestial photographer, and the place became known as the Draper Estate. Edwin Gould purchased the property in 1916 to protect his adjacent estate from commercial encroachment. The mansion was razed before 1953, when Anthony Paterno constructed a 90-family garden apartment development, renovated in 1977 as the Village Green Condominiums.

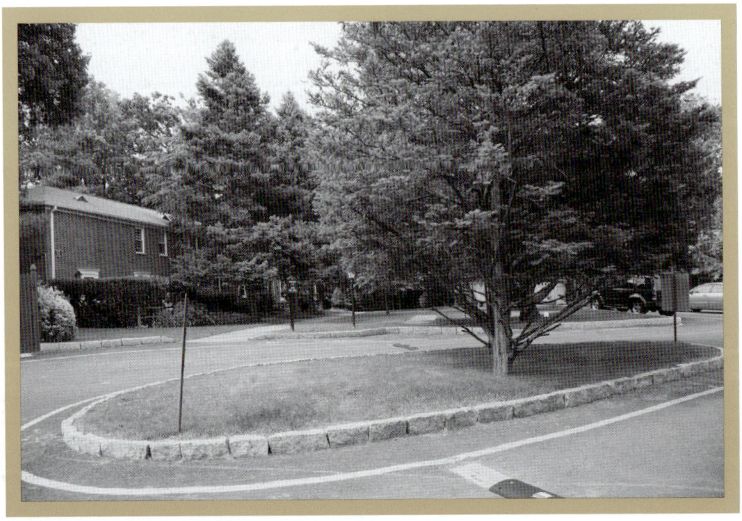

CHAPTER 2

West End
Between Broadway and the Hudson River

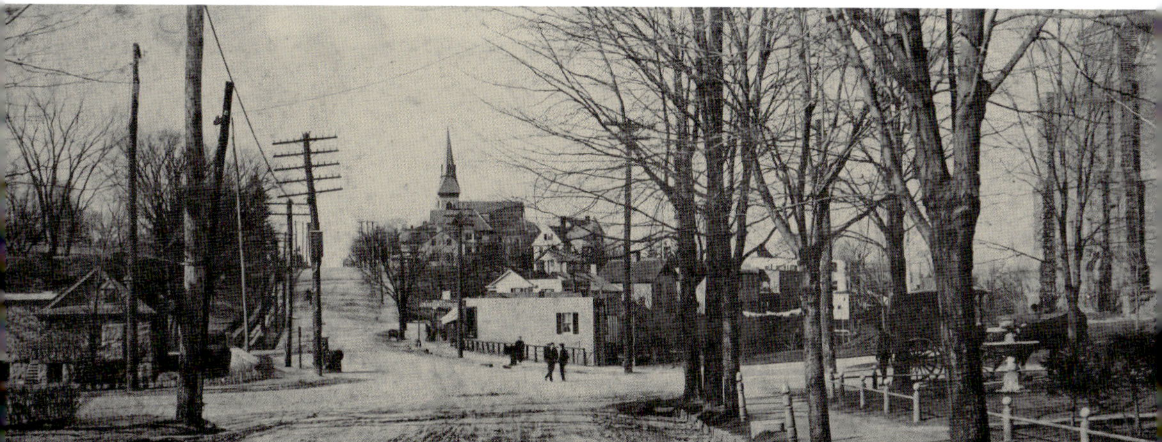

Approaching the Gateway from the east, Ashford Avenue ends at Broadway. From left to right in 1911 are the Masters School Lodge on Estherwood Avenue, the horse trough (at the foot of the utility pole), the steeple of South Presbyterian Church, and Golden's carriage shop. Sacred Heart Church and the front yard of Charles G. Storms's home are on the far right.

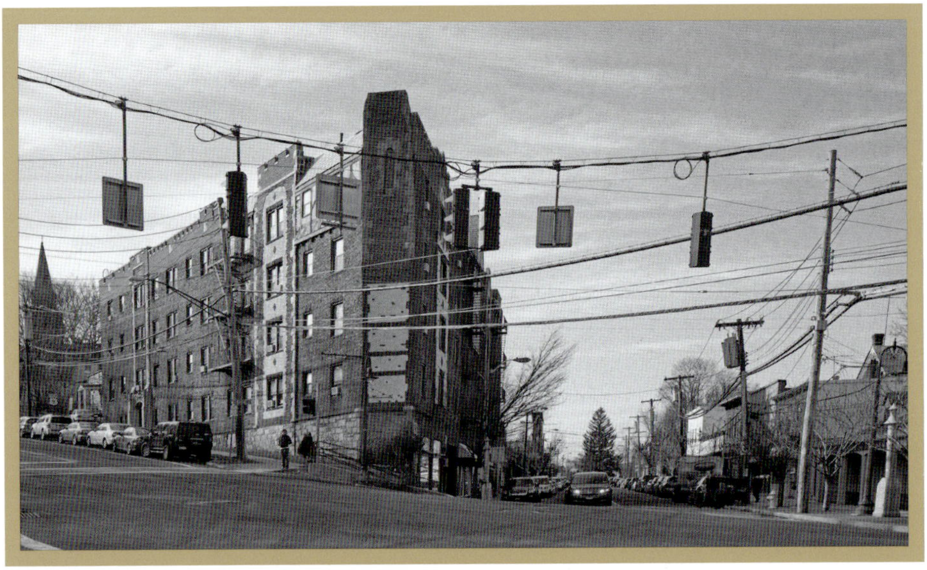

The southwest corner of Broadway and Cedar Street is marked by the Broadway Arms, the first modern apartment building in the village, constructed in 1927. Conveniently near the train station, the virtually universal mode of commuting at that time, it lacked a garage—a feature included in Rosalind Gardens, built a few months later farther south on Broadway. Known as Cedar Crest when this 1950s photograph was taken, it became Dobbs Ferry Manor Condominiums in 2006.

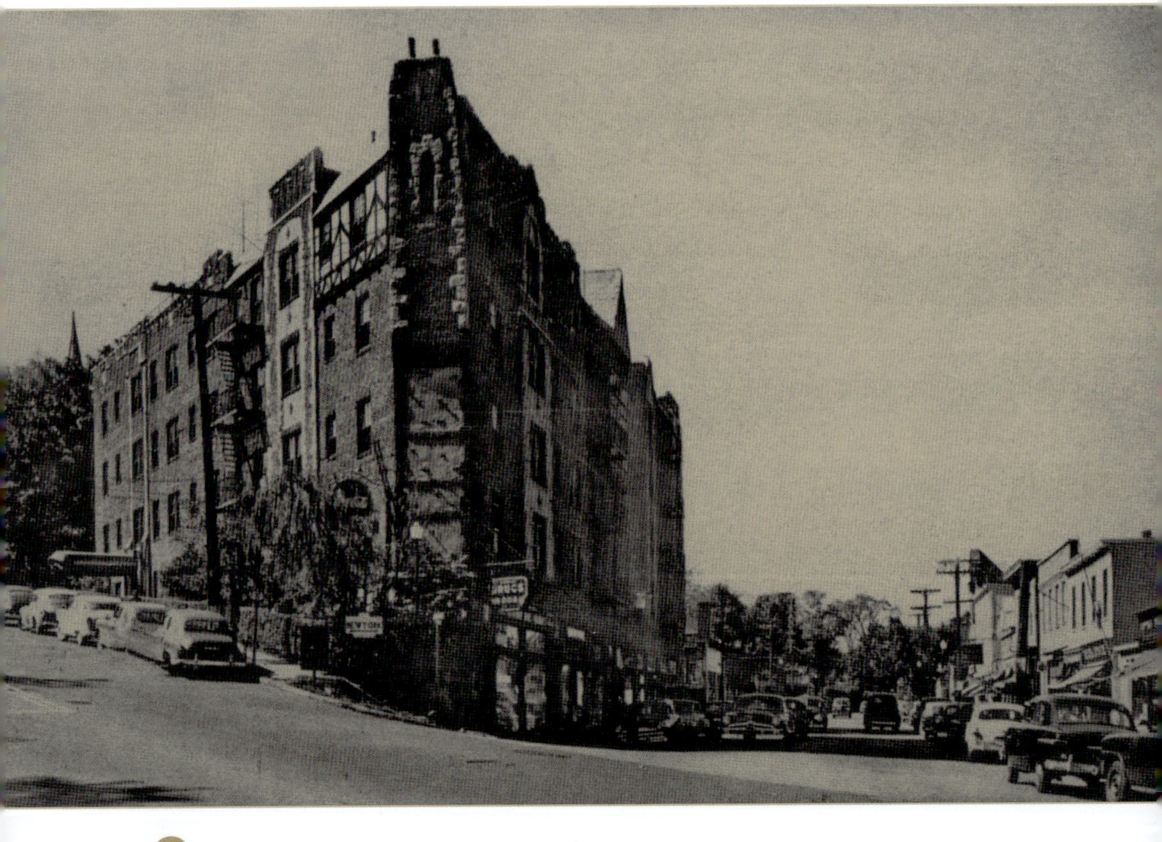

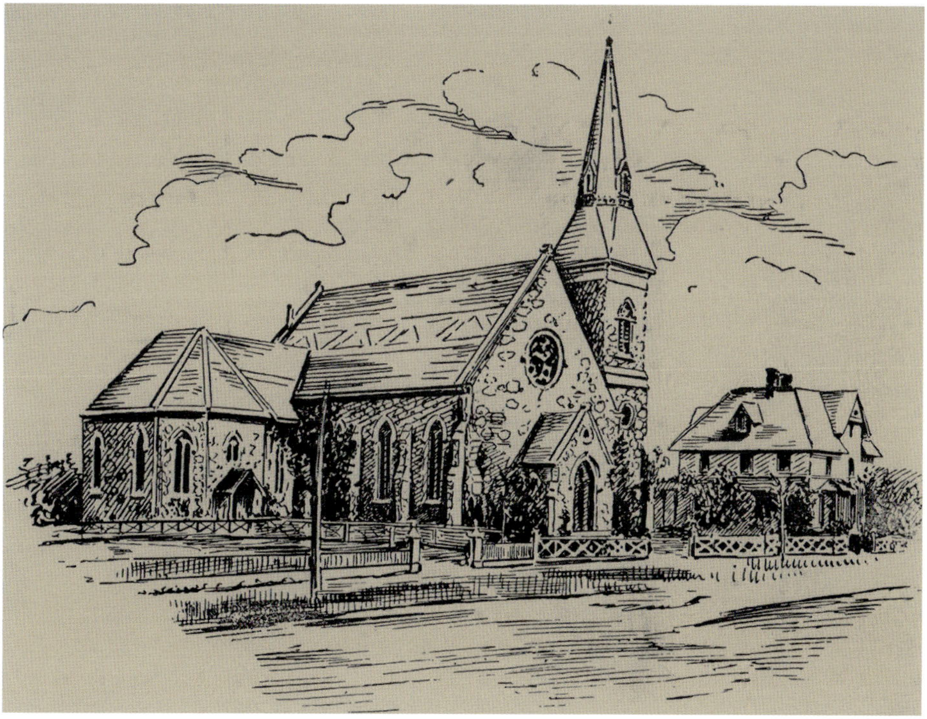

South Presbyterian, the first church organized in Dobbs Ferry, was incorporated in 1823. Until 1843, it shared a pastor with the nearby North Presbyterian Church in Elmsford. The congregation's second building, at 343 Broadway, was erected in 1868 and is seen here in 1880. A long-term and highly influential pastor during the Victorian era, Rev. Thornton Niven was the grandfather of playwright Thornton Wilder, who was often seen riding his tricycle around the church and manse. Both buildings are in the National Register of Historic Places. (Then image courtesy of Patricia Arone.)

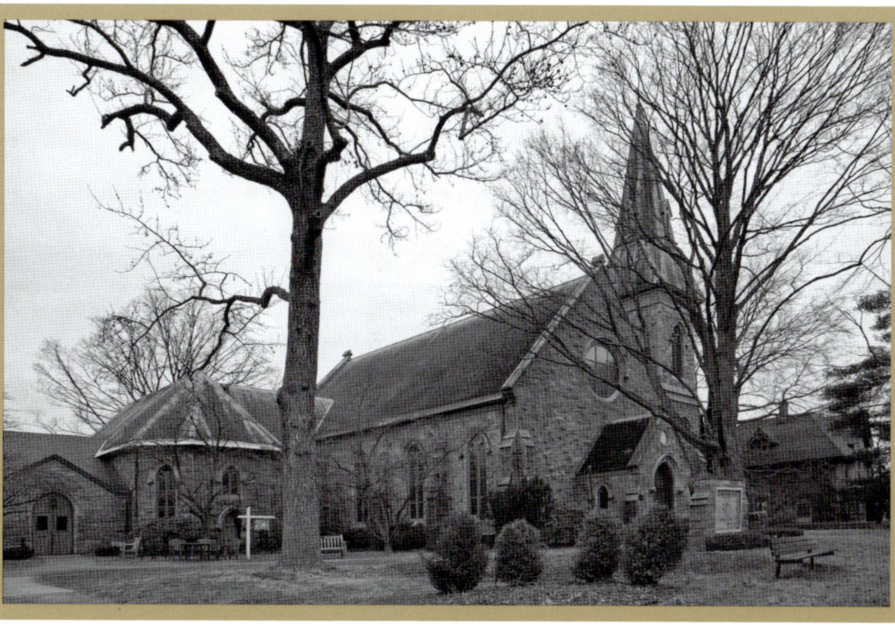

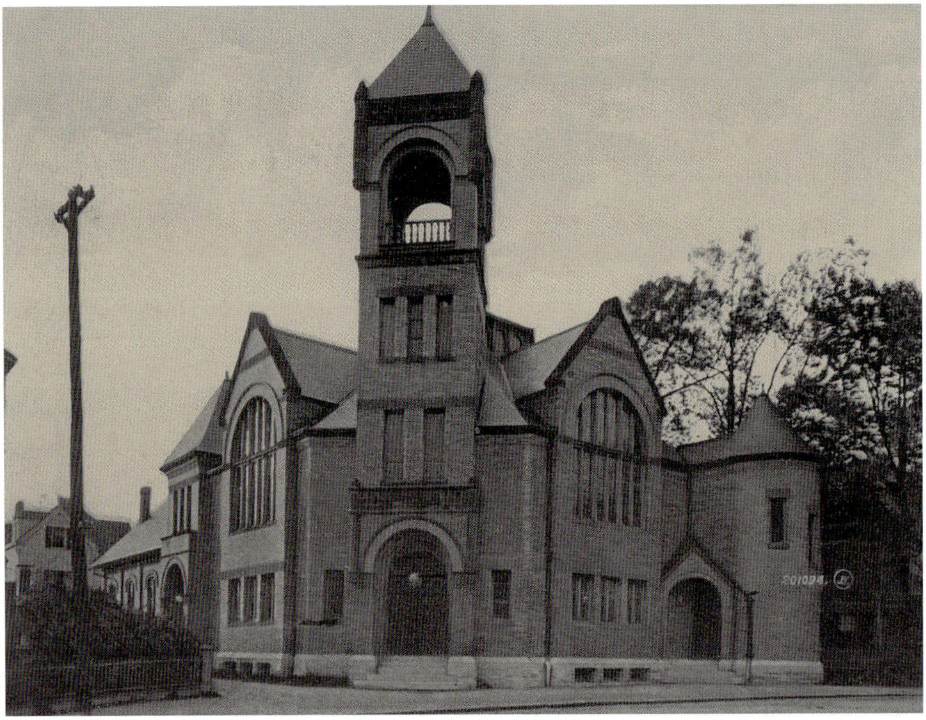

This building, at 303 Broadway, was constructed after a fire in 1894 destroyed the first home of the Summerfield Methodist Church. This second version incorporated the remains of the original 1855 building. It was named for John Summerfield, one of the most popular and eloquent preachers of the 19th century. The congregation left the building in 1927. It has been the home of Chabad of the Rivertowns since 2003. (Then image courtesy of Robert Casino.)

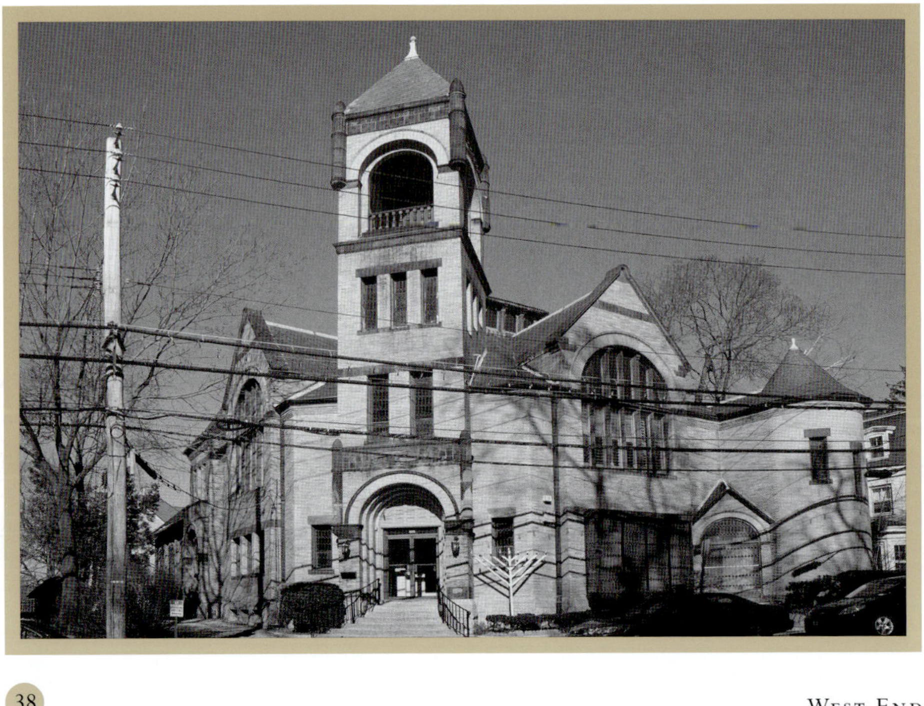

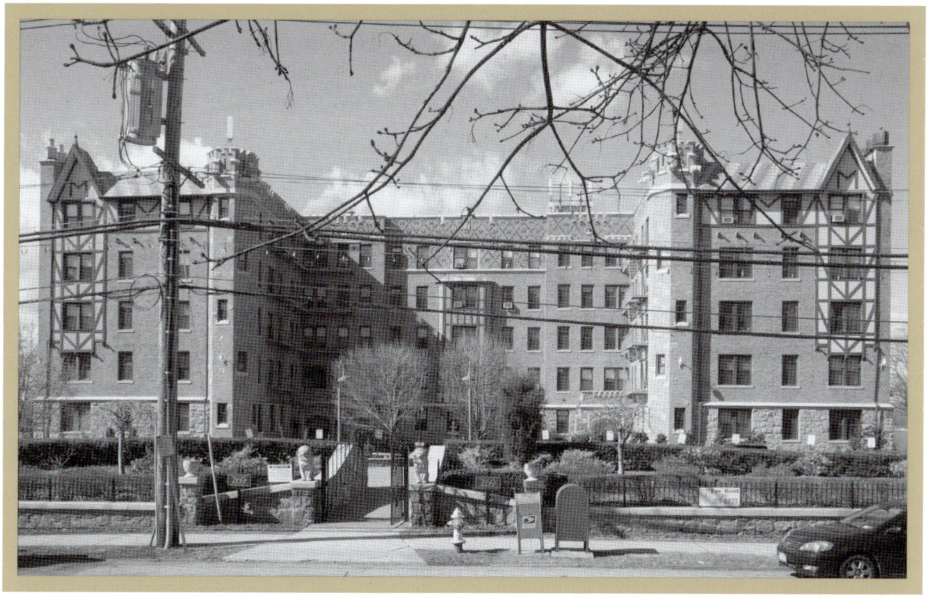

Rosalind Gardens was built in 1927 by Harry Z. Sulchin at 269 Broadway on the site of an estate constructed in 1840 by Rev. Samuel Kellog, the first full-time Presbyterian minister in Dobbs Ferry, who used it as a school. Sulchin, a liquor dealer and bon vivant, was celebrated in *Ripley's Believe It or Not* for refusing to evict Depression-era tenants for inability to pay. Named for Sulchin's daughter, this building was famous for its rose gardens. (Then image courtesy of Robert Casino.)

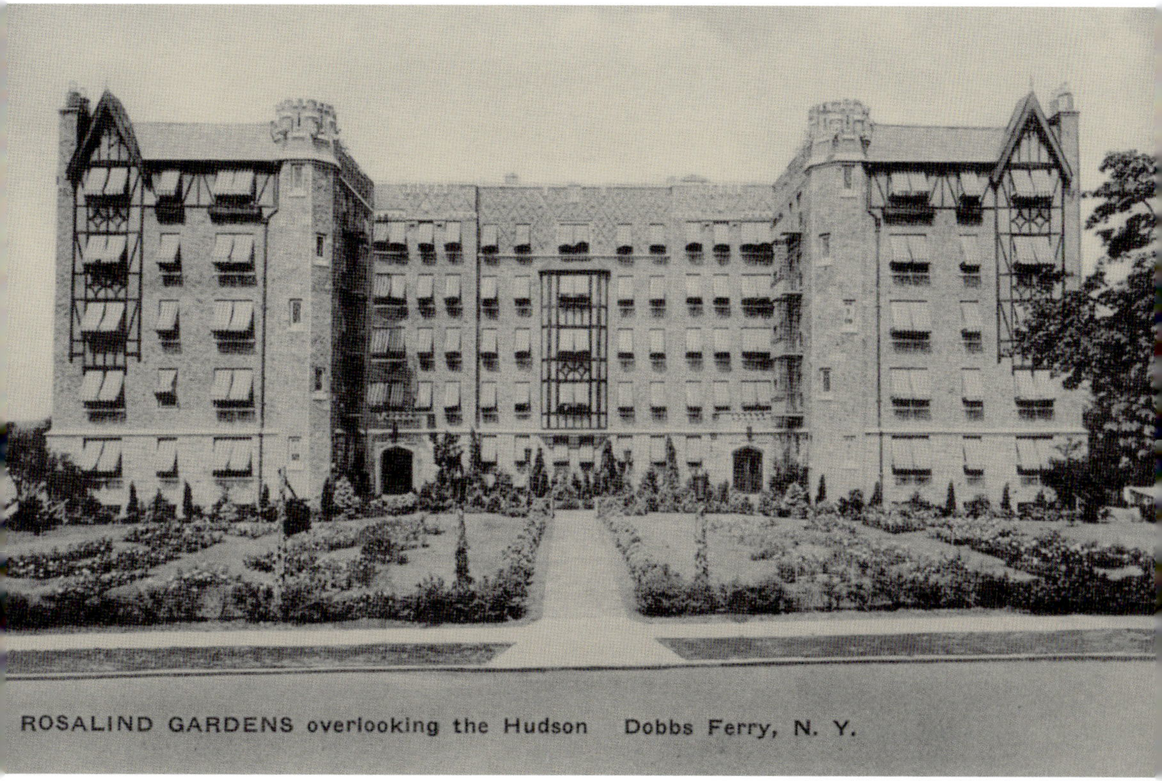

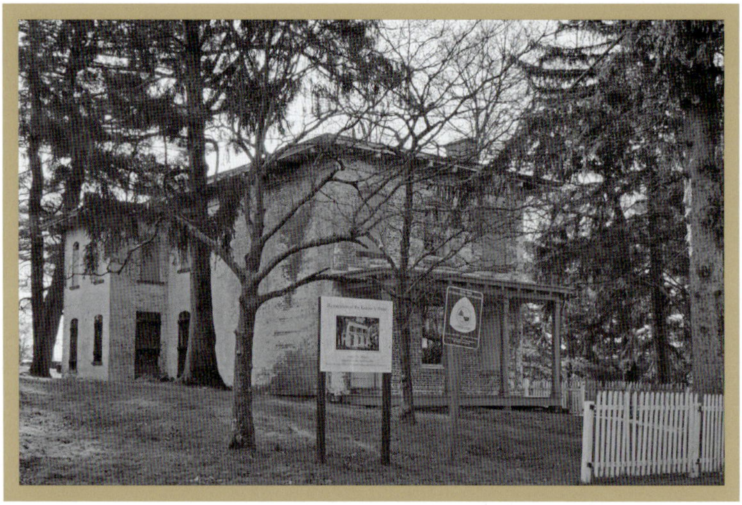

The Old Croton Aqueduct State Historic Park, established in 1968, commemorates New York City's first system of municipal water supply, constructed from 1837 to 1842. A home for the overseer in charge of maintaining Section 50 of the tunnel was built in 1857 near the southwest corner of Broadway and Walnut Avenue. The Friends of the Old Croton Aqueduct are working to restore the Keeper's House, which has stood vacant since 1962. (Then image courtesy of Mavis Cain.)

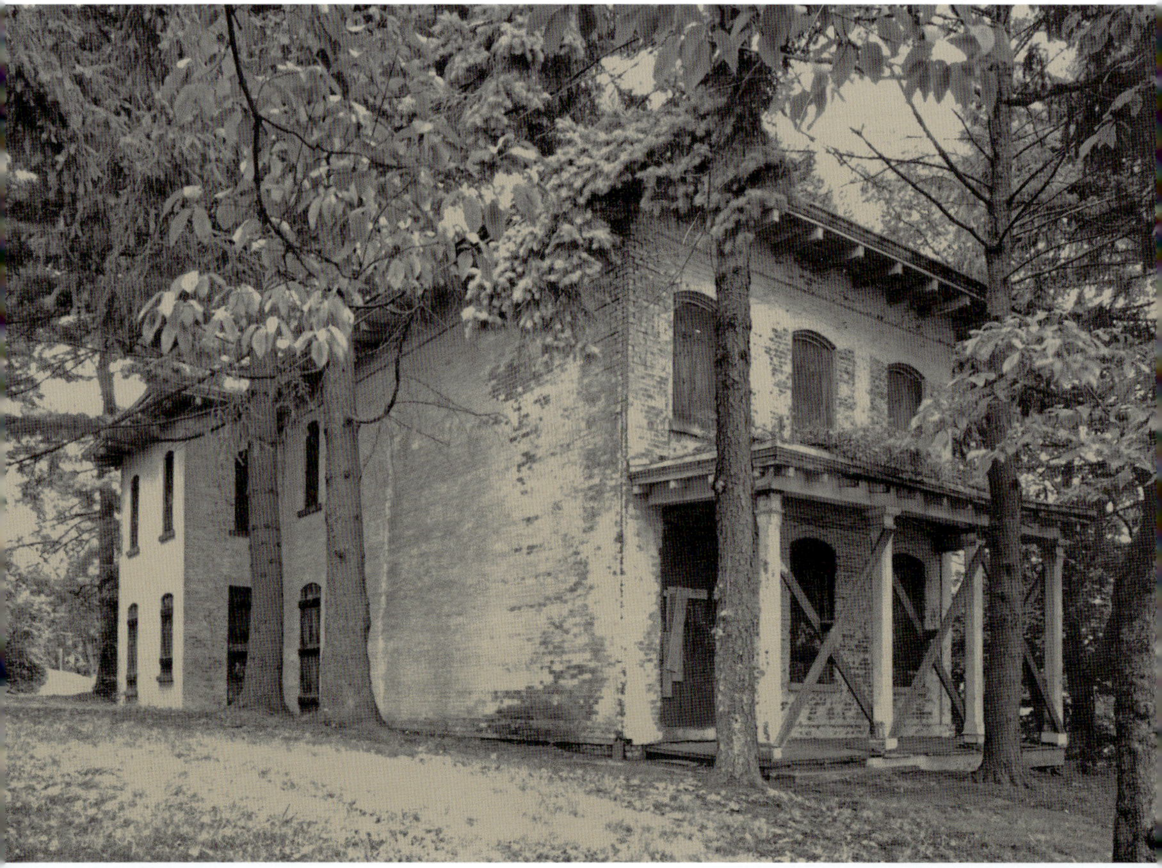

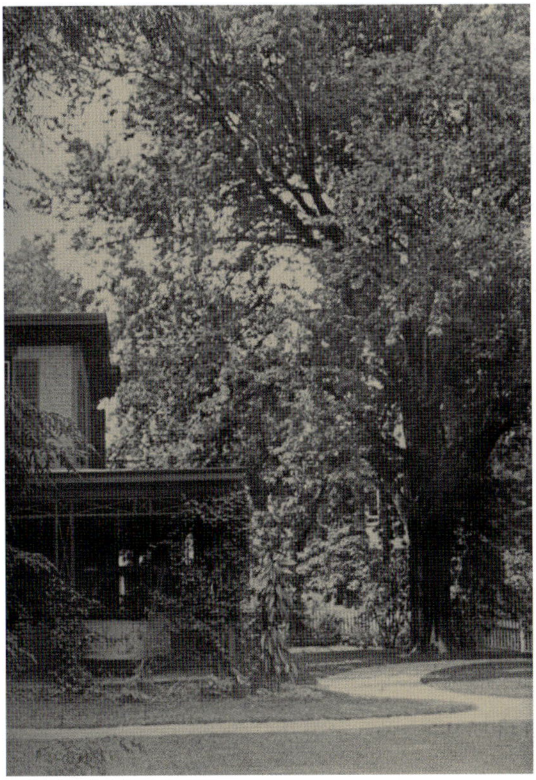

In 1835, George W. Hatch, president of the American Bank Note Company, became the first of several generations of his family to own the land that this house, 189 Broadway, and others stand on. Originally a small cottage, it went through two major additions and in 1905 became the home of Herman Leroy Edgar, a real estate investor and renowned collector of Dickensiana. Yet another substantial remodeling around 2006 adapted it for the 21st century. (Then image courtesy of Ernest Howell.)

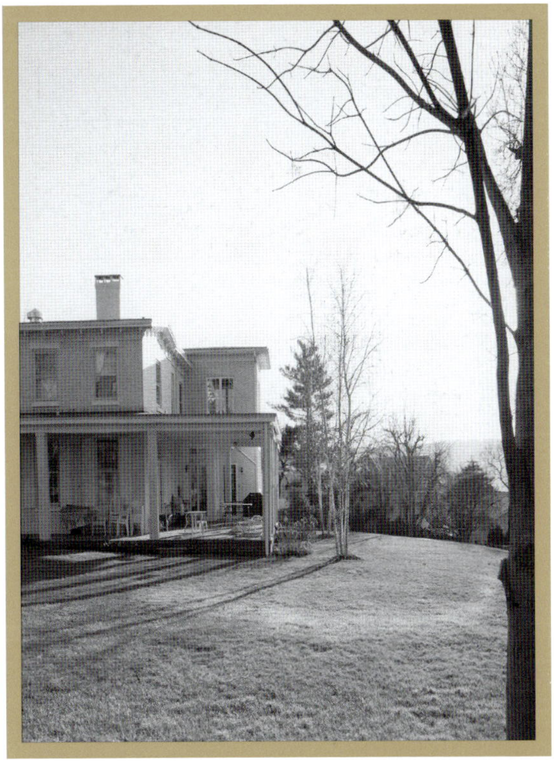

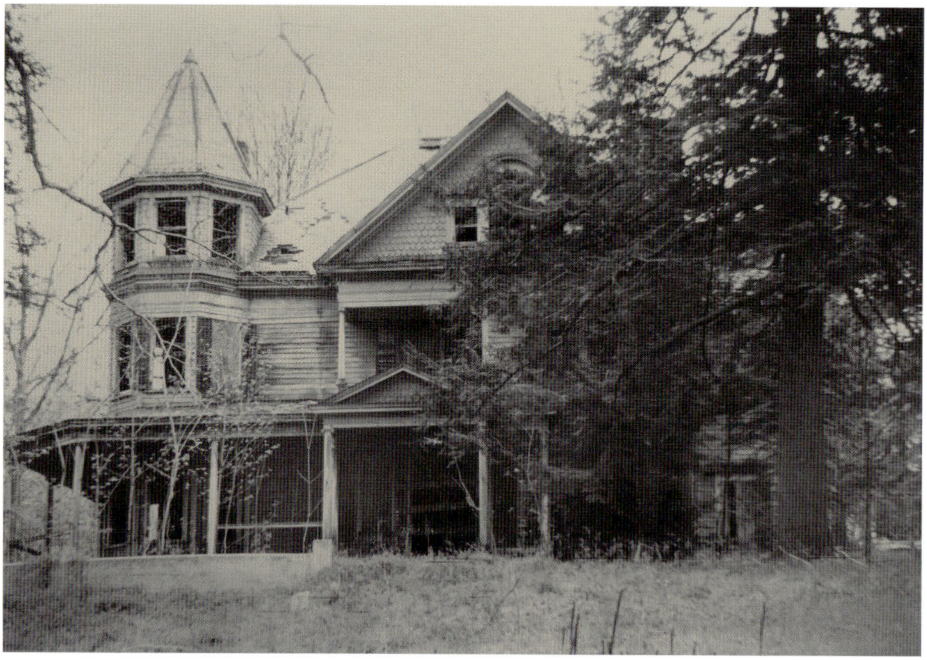

In 1893, William P. Brown retired from land development and manufacturing in New York City and built a home, Redoubt, on an acre of land facing south near the intersection of Broadway and Livingston Avenue. The site was believed to be the site of a Revolutionary-era redoubt—a small wood-and-earth fort dismantled when the Washington-Rochambeau army left Dobbs Ferry in 1781. Shadowy remnants of the earthworks remain to this day.

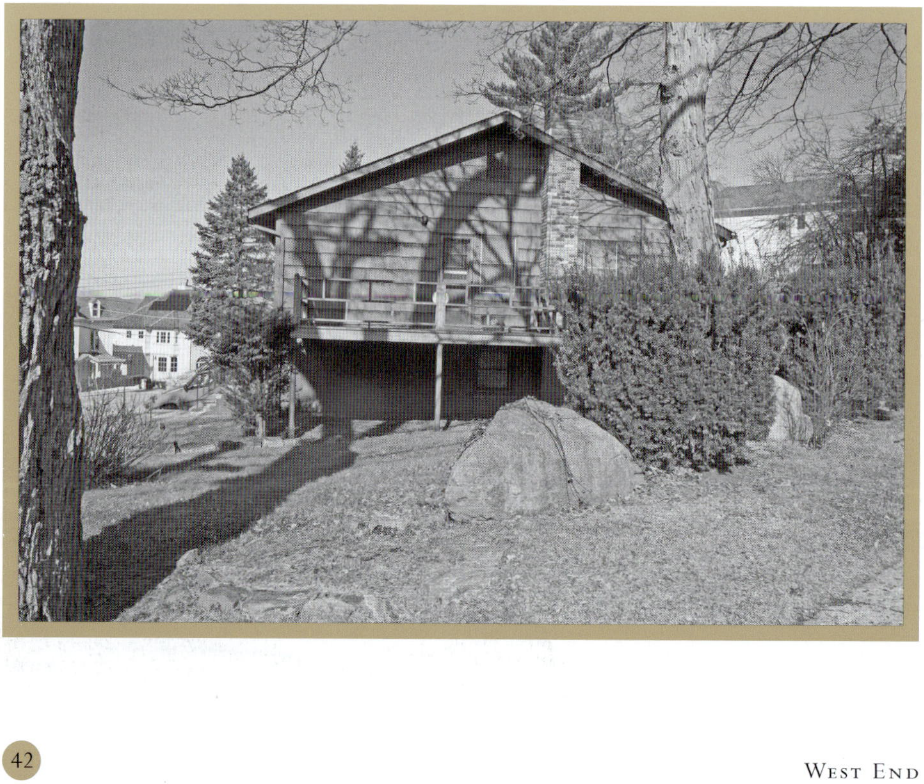

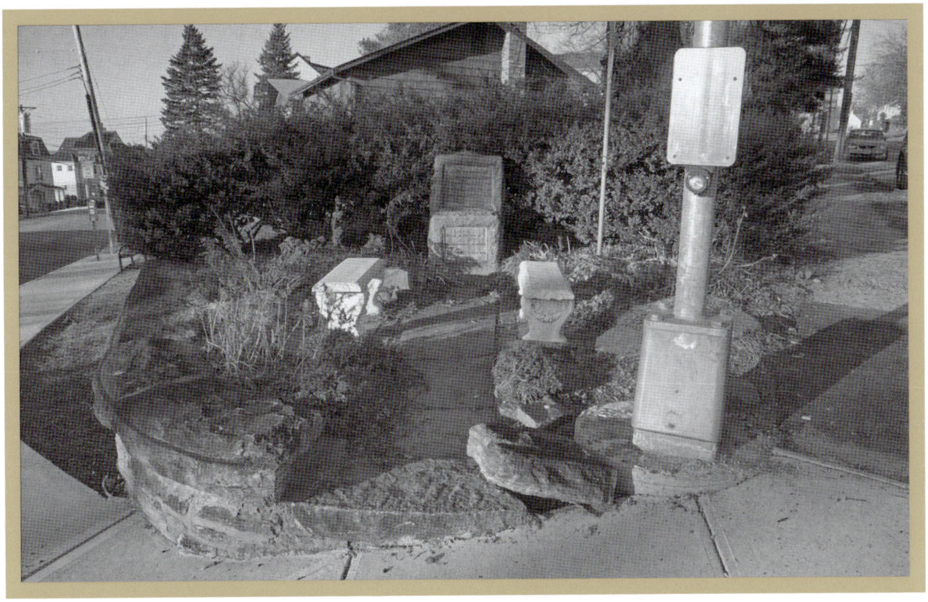

This 19th-century etching depicts the remains of a fort built in 1776 at the south end of Main Street, where it intersects High Street, to monitor and impede the movement of British ships up the Hudson. Or it may depict the 1781 redoubt at the corner of Broadway and Livingston Avenue—expert opinions differ. The contemporary photograph shows the southern tip of the land once occupied by the redoubt, where the meager relics of all the Dobbs Ferry fortifications have been gathered into a tiny park.

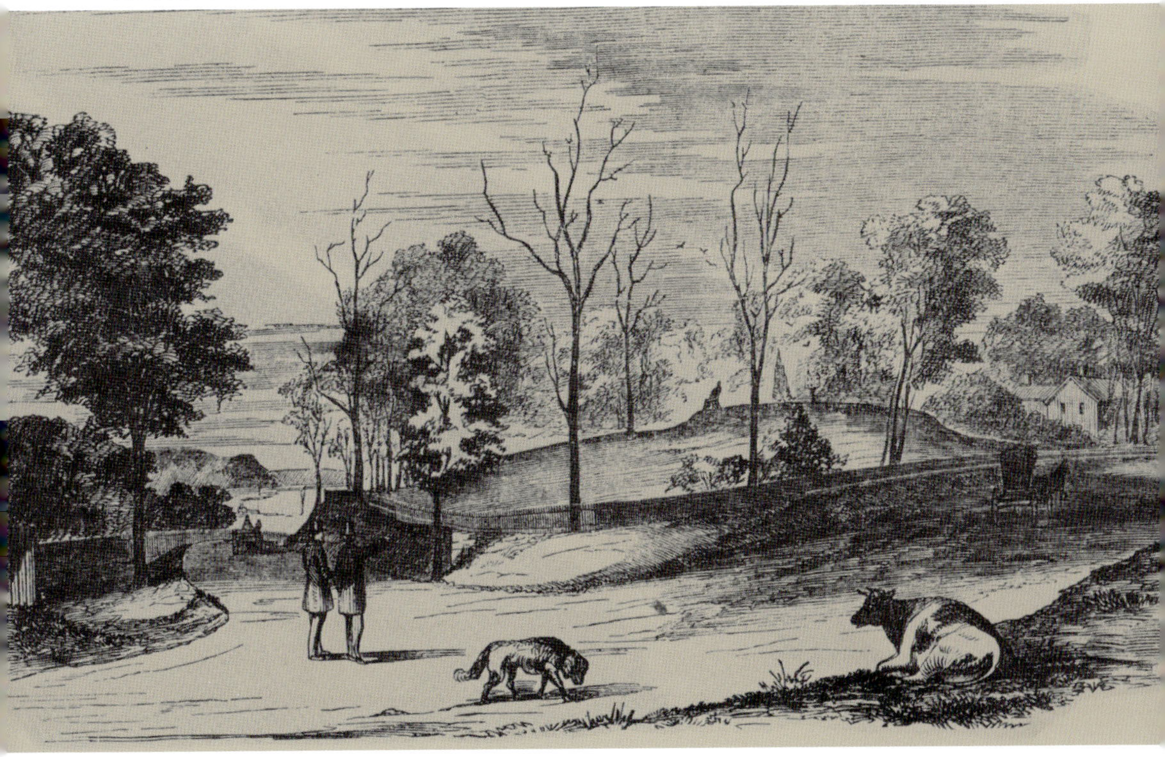

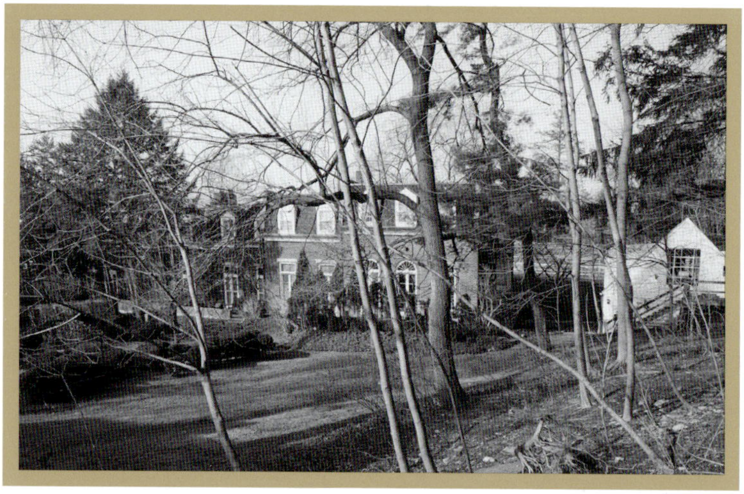

John Hyatt built a four-room tenant farmhouse (far right) on Philipsburg Manor land about 1697. Philip Livingston, a New York City gentleman, purchased the house and the surrounding 233-acre farm in 1785 and added the Georgian-style wing (left, overlooking Broadway) and the connecting five-bay addition. The family's holdings grew to include most of the western part of Dobbs Ferry. The mansion burned in 1974 and was replaced by the Washington Headquarters condominiums at 152 Broadway, whose name preserves a discredited local legend. (Then image courtesy of the Library of Congress.)

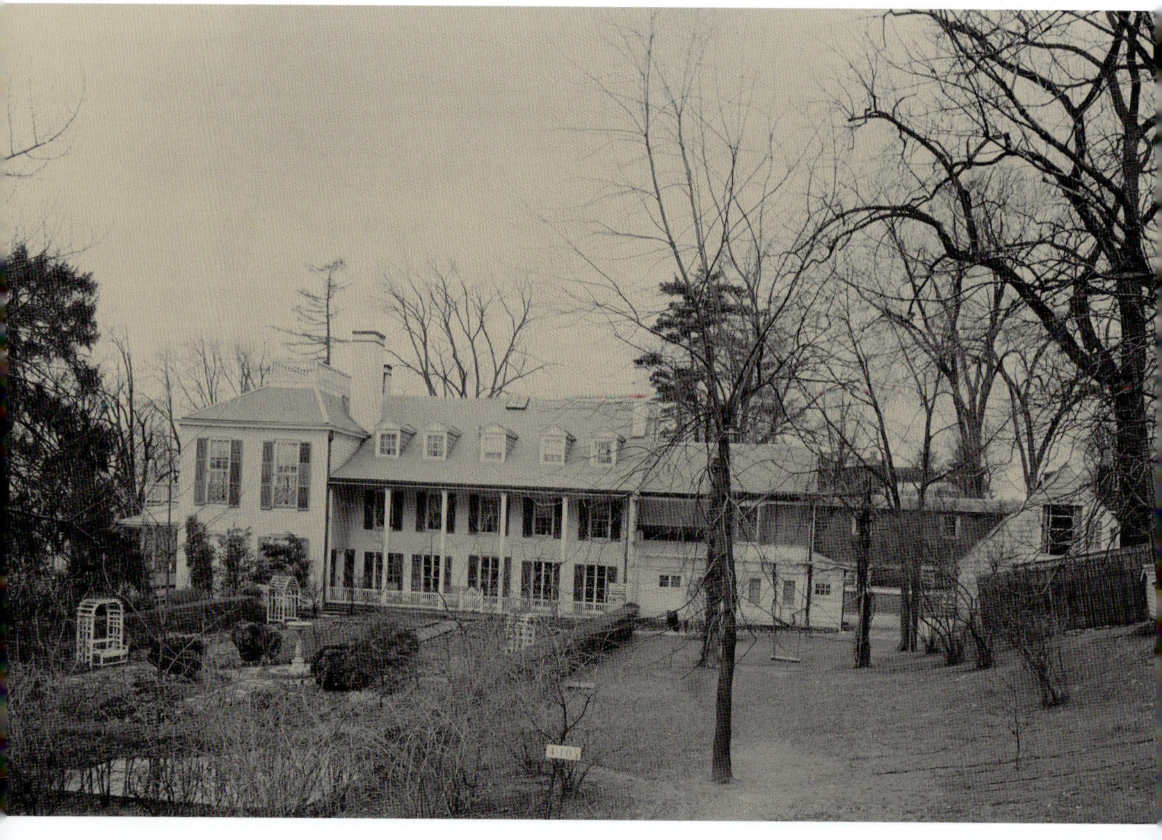

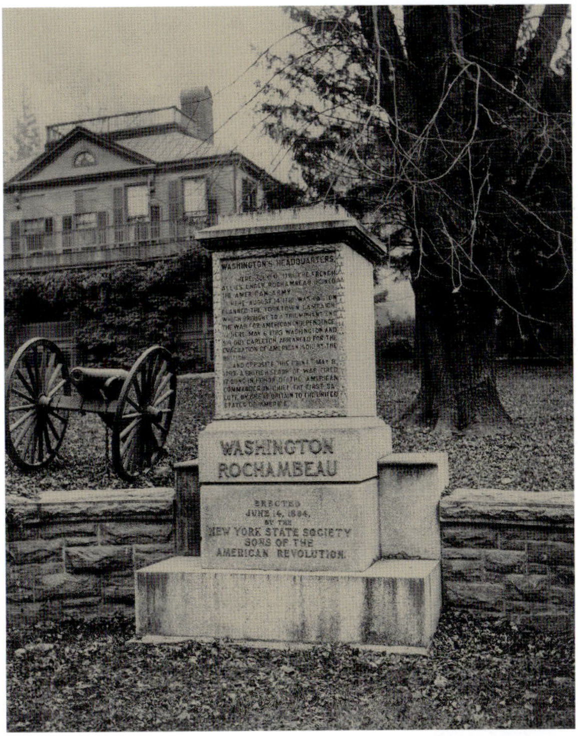

The Hyatt-Livingston house was inherited in 1877 by Sarah Archer and her husband, Dr. Joseph Hasbrouck, a real estate developer and a president of Dobbs Ferry, who fostered the legend that "Washington slept here." This monument was placed facing Broadway in 1894. Following a century of scholarship, controversy, and inscription revision, the consensus now is that the original was substantially correct, except that most of the events occurred over a surrounding area of several square miles, rather than in the house itself.

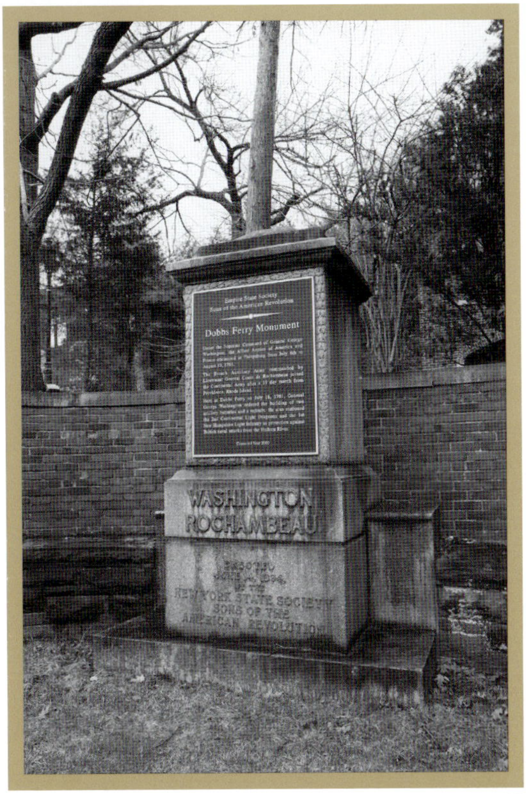

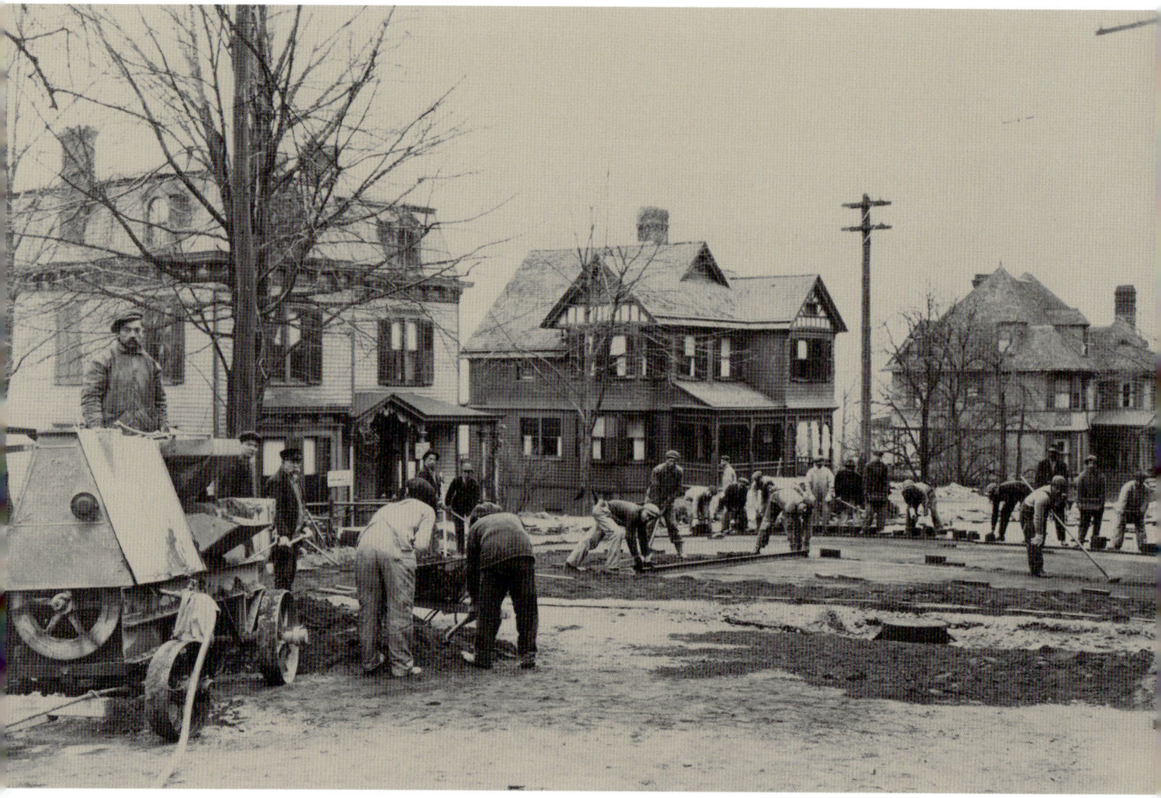

In 1915–1916, Livingston Avenue was paved from Broadway down to Main Street. No. 29 Livingston is on the left, followed by a dwelling renovated beyond recognition except for its roofline in the summer of 2011. These residences were owned in the early 20th century by the Simmons and Achtman families. The Millard Smith (formerly John Besson) home at right was razed in 1999 to accommodate the Livingston Ridge condominiums, at 41–51 Livingston.

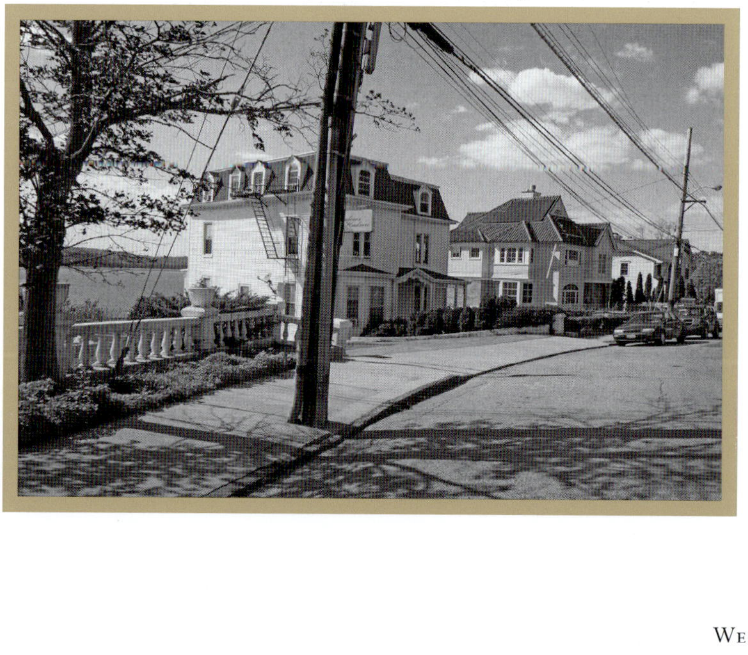

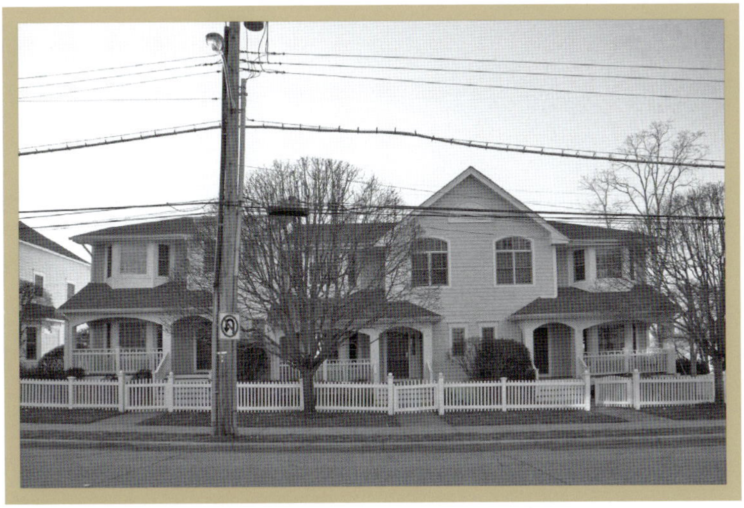

In the early 20th century, John Besson's house stood proudly on Livingston Avenue, separated by a cliff and the railroad tracks from his dock, lumberyard, and coal company. Later, it stood vacant for many years until it was razed in the mid-1990s and replaced with the Livingston Ridge condominiums, which command a rear view overlooking the riverfront. (Then image courtesy of Anne Marie Leone.)

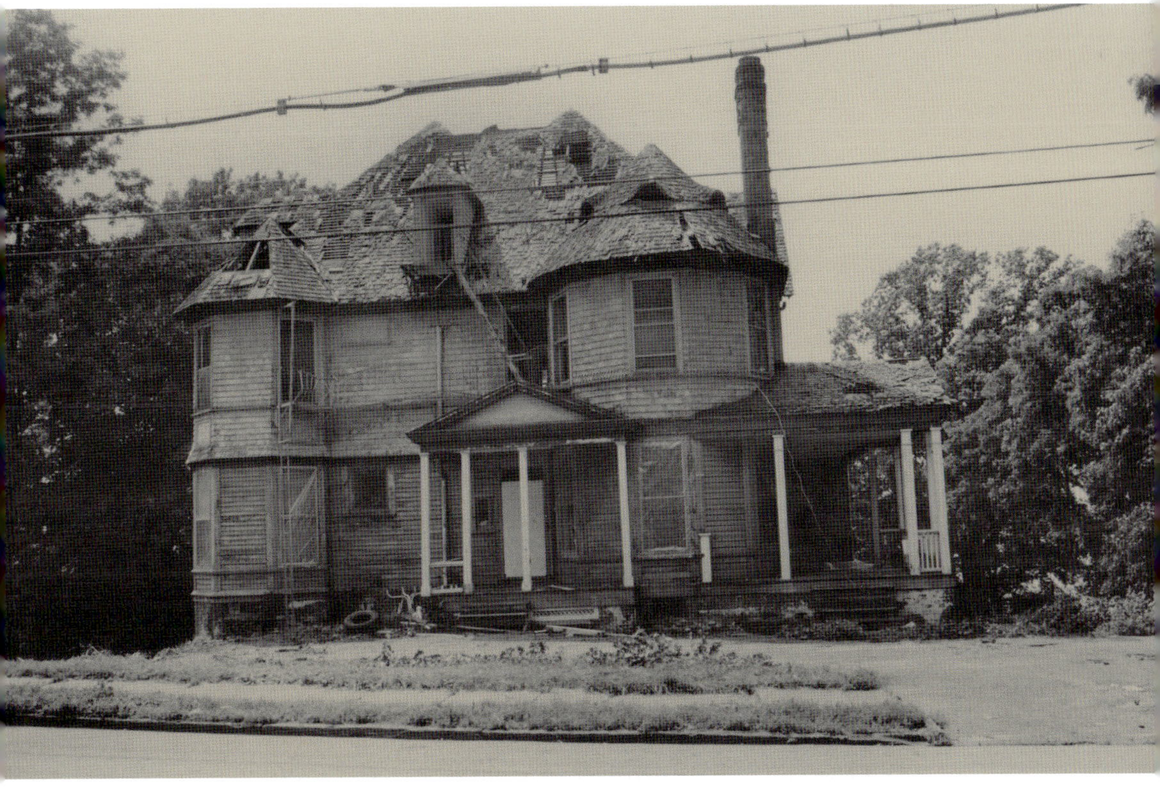

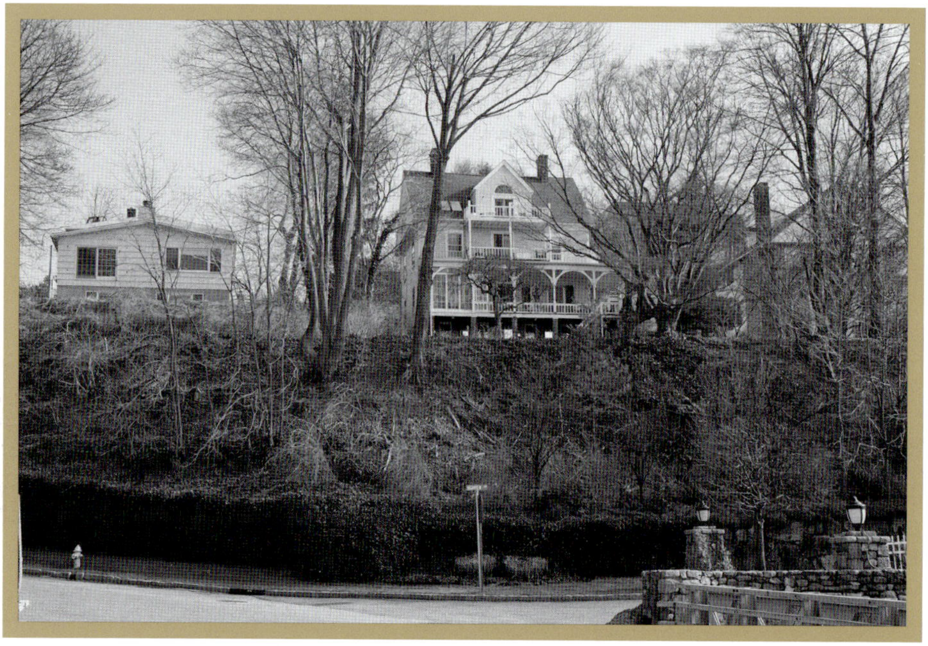

In 1845, William V. Brady, a former New York City mayor, built a house he named Terrace Villa with its back turned to Livingston Avenue. The house stood at the top of a steep terraced hill (hence its name), overlooking the train station, dock, the Hudson River, and the Palisades beyond. It is believed that in 1776 a strongly garrisoned fort was built there, followed in 1781 by several redoubts. About 1885, a third floor was added to the dwelling and the front entrance was relocated to 63 Livingston Avenue. (Then image courtesy of Mary S. Donovan.)

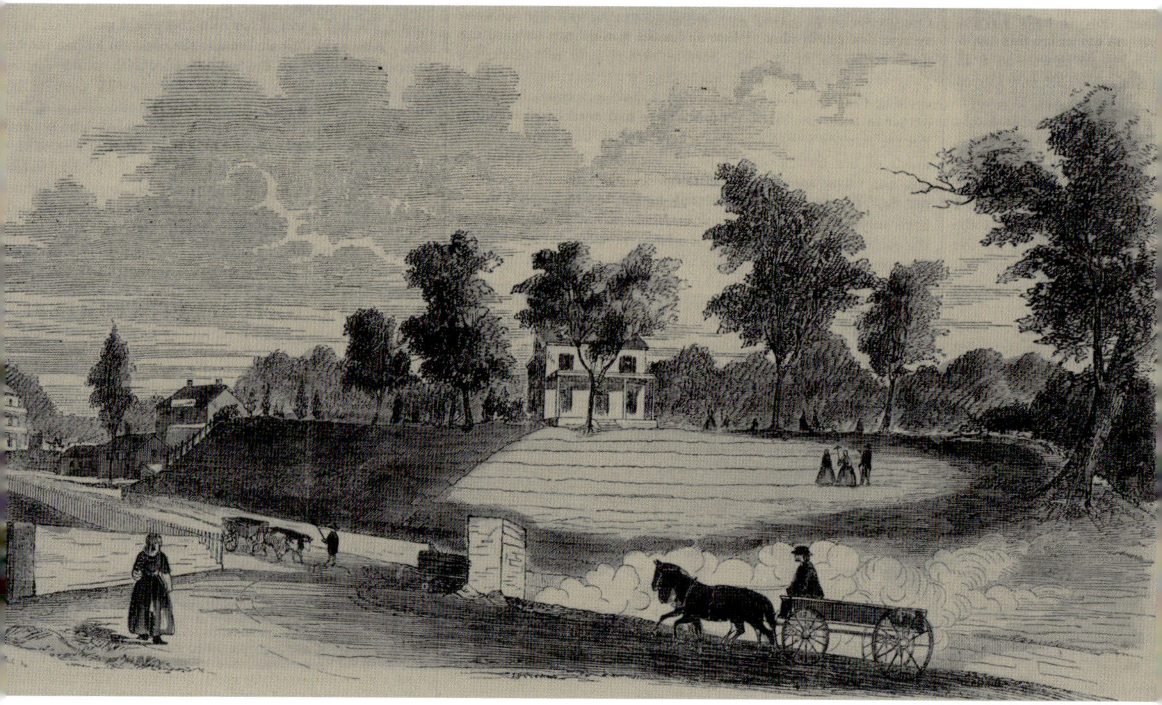

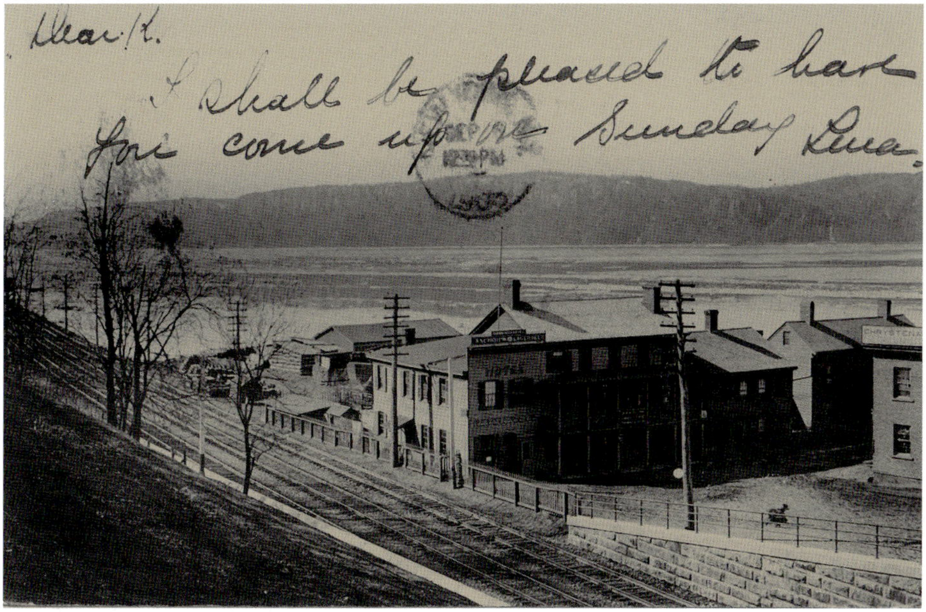

From the earliest days, a public dock extended from the westernmost point of land along the river. By 1849, landfill west of the railroad tracks provided space for a depot and a commercial dock; a hotel and lumber and coal yards soon followed. In the 1980s, the industrial area was cleared for an upscale restaurant and bar, the Chart House (now the Half Moon). (Then image courtesy of Patricia Arone.)

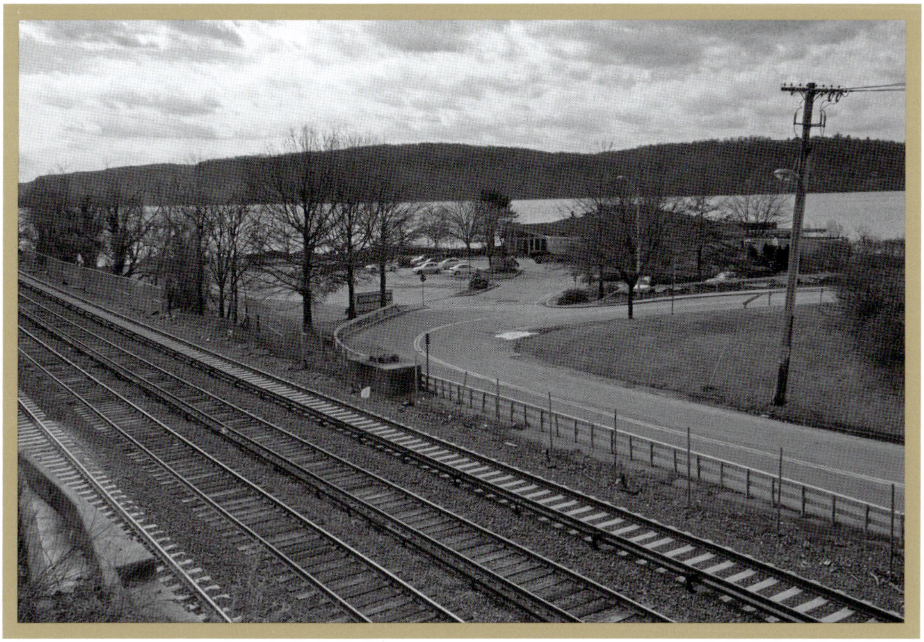

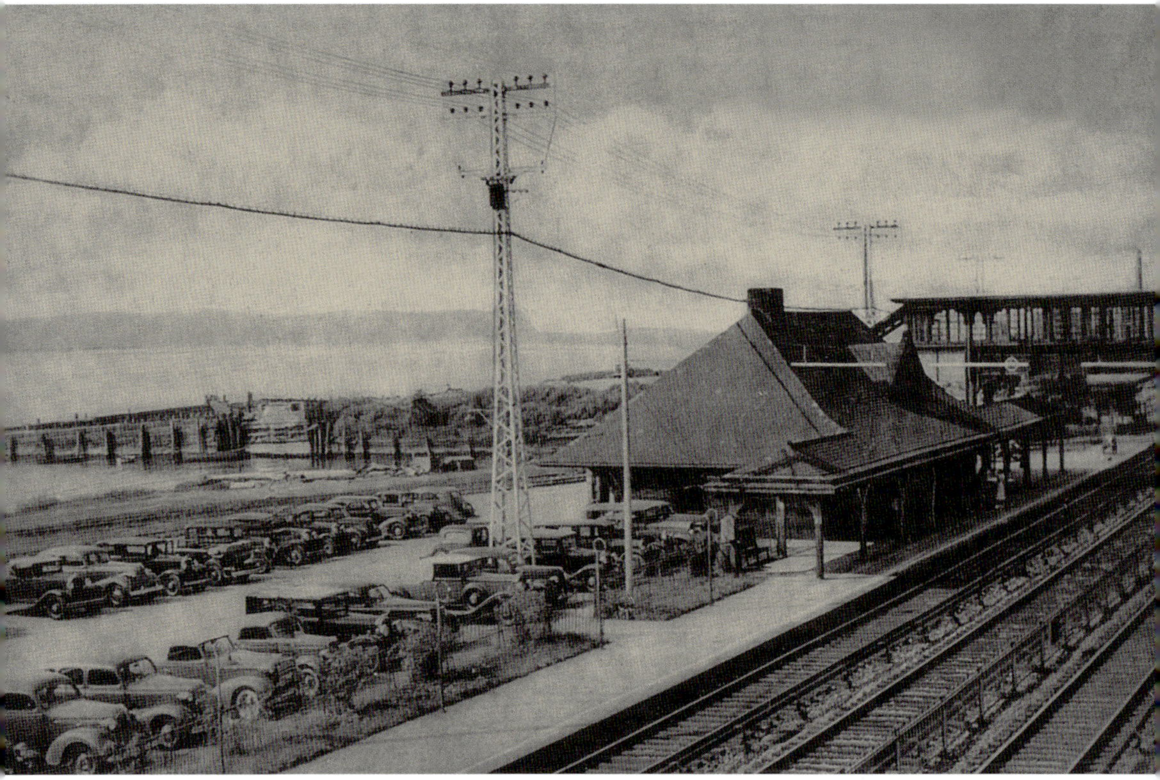

The Hudson River Line laid railroad tracks along the riverbank and erected a small wooden depot on landfill west of the tracks in 1849. In 1869, it merged with the New York Central and built this Romanesque-style station north of the depot in 1890. The average commute time was 65 minutes, but the discomfort and uncertainty of the journey caused many commuters to prefer traveling by sloop or steamship until double-tracking and electricity were introduced in 1911. (Then image courtesy of Patricia Arone.)

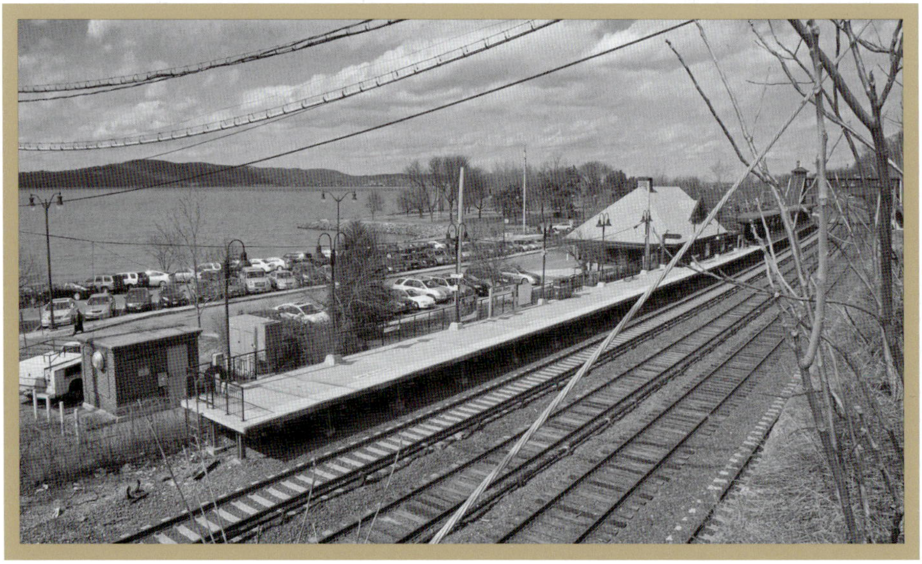

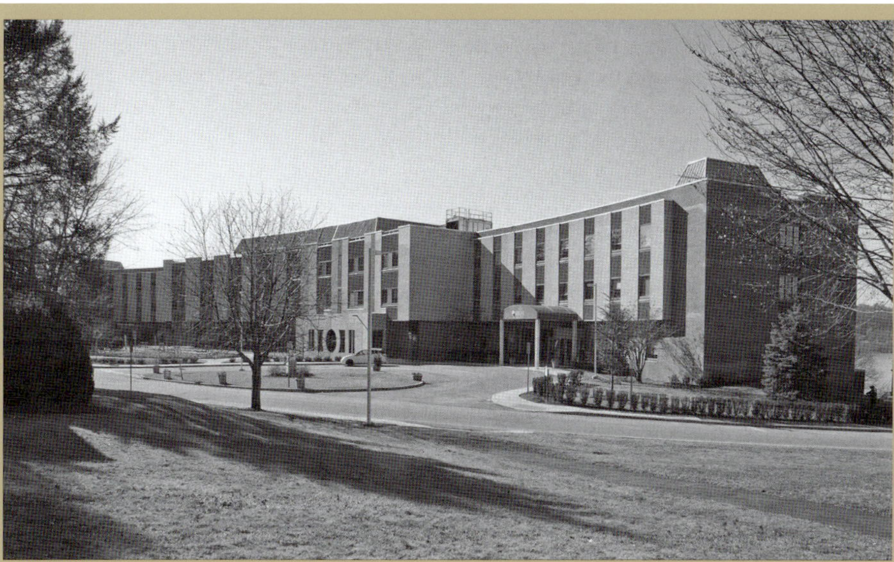

In 1865, T.H. Hardcastle built Glen Tower on riverside acreage south of Livingston Avenue. In 1886, a 65-foot-by-80-foot addition was erected facing Broadway that housed the Westminster Classical School for Boys until 1891. Rev. James Mackenzie operated Mackenzie School there until he sold the premises to Mother Francis Cabrini in 1913. Cabrini Health Care Center now occupies the site. The ruined towers and loggia still facing the river are from the original mansion. (Then image courtesy of Robert Casino.)

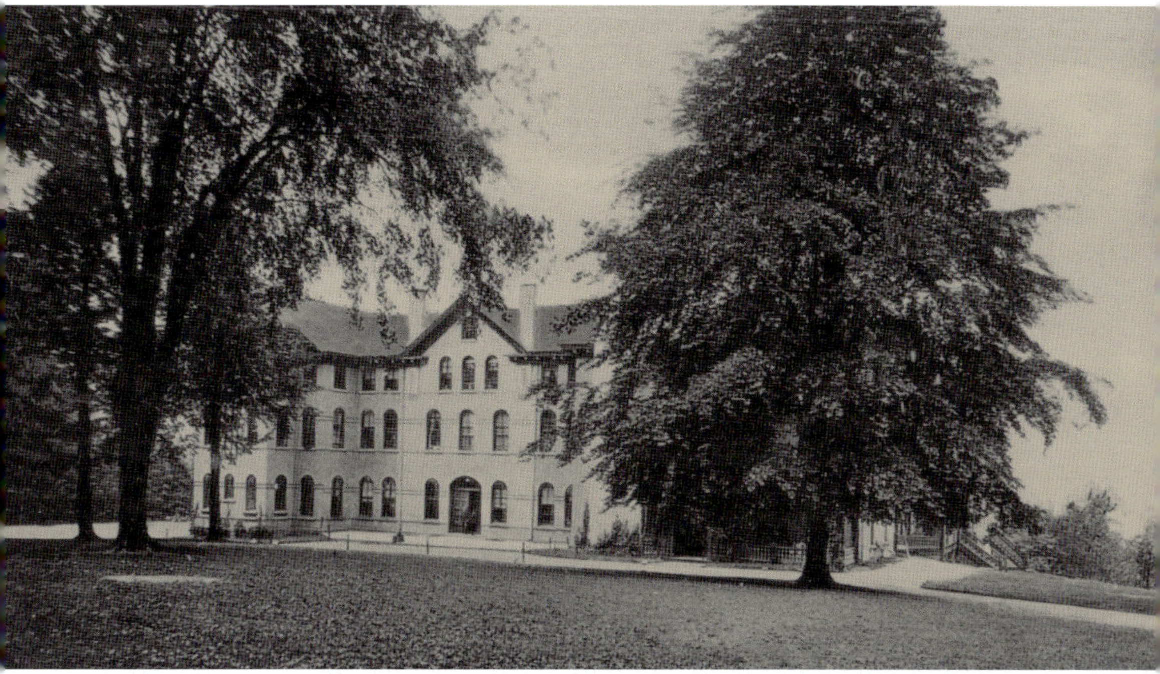

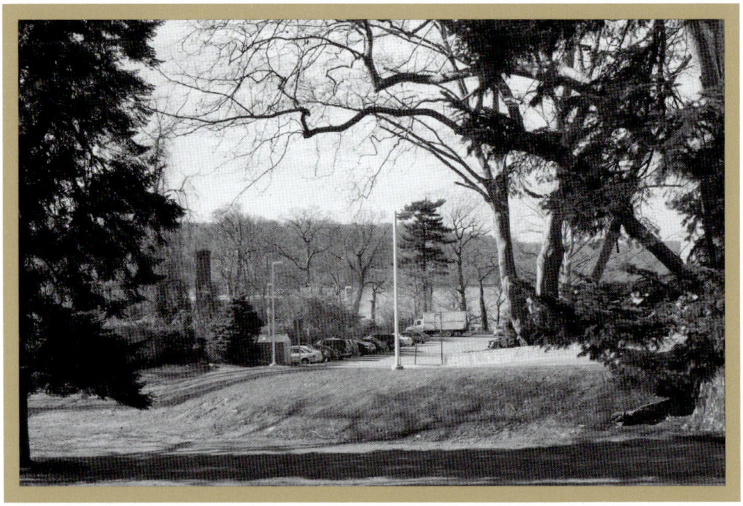

This Broadway estate was owned by T. Foote in 1860, William J. Syms in 1865, Julius Nathan in the 1880s, and Maj. Orlando Jay Smith and his heirs from 1891 to 1914. Major Smith (1842–1908) founded the American Press Association in 1882. By 1930, the mansion and four-acre estate belonged to the Missionary Sisters of the Sacred Heart. The site is now a parking lot for the Cabrini Health Care Center.

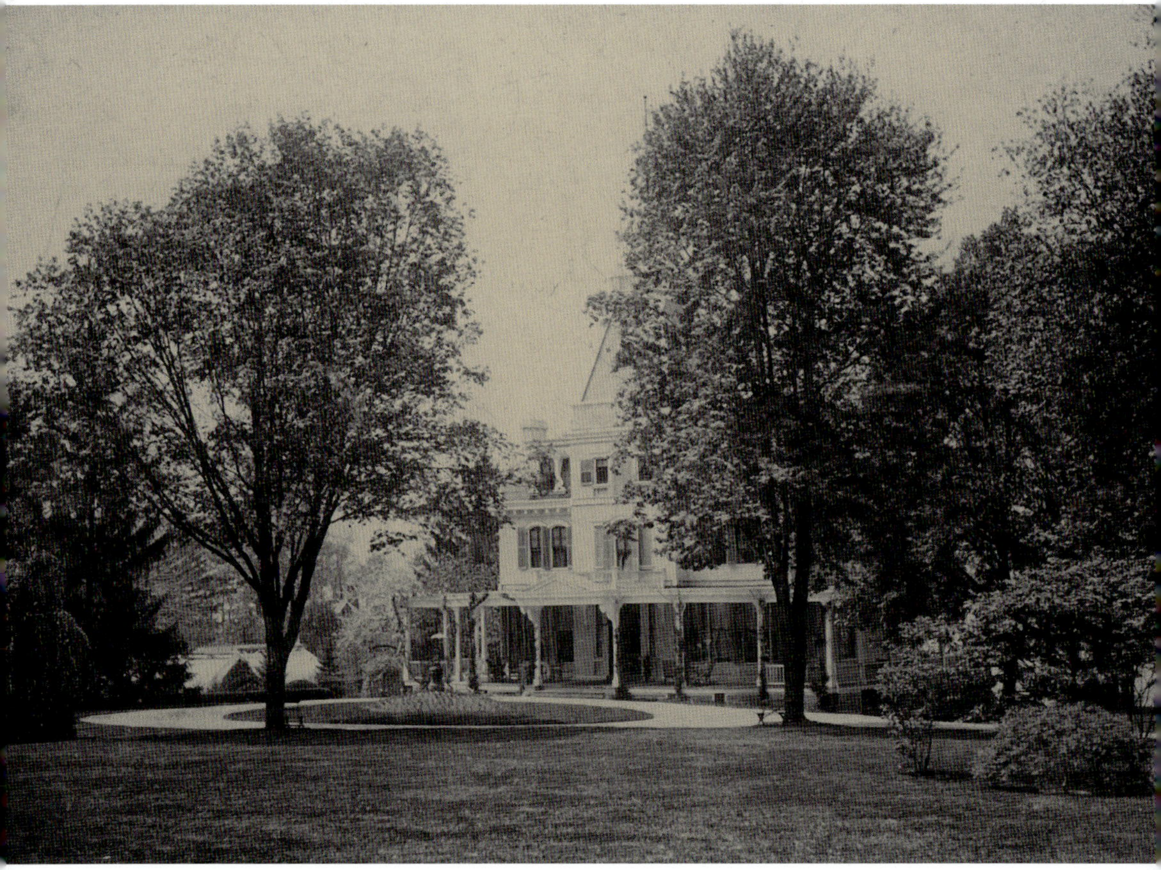

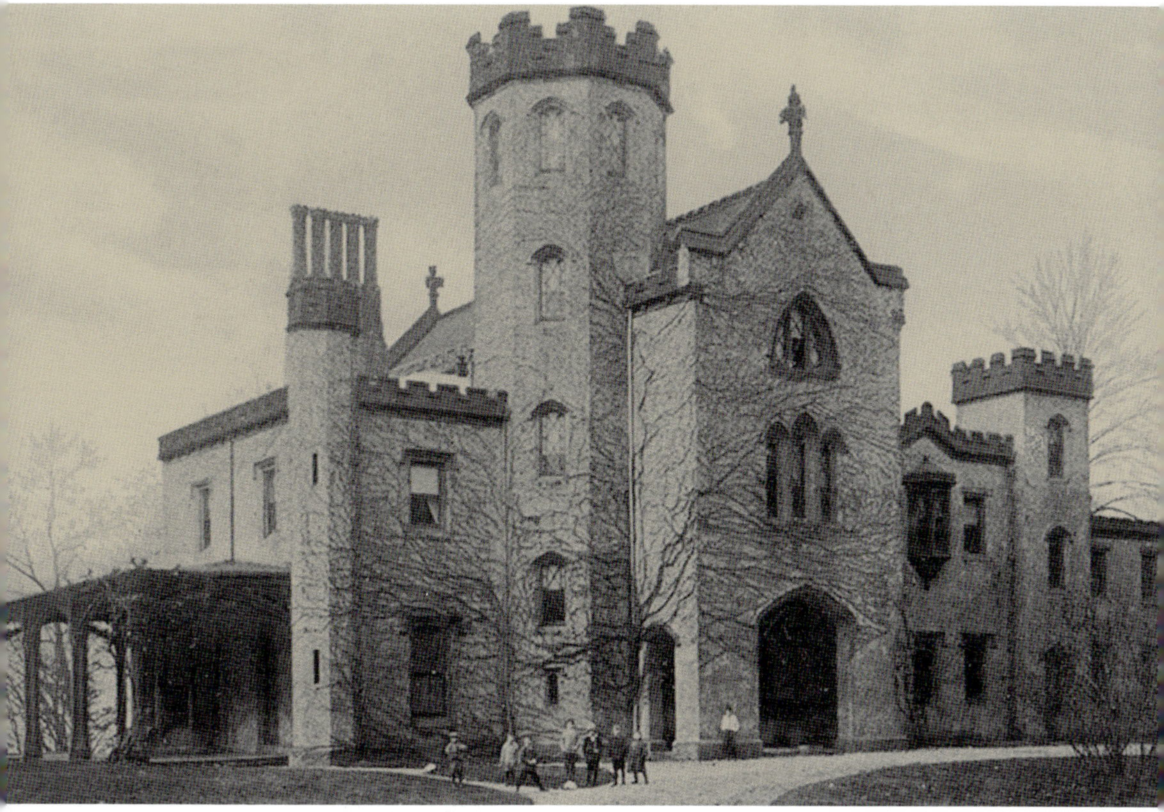

Designed by Alexander Jackson Davis, Ingleside was built for Albert and Edward Bruton Strange and their mother from 1854 to 1857. Born to an unmarried cloth picker, the brothers came to America from England about 1839, started in business as feather importers, and amassed a fortune as silk merchants. They sold the estate in 1890 to St. Christopher's, the private school and child welfare agency that continues there today.

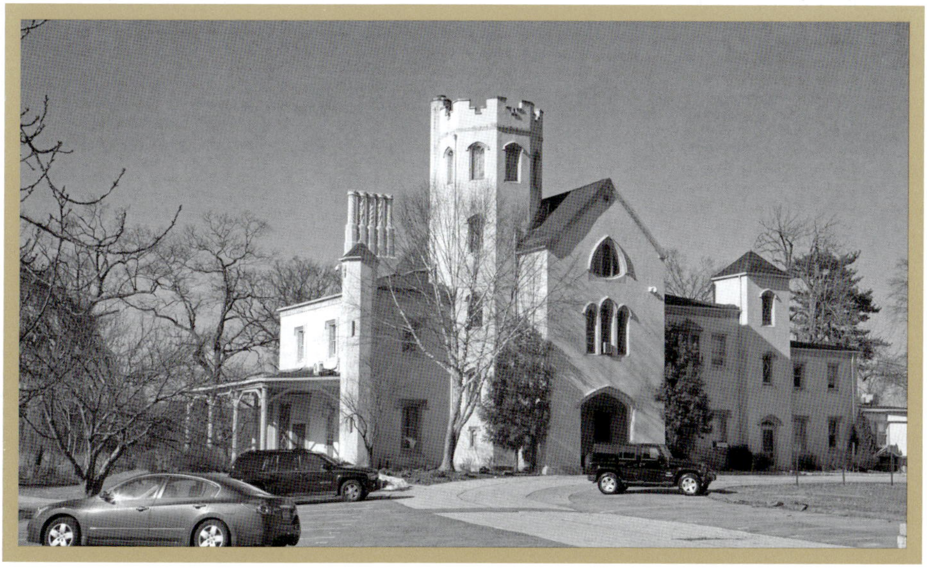

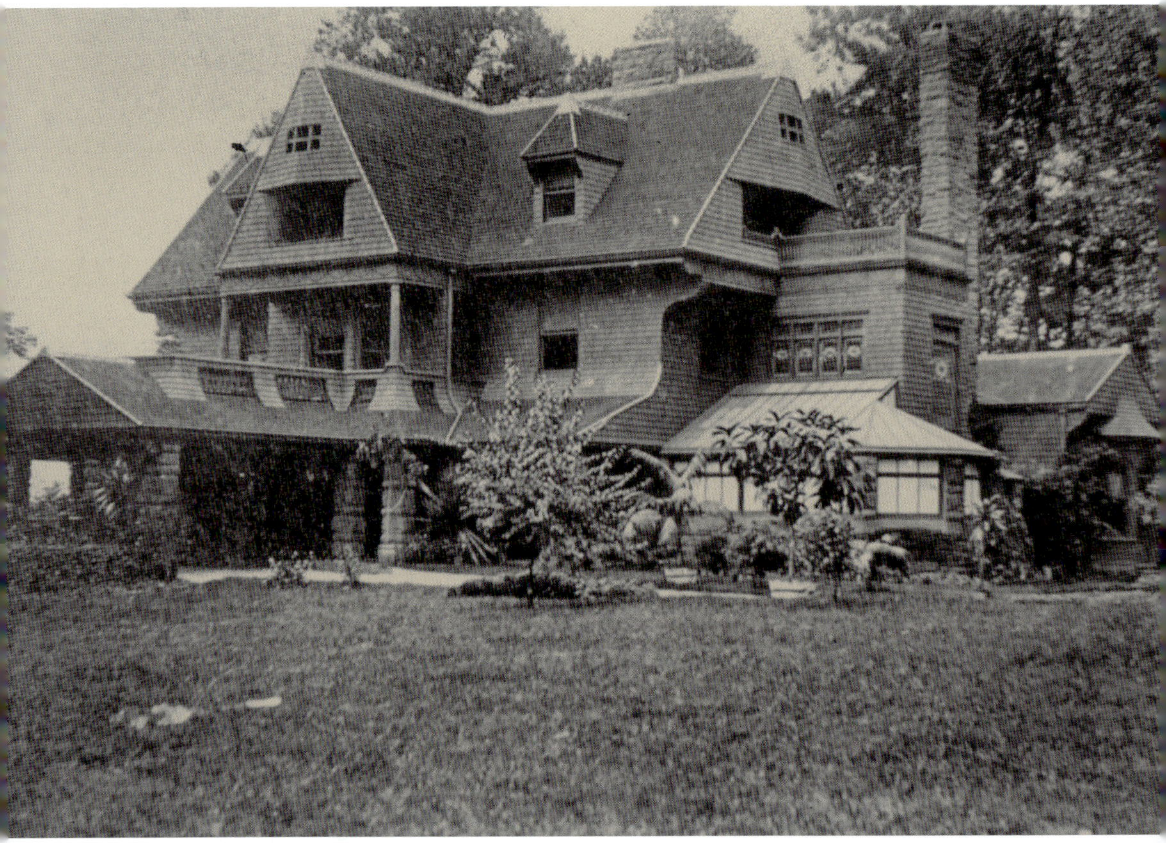

Fairmead, a red sandstone mansion on 14 riverside acres straddling the Hastings border, was built about 1884 for Gen. James Bowen, president of the Erie Railroad. Although subdivided in 1924, the land remained rural until 1971, when public utilities were installed. Dr. Henry Barrow operated the mansion as Barrow Manor Convalescent Home from 1924 to 1971. The mansion was demolished after it was purchased in 1971 by St. Christopher's, which sold the land in 2005. It is now being developed as The View at Dobbs Ferry.

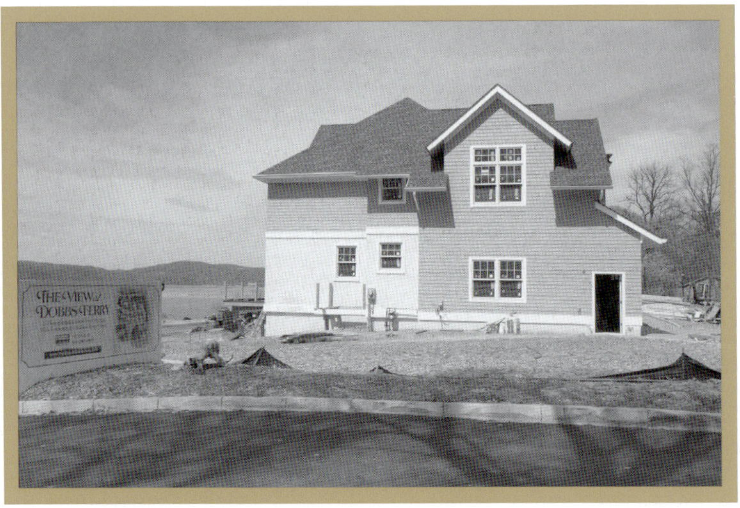

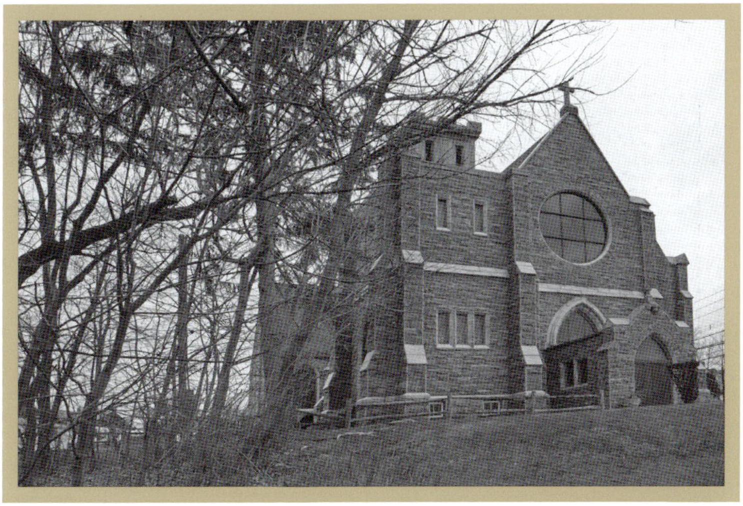

Completing the Gateway on the northwest corner of Broadway and Ashford Avenue is the second church of Sacred Heart parish. It was erected in 1894 on land purchased from Mrs. John J. Storms, a relative of Charles G. Storms, who at that time occupied the former Anthony Inn on the east side of Broadway. Shown here in 1904, the building was dedicated in 1896. (Then image courtesy of Robert Casino.)

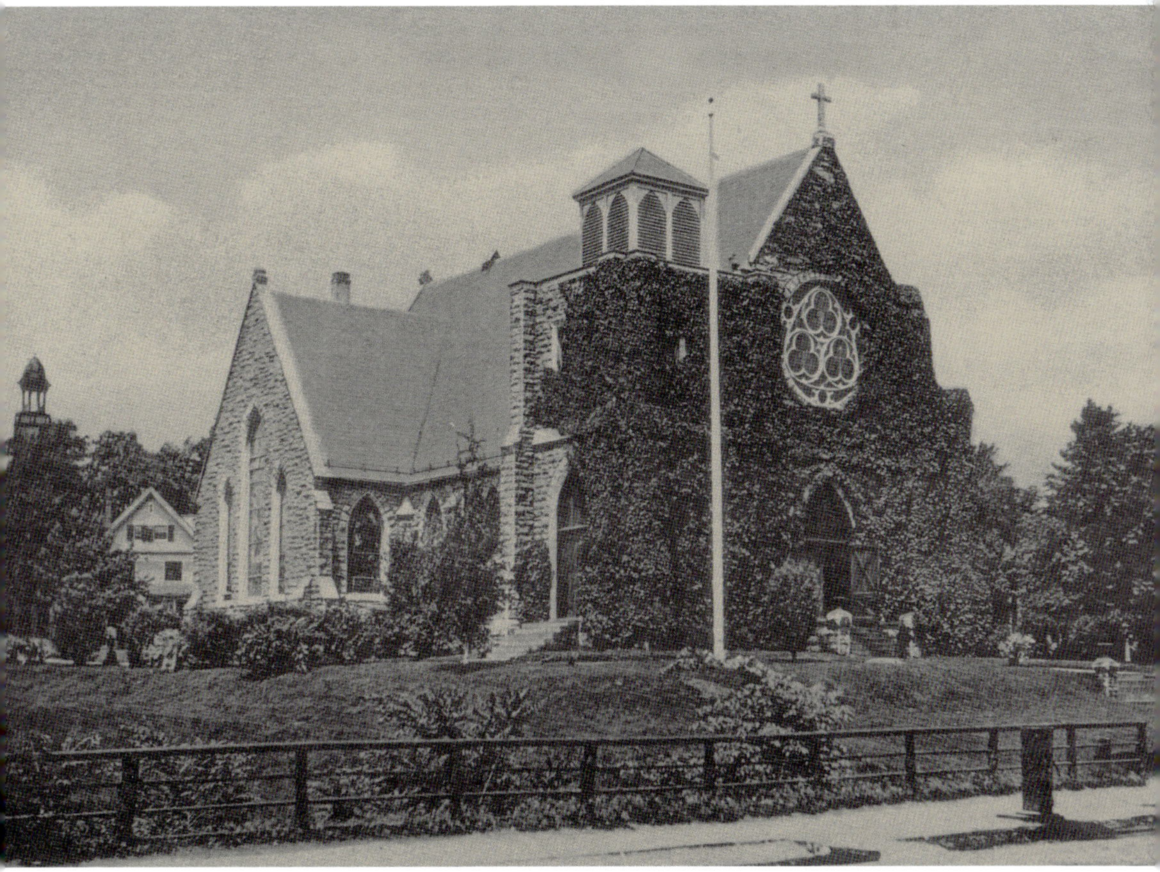

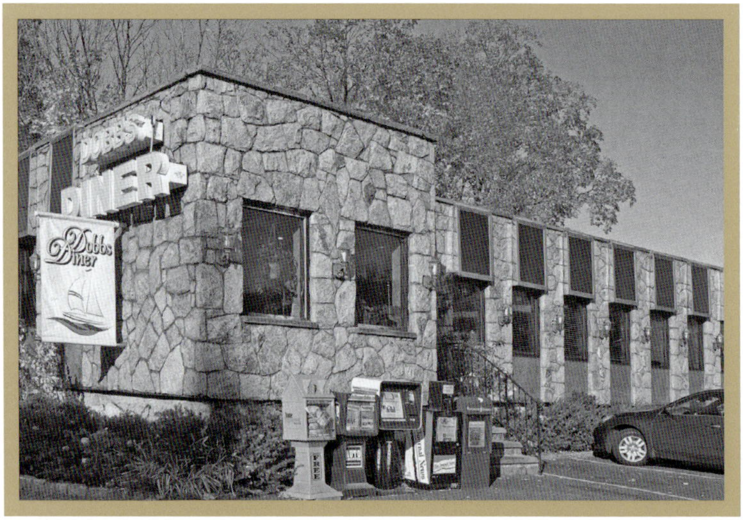

Frank Otero, a World War II veteran, moved to Dobbs Ferry after the war. In 1953, he bought the Mayflower Diner, which had been built in 1923 on a parcel subdivided from the Anthony Inn/Storms homestead along Broadway. In 1956, Otero replaced the old diner with a parking lot and constructed this new steel and glass Kullman Dining Car at 434 Broadway. In 1987, the title passed to the current owners, Aristede and Eleni Garganourakis, who remodeled the structure and renamed it Dobbs Diner.

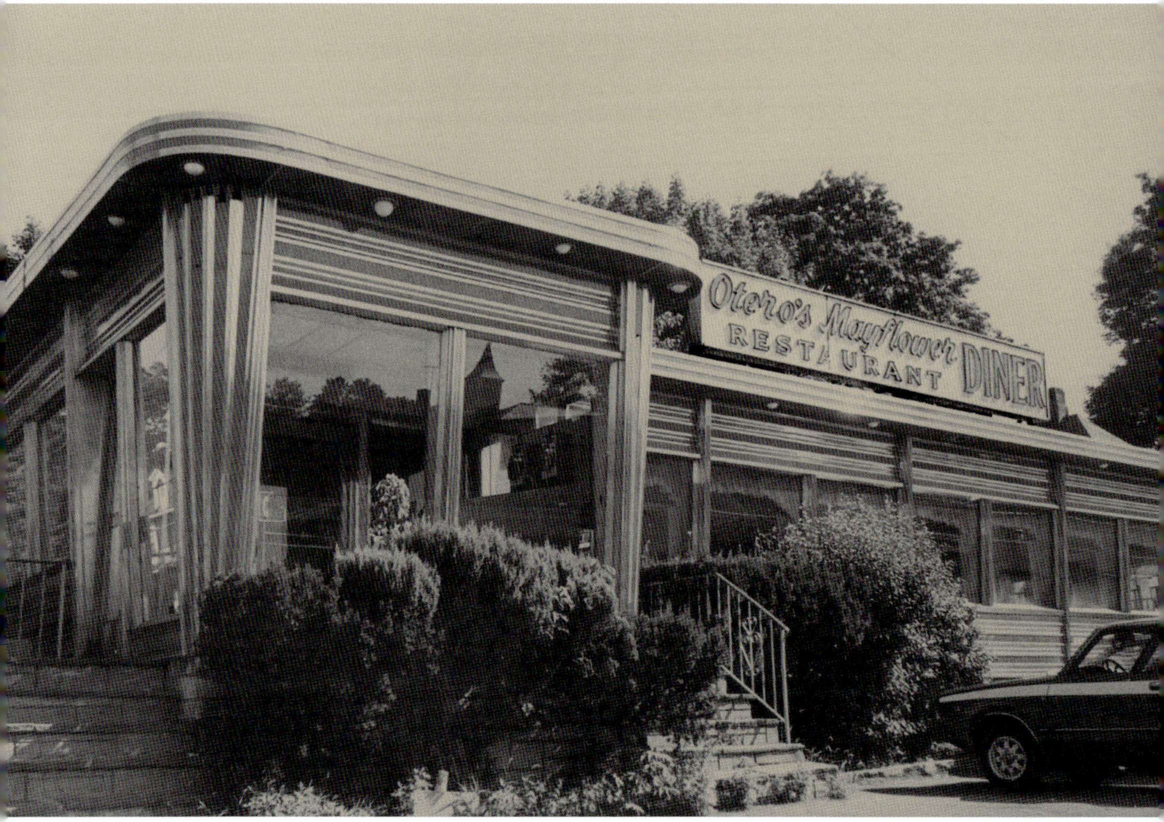

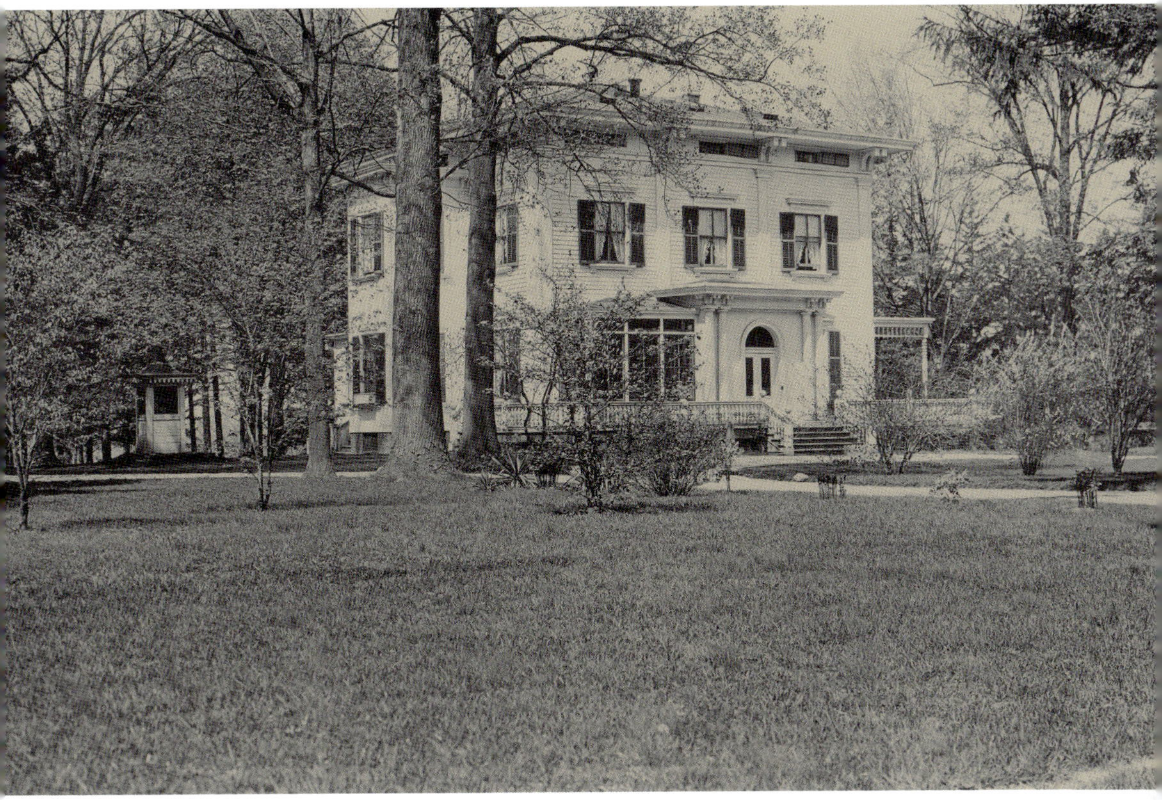

By 1860, the twin estates of T.S. and John William Cooper stood on the west side of Broadway north of the Gateway. In 1897, a new building for the Dobbs Ferry grammar and high schools was erected on the T.S. Cooper estate. The 1897 building became the junior high school in 1934, when a new high school was constructed with help from the Works Progress Administration (WPA) at 505 Broadway. The 1897 building was razed when a new middle school was erected in 1972. Subsequent wings and playing fields have now extended the campus over the John William Cooper estate as well; his mansion, shown here, was located somewhere under the present high school.

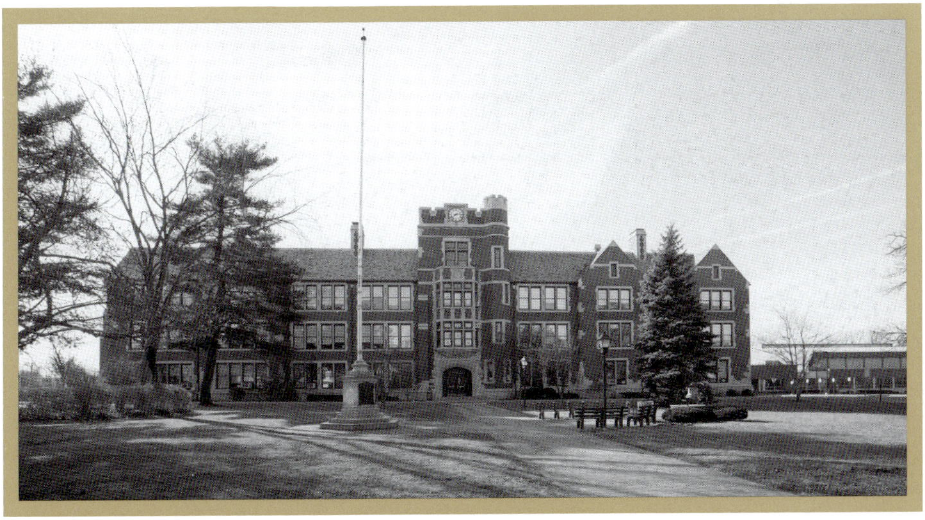

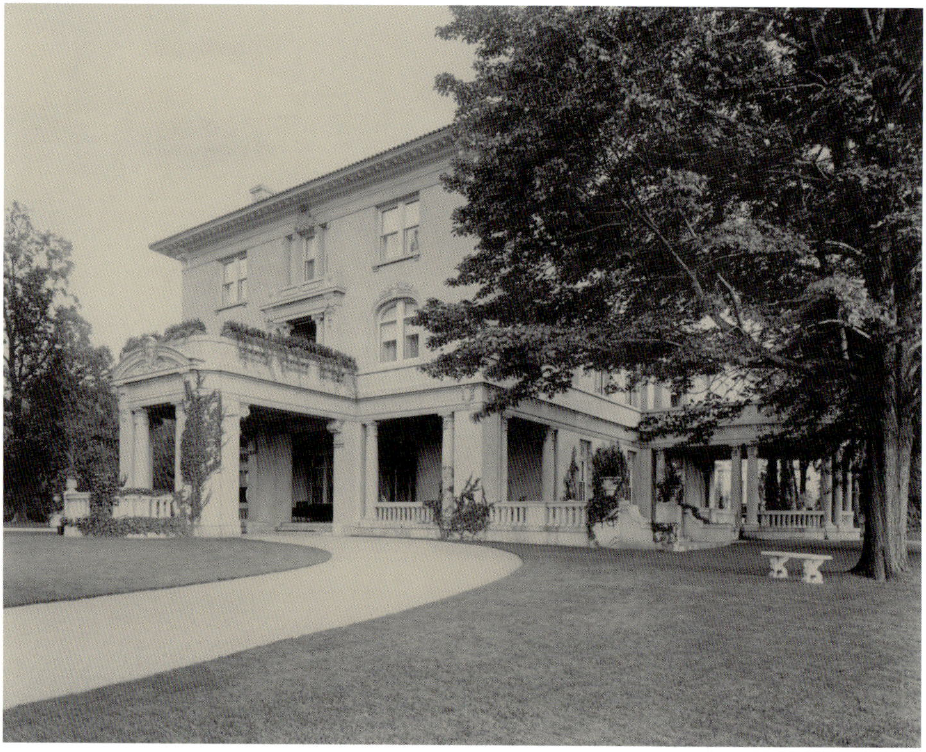

James Wilde Jr., a clothier and the first president of the Greenburgh Savings Bank, established Midgrove in 1850 on property now occupied by Mercy College and The Landing condominiums. Samuel Thomas, a Civil War brigadier general, railroad builder, and founder of the Ardsley Club, purchased the estate in 1882. In 1902, it passed to industrialist Jay Gould's son Edwin who remodeled it. Dormitories now occupy the site.

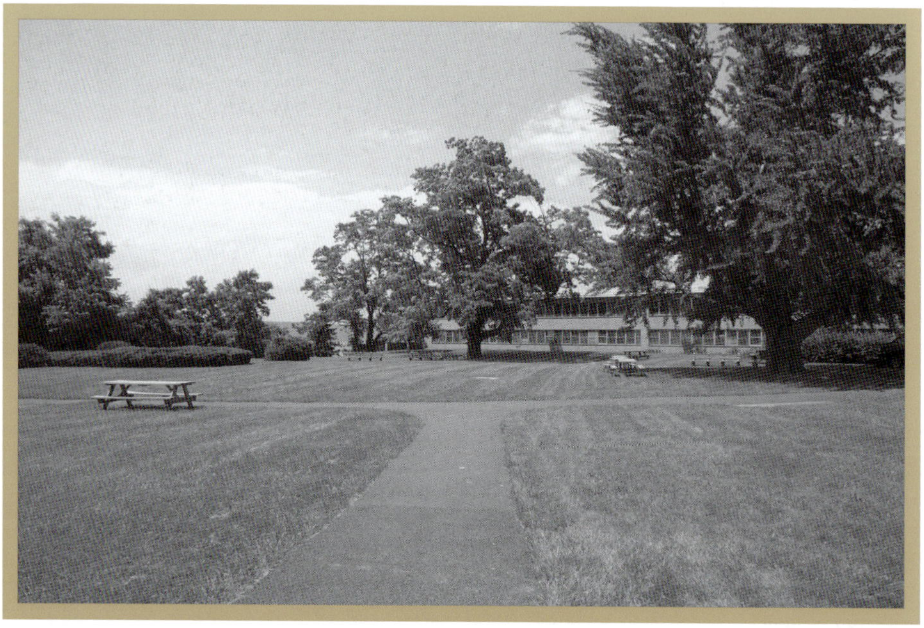

CHAPTER 3

NORTH AND EAST ENDS

BELDEN PARK AND ARDSLEY PARK, ASHFORD AVENUE, AND CHAUNCEY

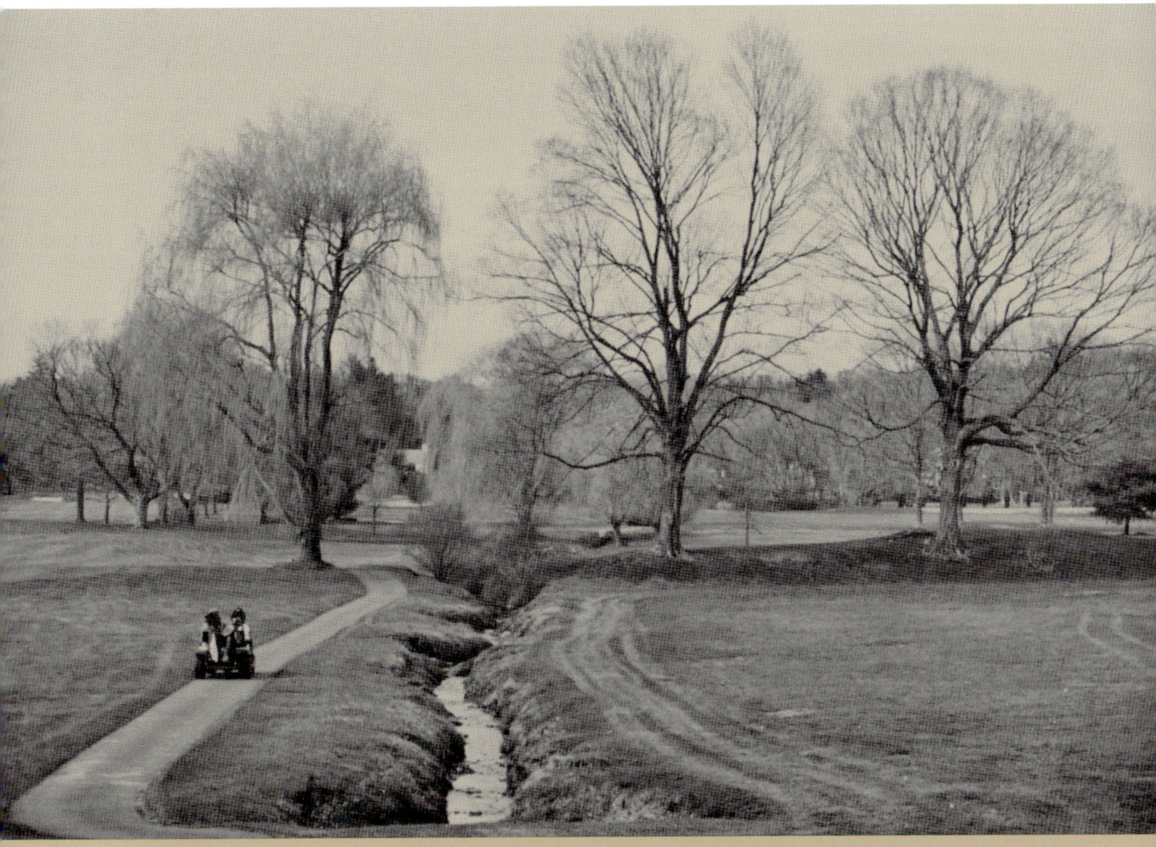

The second nine of the Ardsley Club golf course was laid out in 1897 in the Dobbs Ferry portion of Cyrus W. Field's vast estate. The northeast end of the village soon became part of the Ardsley Park development, except for the estate therein, which since 1865 had belonged to Field's brother David Dudley Fields and his wife, Laura Belden Fields. It was subdivided in 1880 into Dudley Park, which was later changed to Belden Park. The remainder of the northeast end lies along Ashford Avenue and the Saw Mill River Parkway. (Then image courtesy of Anne Marie Leone.)

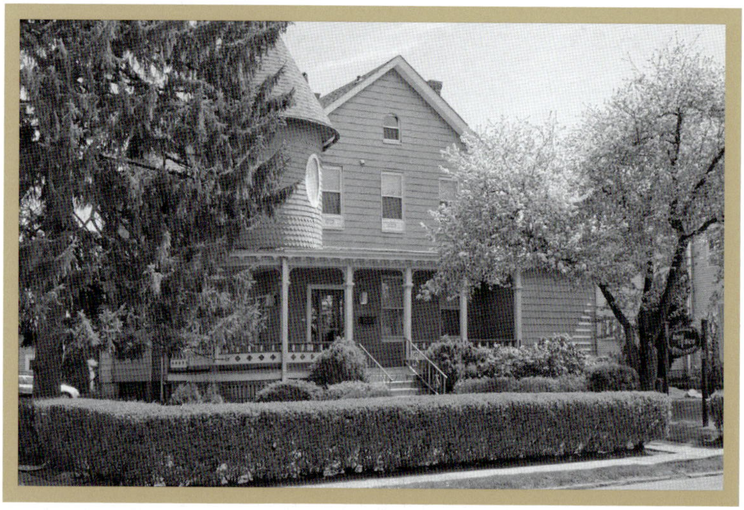

This 1890 Belden Park dwelling, which served as the third rectory of the Sacred Heart Church from 1905 to 1970, stands at 468 Broadway, with Terri Optics on the first floor and living quarters above. The rectory was purchased in 1970 by Dr. Joseph Gelsi, an optometrist who conducted his practice in the building. (Then image courtesy of Teresa Gelsi.)

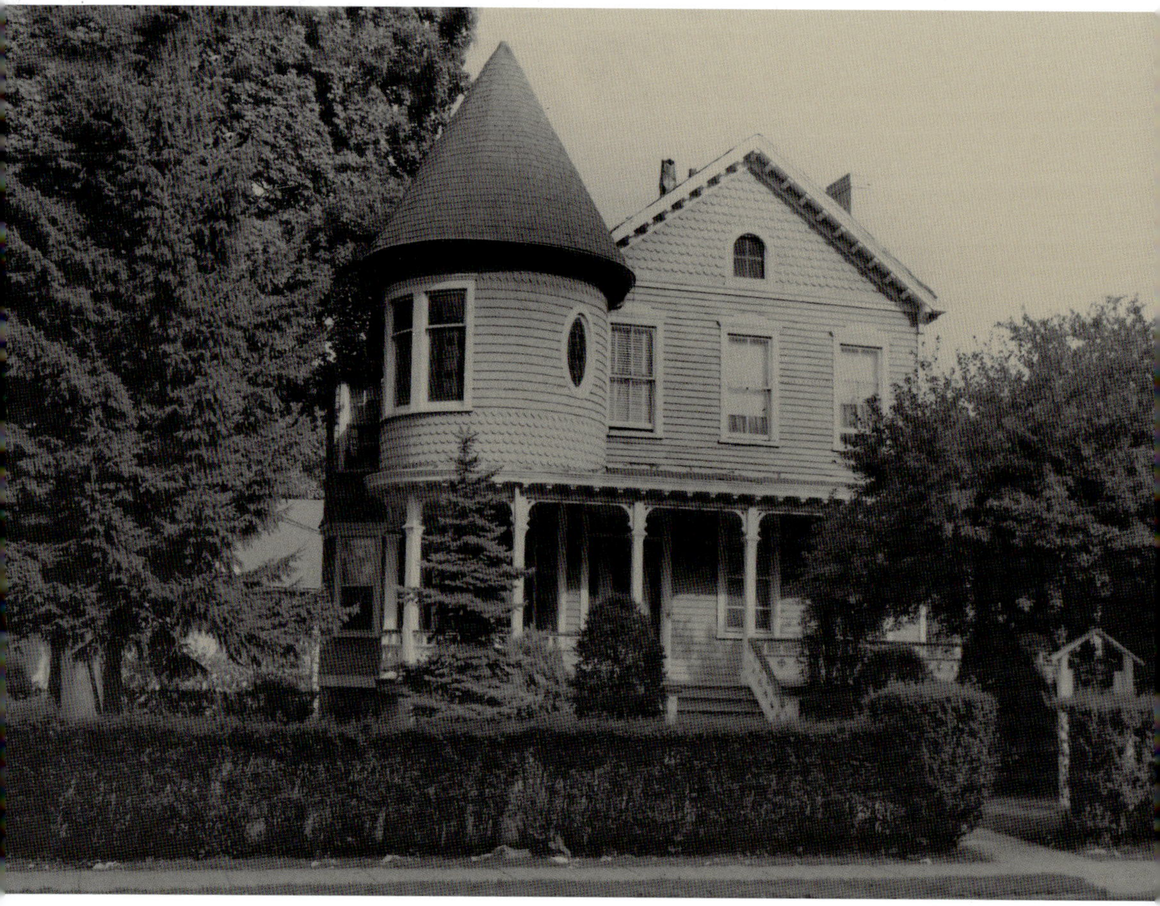

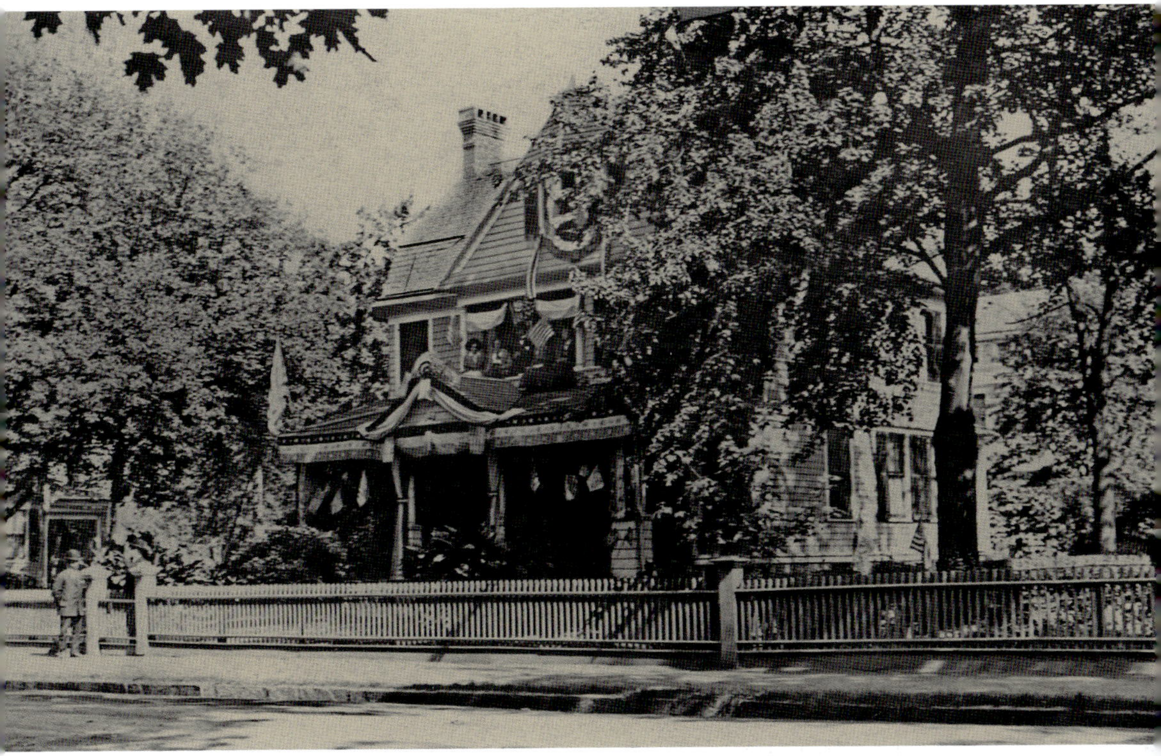

Grocer Thomas Losee Jr., a member of a large clan of local businessmen and bankers, and his heirs owned this 1892 residence at 480 Broadway in Belden Park until 1954, when it was purchased by Samuel Untracht, a pediatrician and allergist who used it as his home and office for half a century.

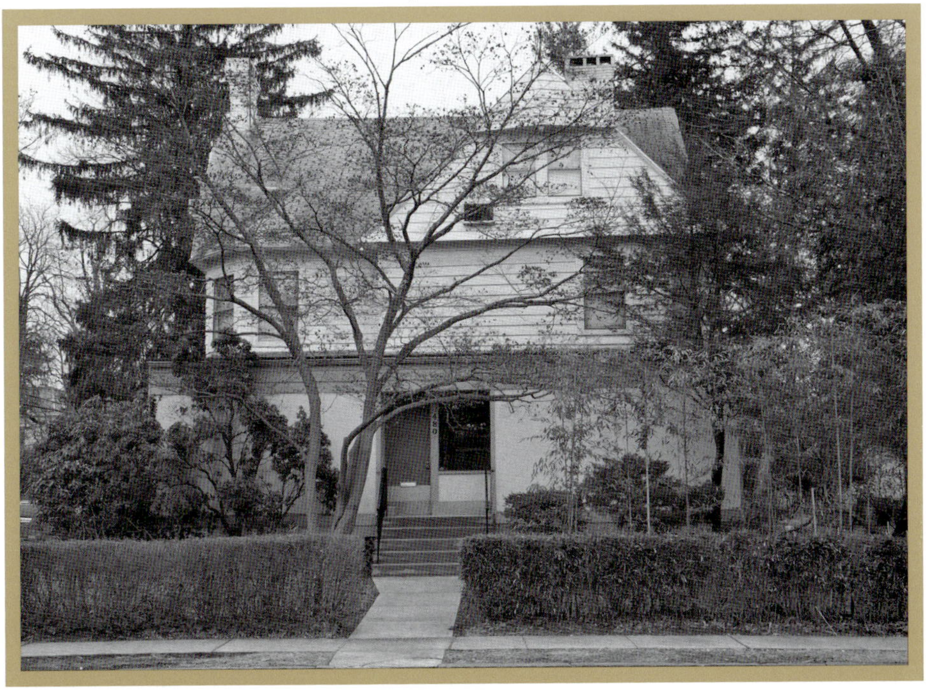

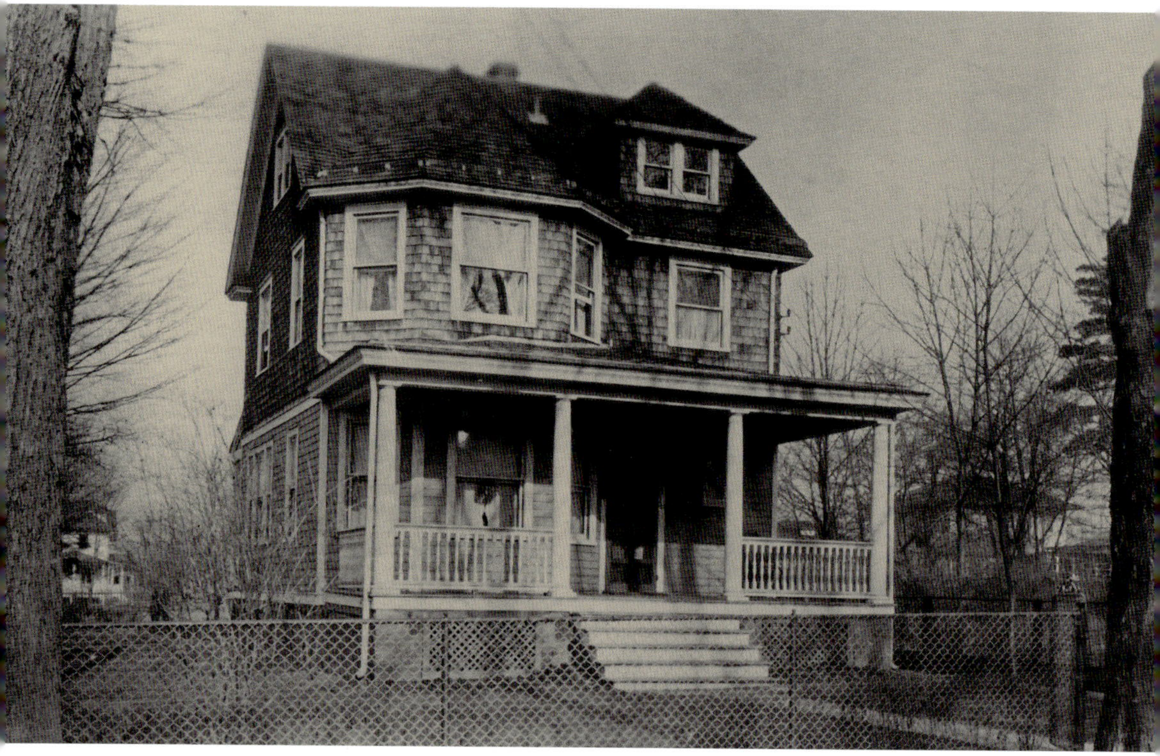

In 1917, this house was built at 17 Belden Avenue for John and Margaret Monahan, who worked on the property of the Masters School. After Margaret died in 1946, their son Raymond moved in with his wife, Kay, and their family. Brian Monahan, who grew up to be a Dobbs Ferry mayor, was born to them two years later; he remembers breaking his collarbone in the backyard while practicing to be an acrobat. (Then image courtesy of Brian Monahan.)

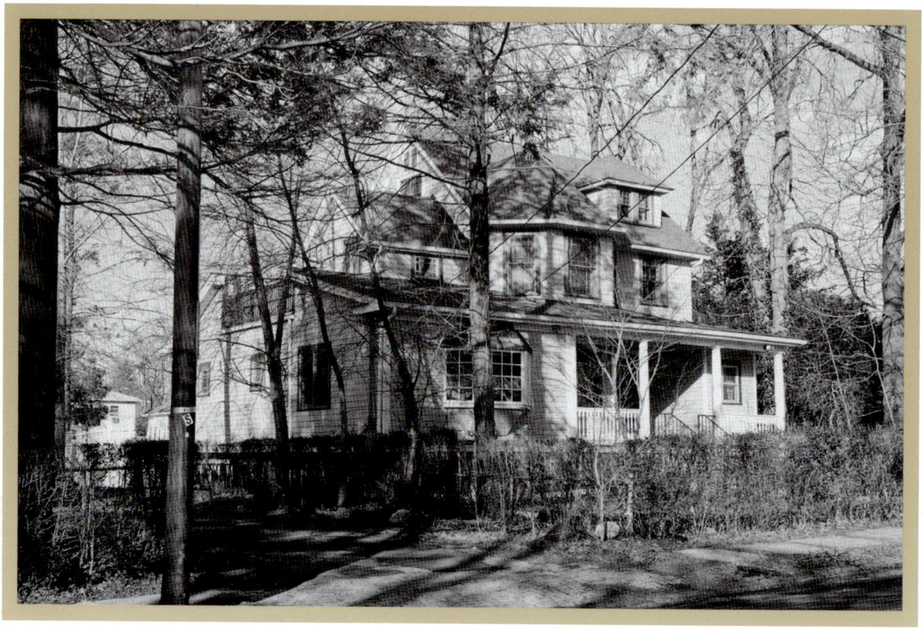

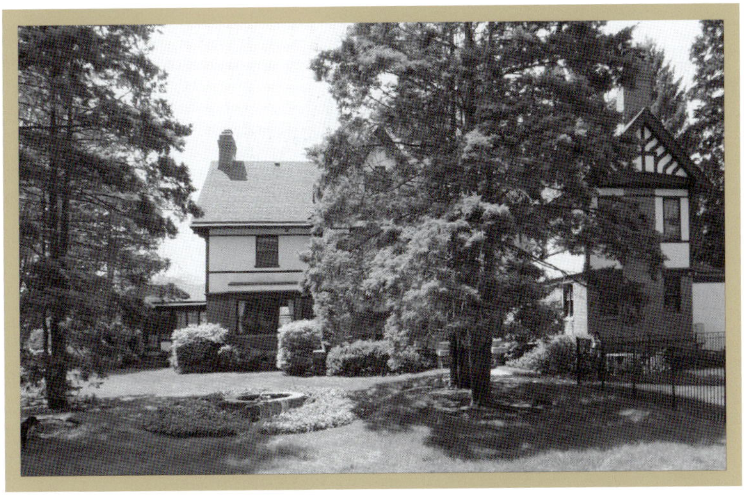

The first residence in Ardsley Park, 130 Washington Avenue, was built in 1899 on property leased to the Ardsley Country Club by the Dobbs Ferry Land and Improvement Company. It served as a model home for the development, which overlapped the Dobbs Ferry border with Irvington, and as guest quarters for the club until it was sold to Isabel and Edward Morrison in 1904. The design has been attributed to Samuel Breck Trowbridge, designer of the Newport Casino. The rear view is seen here. (Then image courtesy of Eden Anker).

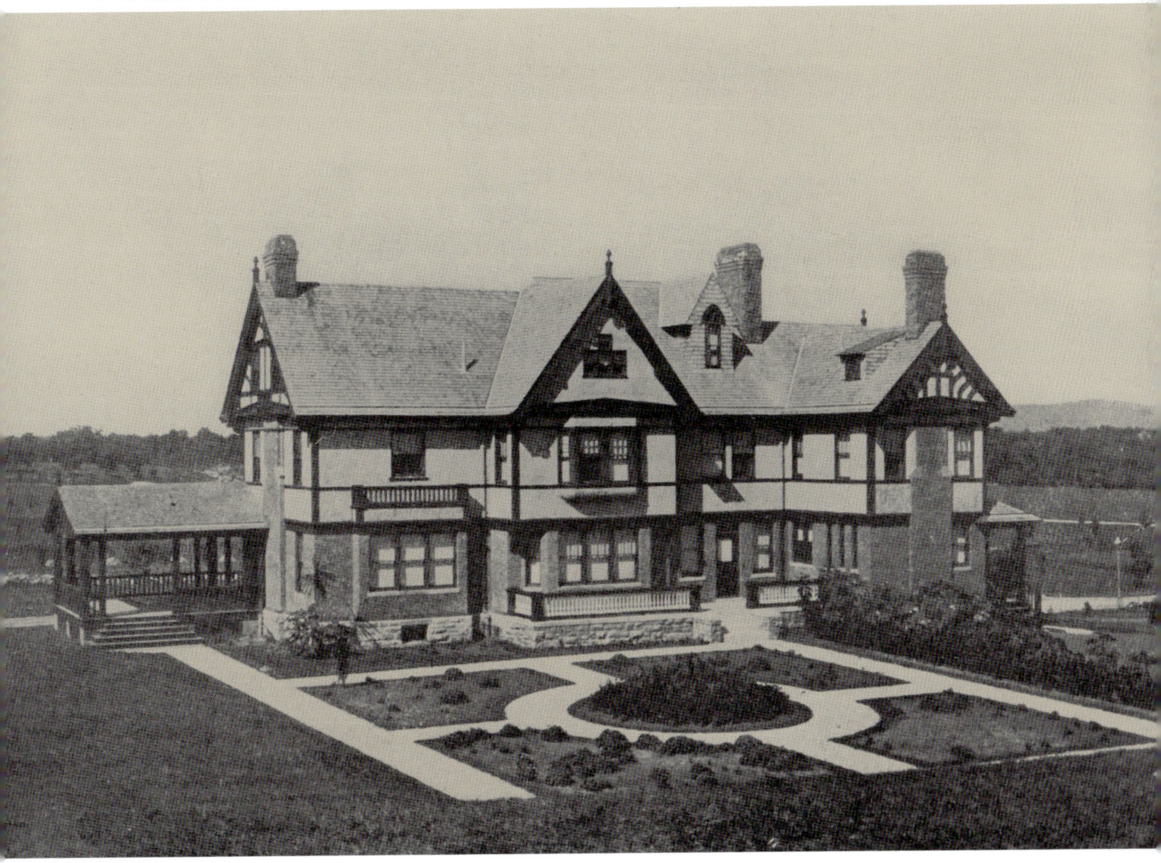

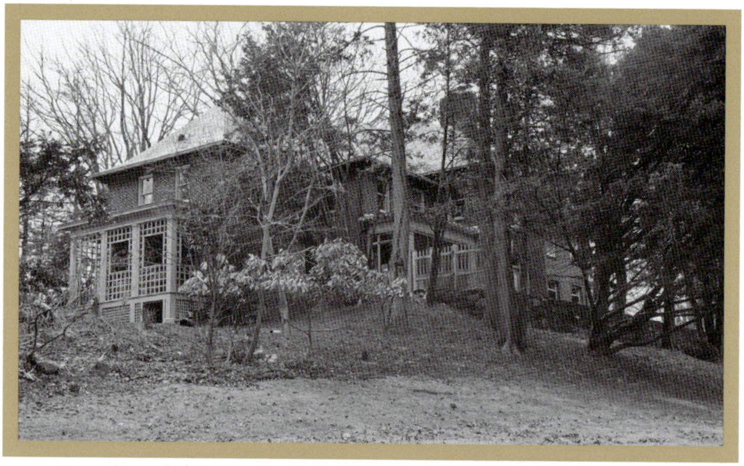

The mansion at 86 Belden Avenue, at the end of a private driveway off Washington Avenue, in Ardsley Park was built in 1917 for Robert J. Eidlitz, the nephew and cousin of famed architects Leopold and Cyrus Eidlitz. Robert and his father were partners in Marc Eidlitz and Son Builders. The vintage photograph records the topping-out ceremony, when the framing of the roof was completed. Note the small tree nailed to the ridgepole. (Then image courtesy of Tracy Halpern.)

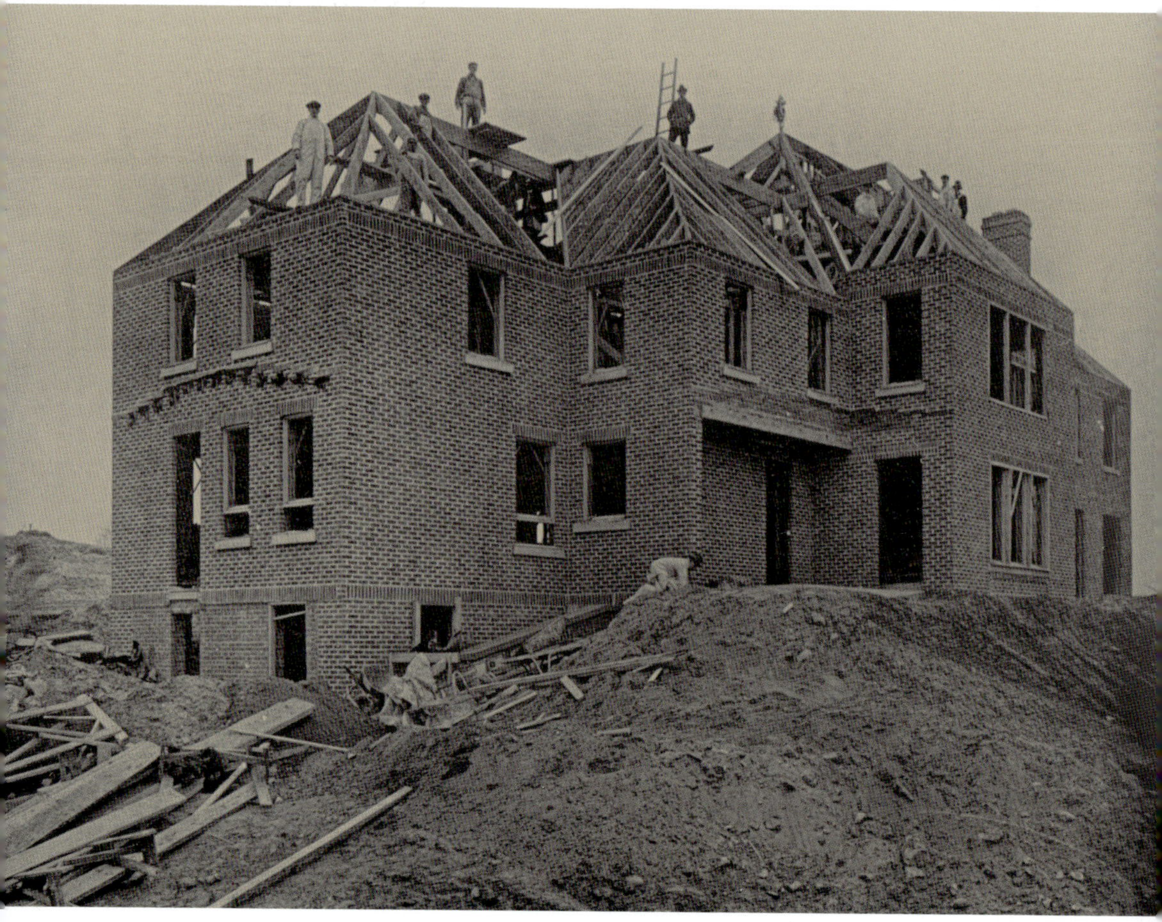

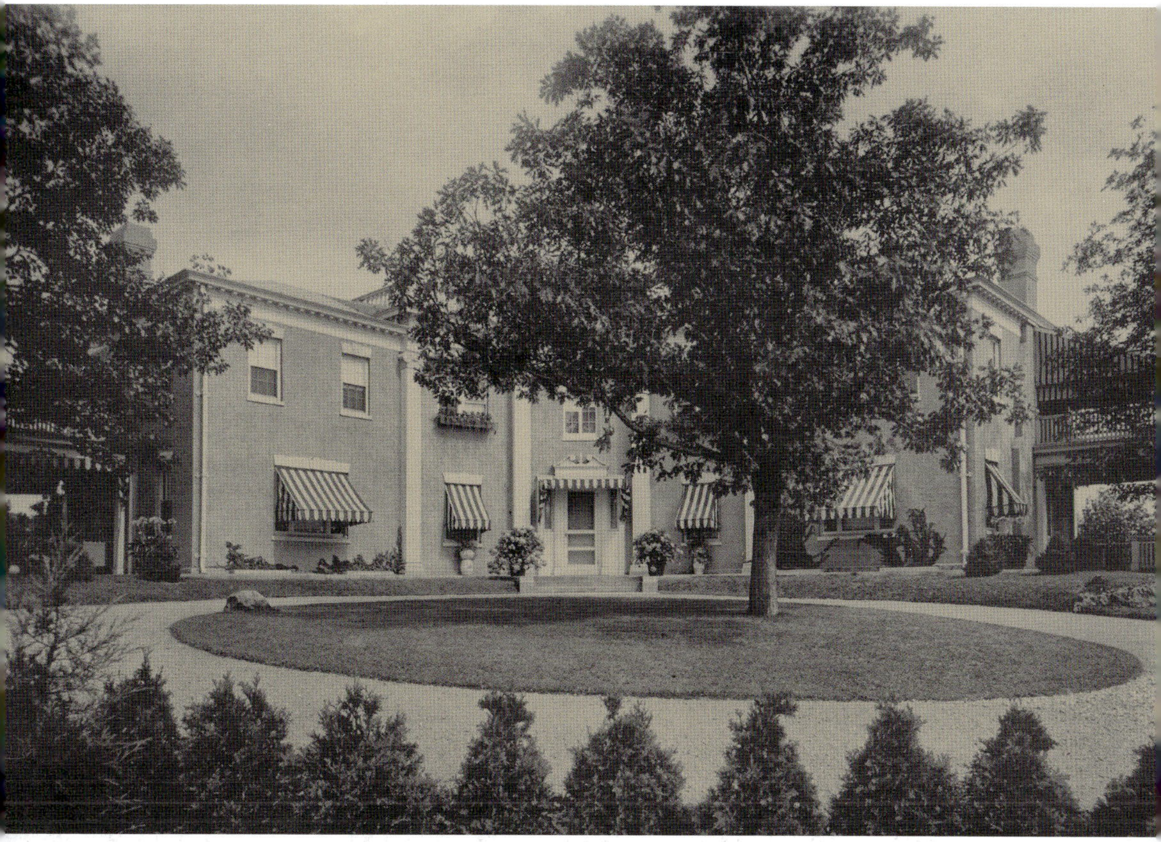

In 1902, Dr. George F. Shrady, the father-in-law of Edwin Gould, converted an old estate into his summer home, Upaway. Dr. Shrady, for whom a street in the Bronx is named, edited the *NY Medical Record*. The residence burned in 1931 and was demolished in 1941. Its site was annexed to land dedicated in 1996 as the Juhring Estate Woodland Preserve, named for John C. Juhring, a wholesale grocer, and his son of the same name, a landscape architect, who owned most of the property from 1909 to 1958.

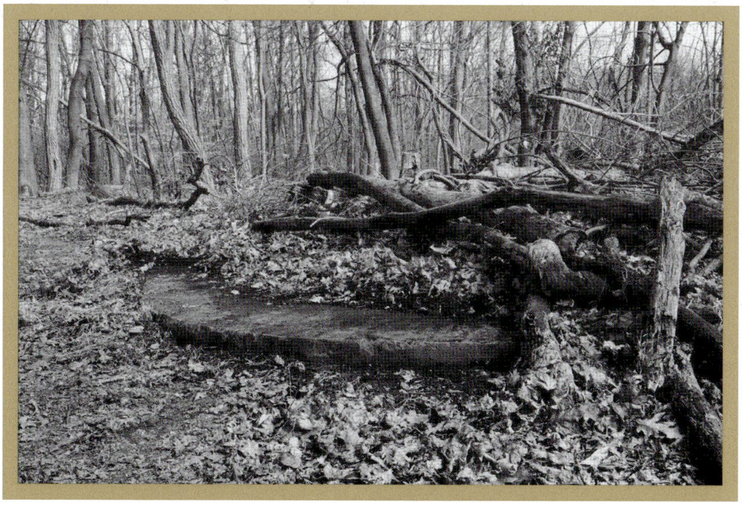

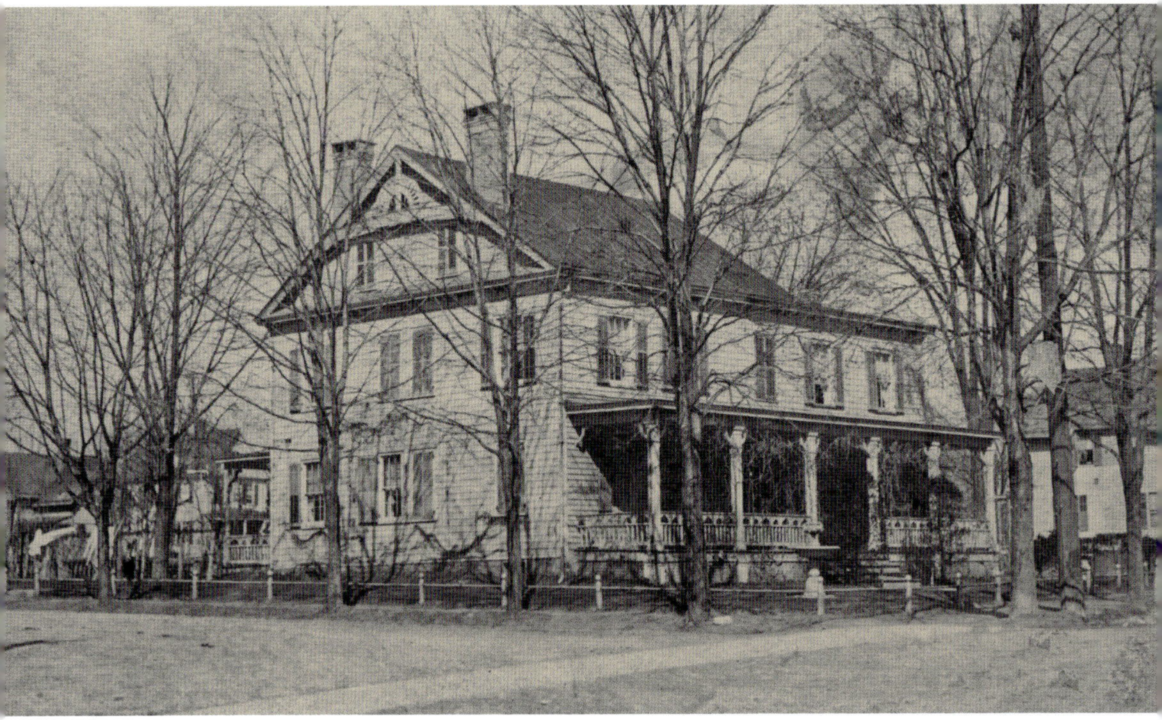

Jacob Storms acquired 329 acres of Philipsburg Manor in 1785, and in 1820, his grandson Anthony built the Anthony Inn on the northeast corner of Broadway and Ashford Avenue to serve travelers between New York City and Albany and for use as a post office and community center. By 1900, the inn had become the home of Charles G. Storms, the village president. In 1933, it was replaced by a gas station adjoined by a Mayflower Diner and an A&P.

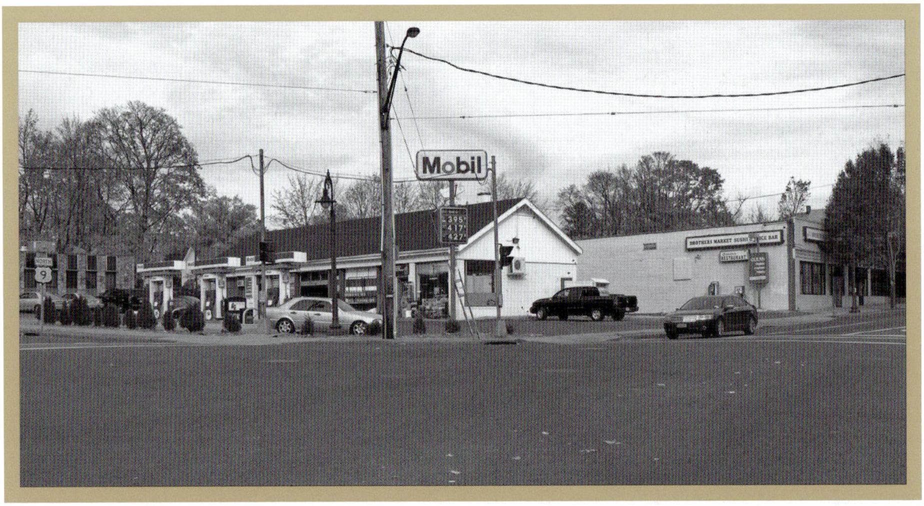

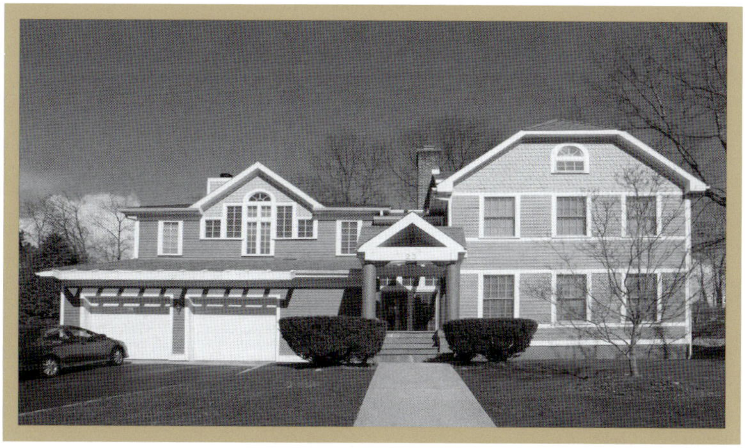

David Ravekes, whose father, John Henry Ravekes, had established a tailor shop on Main Street in 1874, moved his 1880 house from 17 Ashford Avenue to 23 Bellewood Avenue in 1954. David married Lily Storms, a member of Dobbs Ferry's oldest family, and became a vice president of the Dobbs Ferry Bank. The house on its new site was purchased in 1986 by Dobbs Ferry mayor Charles Lester, an architect, who remodeled the old house and more than doubled it in size.

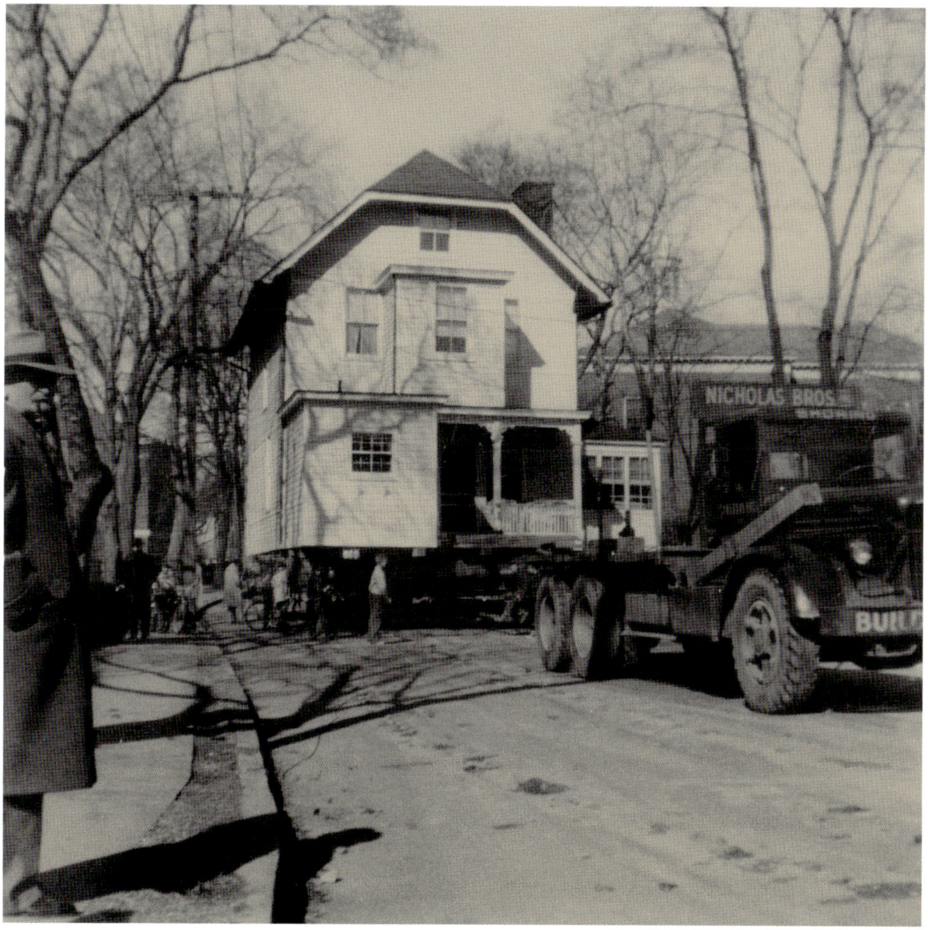

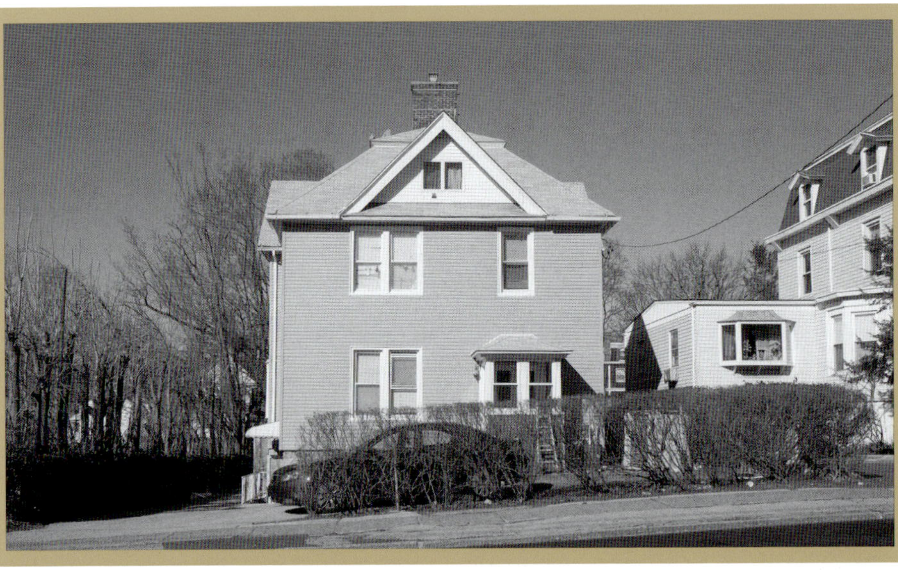

The 10-room William H. Wright family home at 23 Ashford Avenue is typical of the commodious single-family middle-class homes built along Ashford Avenue after the Civil War. Wright, a county Democratic committeeman, died in 1919, and the house was sold to Charles E. Miller. It now accommodates five families. At left in the vintage photograph is the Ravekes home, moved in 1954 to make way for a parking lot. (Then image courtesy of Patricia Arone.)

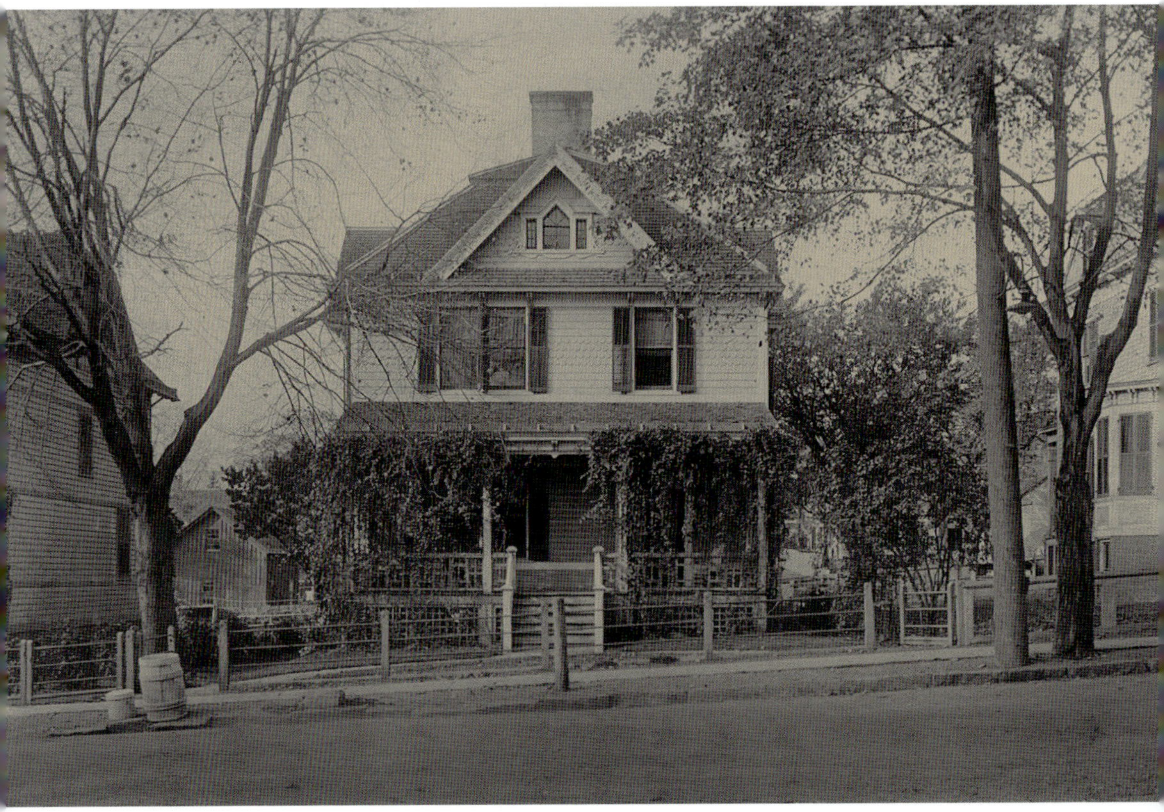

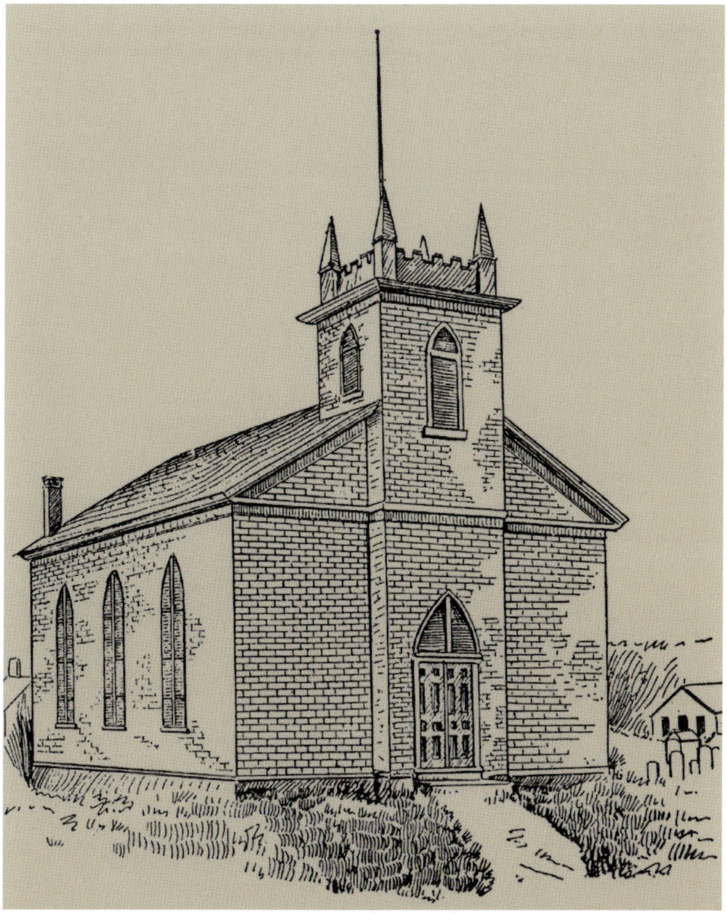

This etching depicts the first building of the South Presbyterian congregation, constructed in 1823 facing Ashford Avenue east of Storm Street, as brick, whereas records describe it as a wooden building painted white, hence its popular name, the Little White Church. Used until 1869, when the congregation moved to Broadway, the church was dismantled in 1883 and the land was sold to Jane Sarah Mabie, wife of Dr. Champion Judson, for a hospital site. The Dobbs Ferry Lutheran Church stands there today.

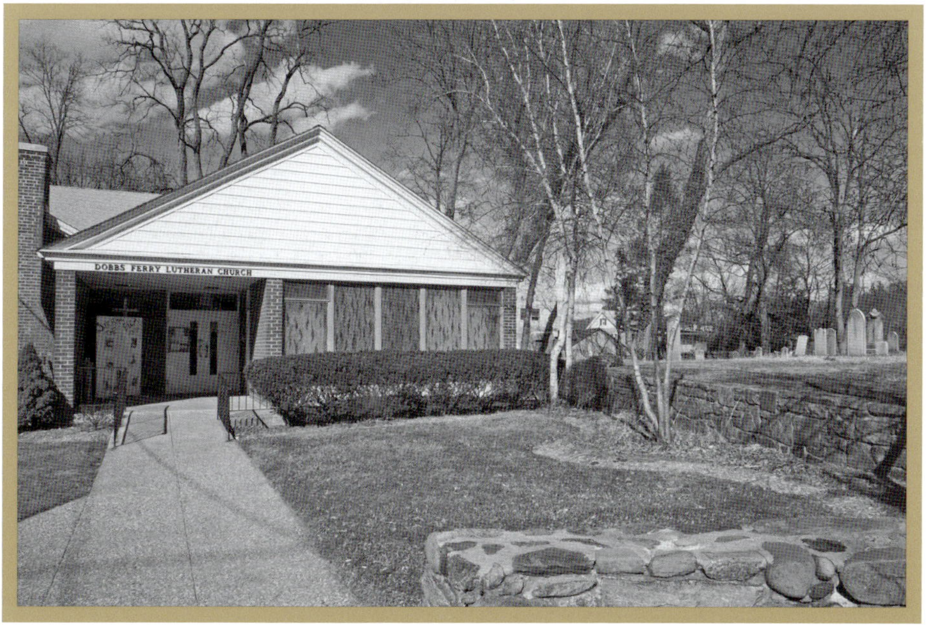

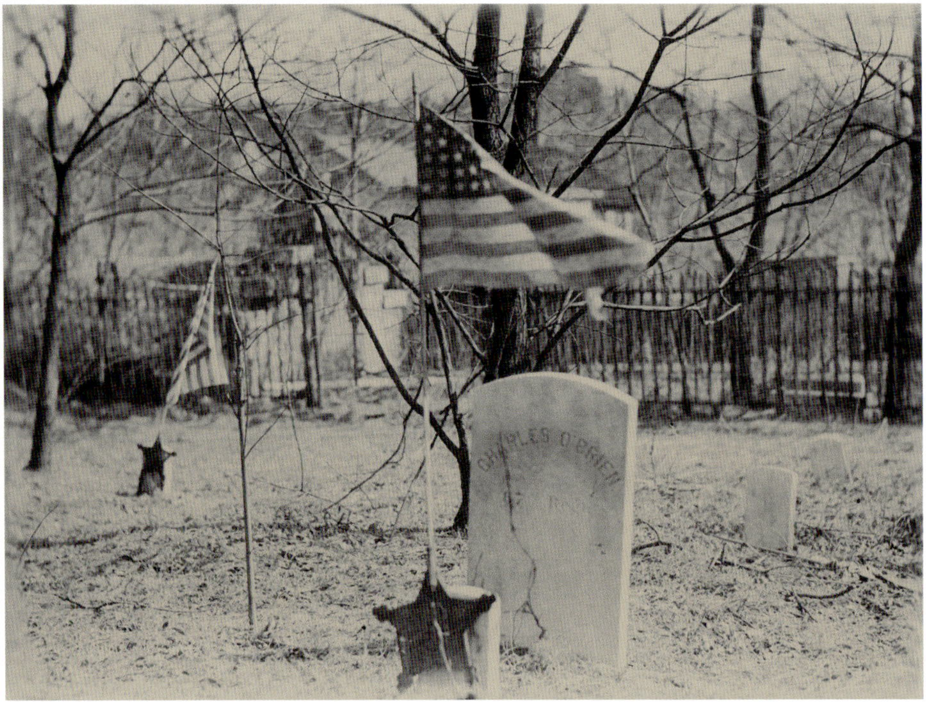

Martin Lefurgy, who had owned this ancient community burying ground on Ashford Avenue adjoining the Little White Church near the corner of Storm Street since 1785, donated it to the Presbyterian congregation in 1823. The Presbyterians deeded it to Dobbs Ferry in 1962. The last burial occurred in 1886. Civil War grave markers and 48-star flags appear in the vintage photograph, from about 1930. Charles O'Brien's headstone could not be found in 2012.

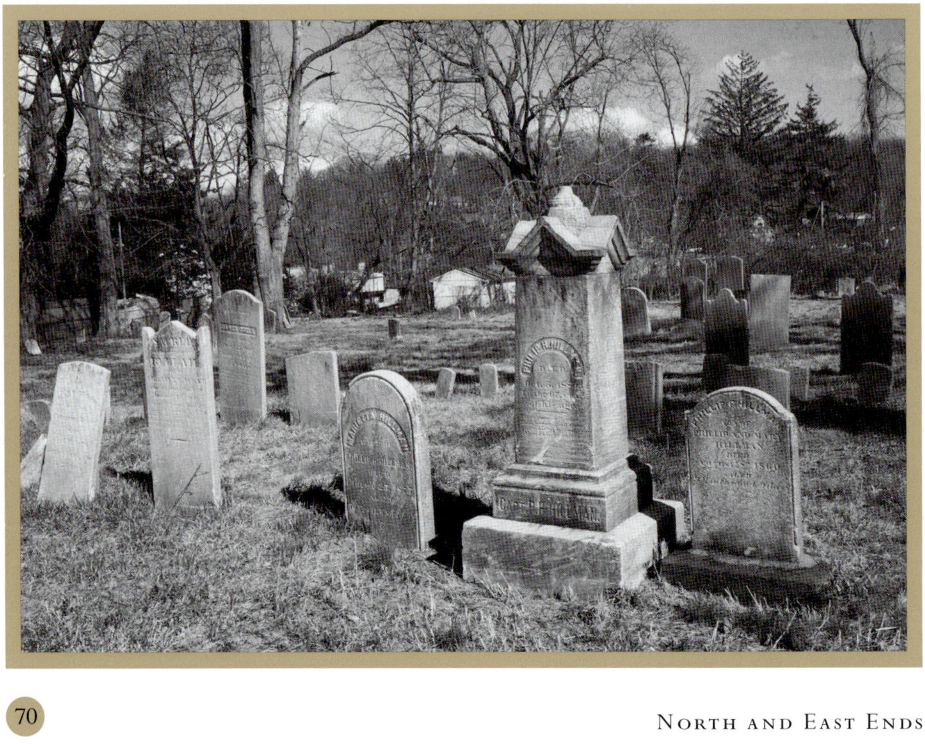

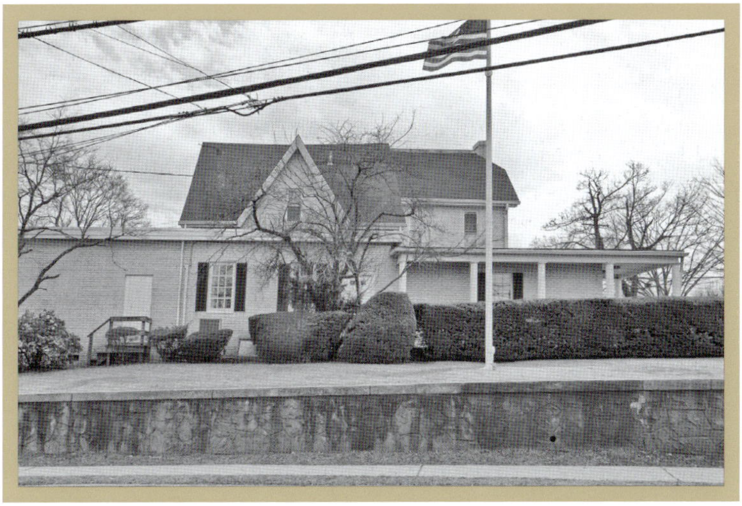

Ogden S. and David Ogden Bradley owned this residence at 64 Ashford Avenue and many surrounding acres in the 19th century. M.J. Francis was the homeowner when this photograph was taken in the early 20th century. Bertsil Edwards founded a funeral home in the dwelling in 1927. A remodeling around 1960 eliminated the Carpenter Gothic porch and trim, but the original gables and roofline can still be discerned. It has been the Edwards Dowdle Funeral Home since 1989. (Then image courtesy of Patricia Arone.)

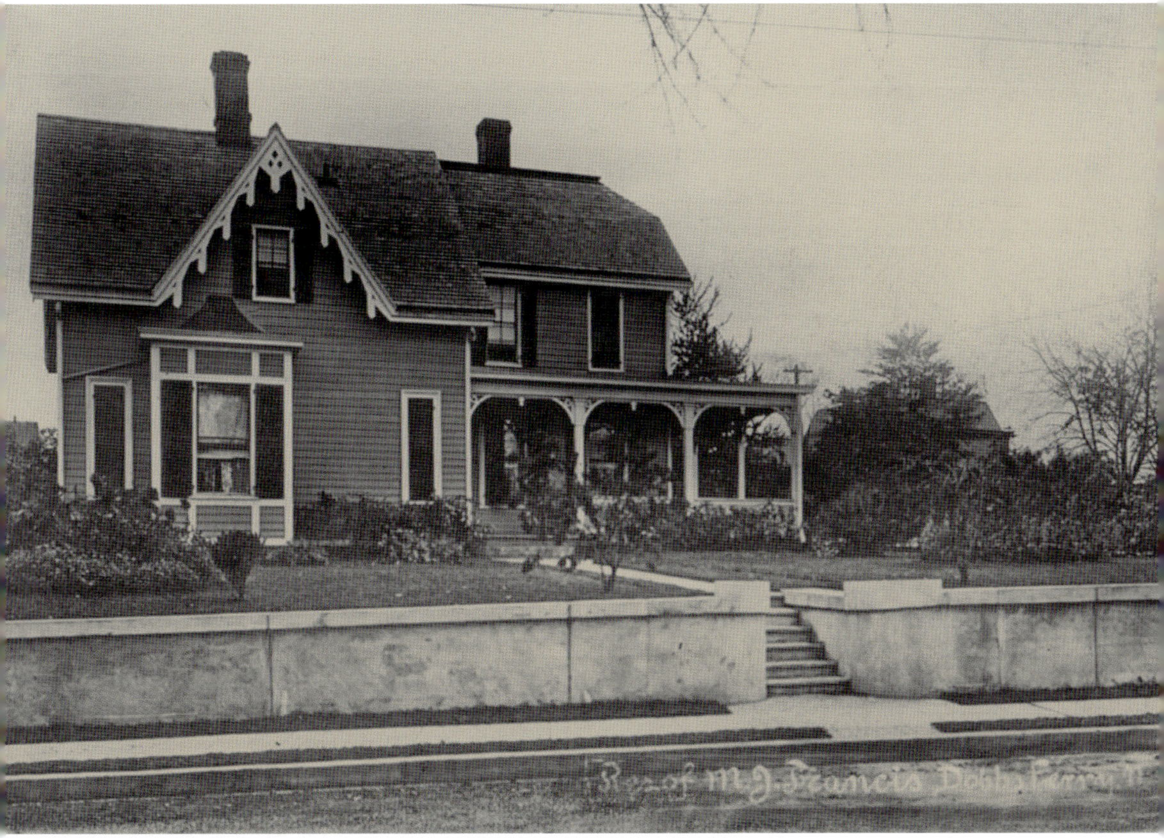

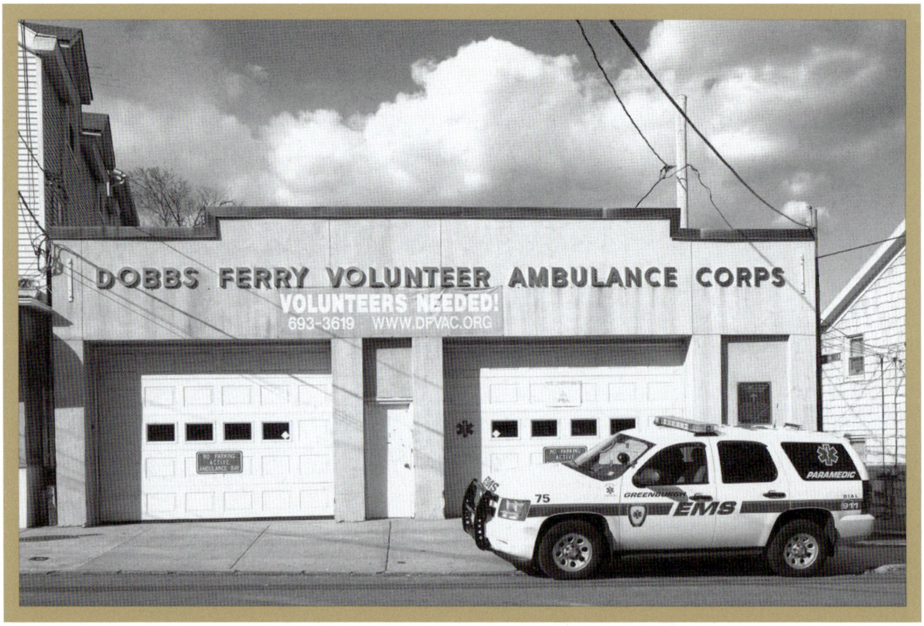

Edwards Funeral home made its 1948 Cadillac hearse available to transport any patients in need of a stretcher. George Keiling was the volunteer driver from 1953 until 1962, when the Dobbs Ferry Volunteer Ambulance Corps was established in the bicycle shop that housed the hearse. Nurse Peggy Moynihan (second from left) spearheaded the project and was the first captain. The Ambulance Corps' own building was constructed at 81 Ashford Avenue in 1963. (Then image courtesy of Dobbs Ferry Ambulance Corps.)

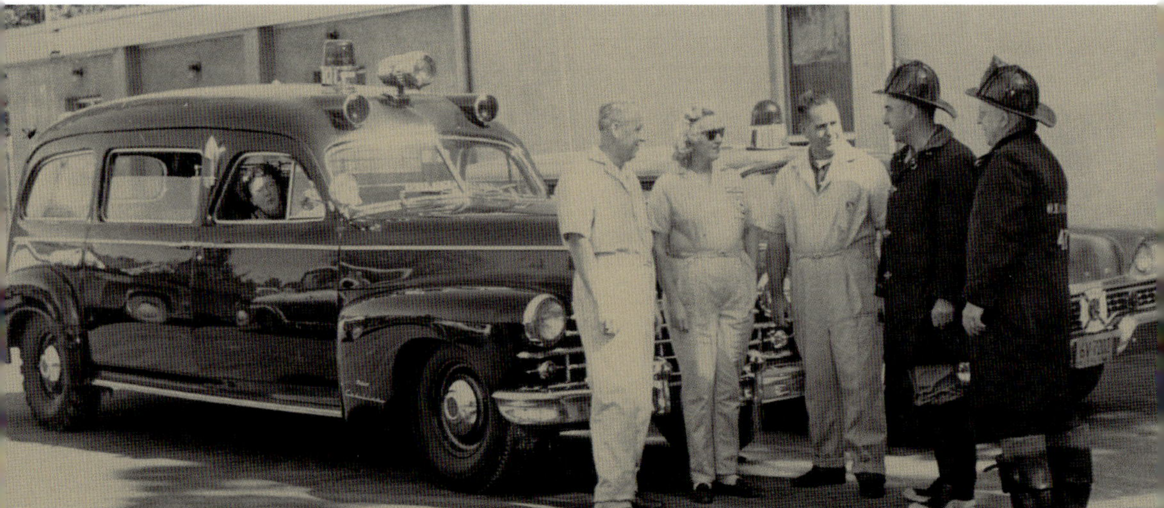

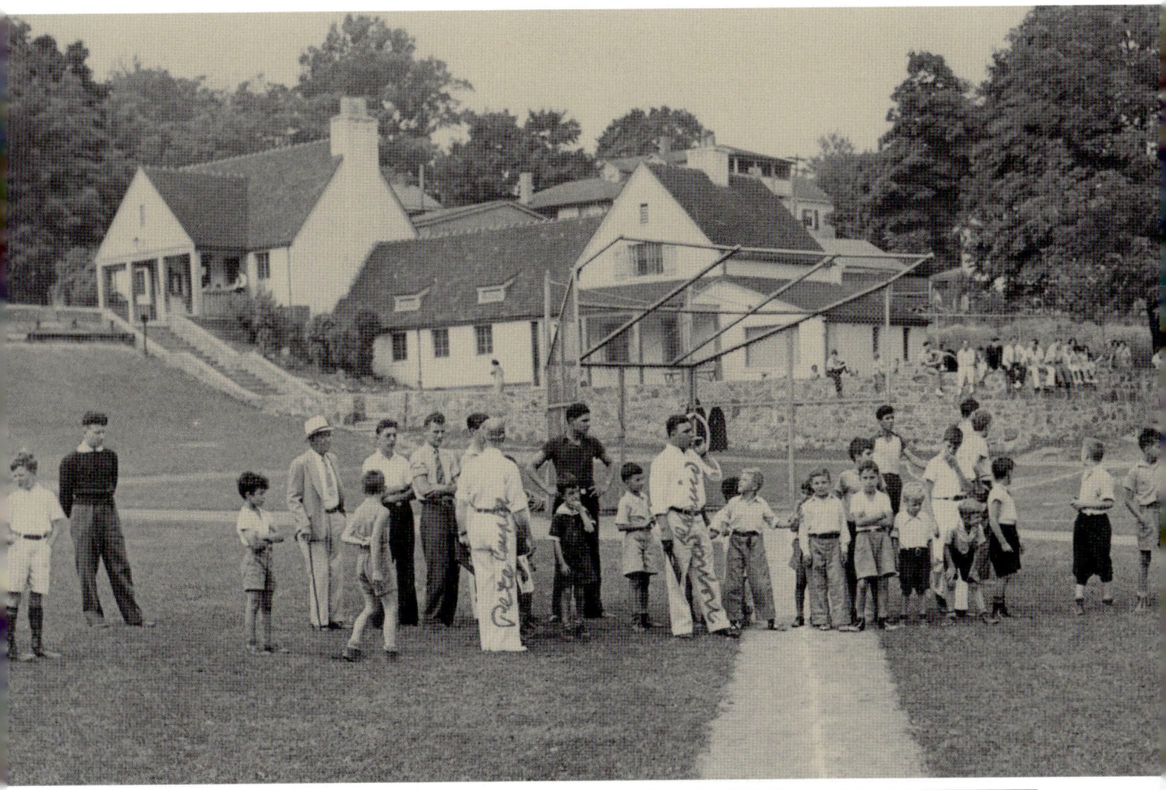

Edwin Gould, the owner of a riverfront Dobbs Ferry estate and the son of robber baron Jay Gould—the master of Lyndhurst in Tarrytown—donated 6.5 acres of prime Belden Park land for Gould Park on Ashford Avenue in 1924. By 1936, when this photograph was taken, the park contained spacious playing fields and an expanded field house.

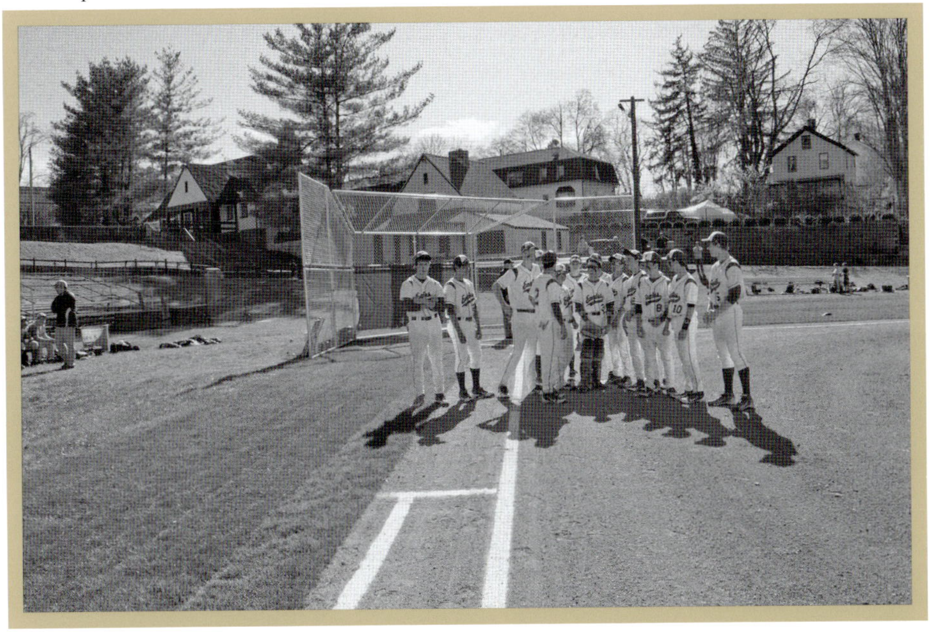

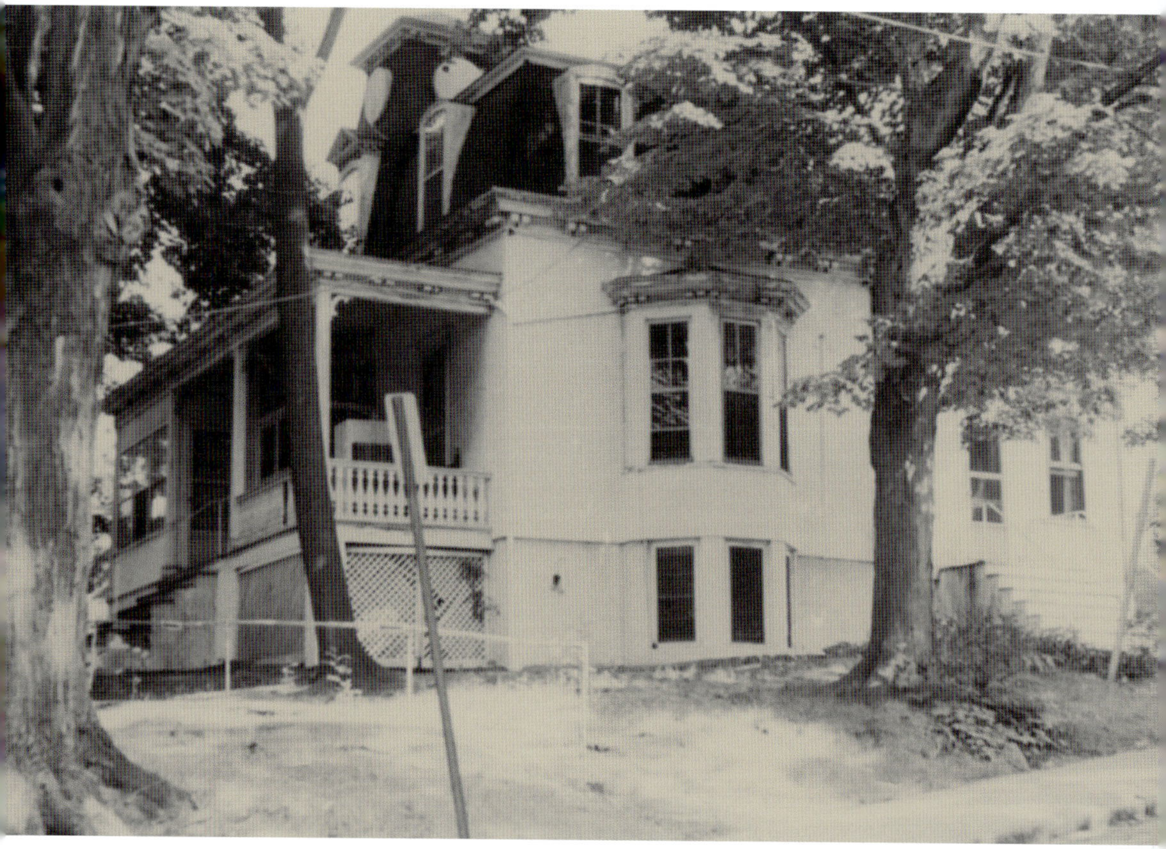

Dobbs Ferry Hospital originated in 1893 when Dr. Champion H. Judson outfitted a small building at Ashford Avenue and Storm Street with four beds for indigent patients. The cornerstone was laid for a new building across the street in 1902. The adjacent 1870 residence of Ogden S. Bradley, the superintendent of the Greenburgh section of the Croton Aqueduct, was acquired at the same time. The house was razed in 1981, and new buildings were constructed for what is now the Dobbs Ferry Pavilion of St. John's Riverside Hospital.

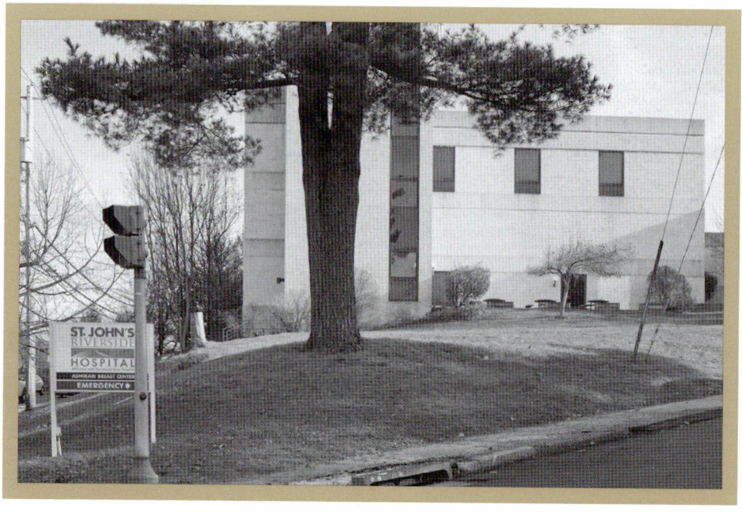

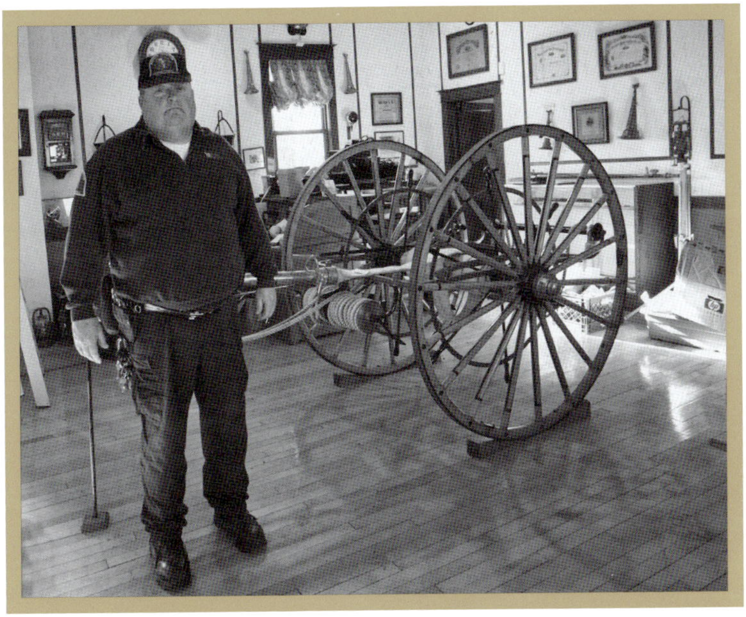

This hand-pulled jumper was the first piece of apparatus owned by Ogden Hose Company No. 3, founded in 1898. The company, now Ogden Engine No. 1, took its name from the neighborhood, largely owned in the 19th century by David Ogden Bradley, a proud descendant of John Ogden, "the Wandering Puritan," who settled several communities in New Jersey. Capt. Jerry McIlvain poses with the jumper in 2011 in the Museum of Firefighting on the second floor of the Ogden firehouse at 203 Ashford Avenue.

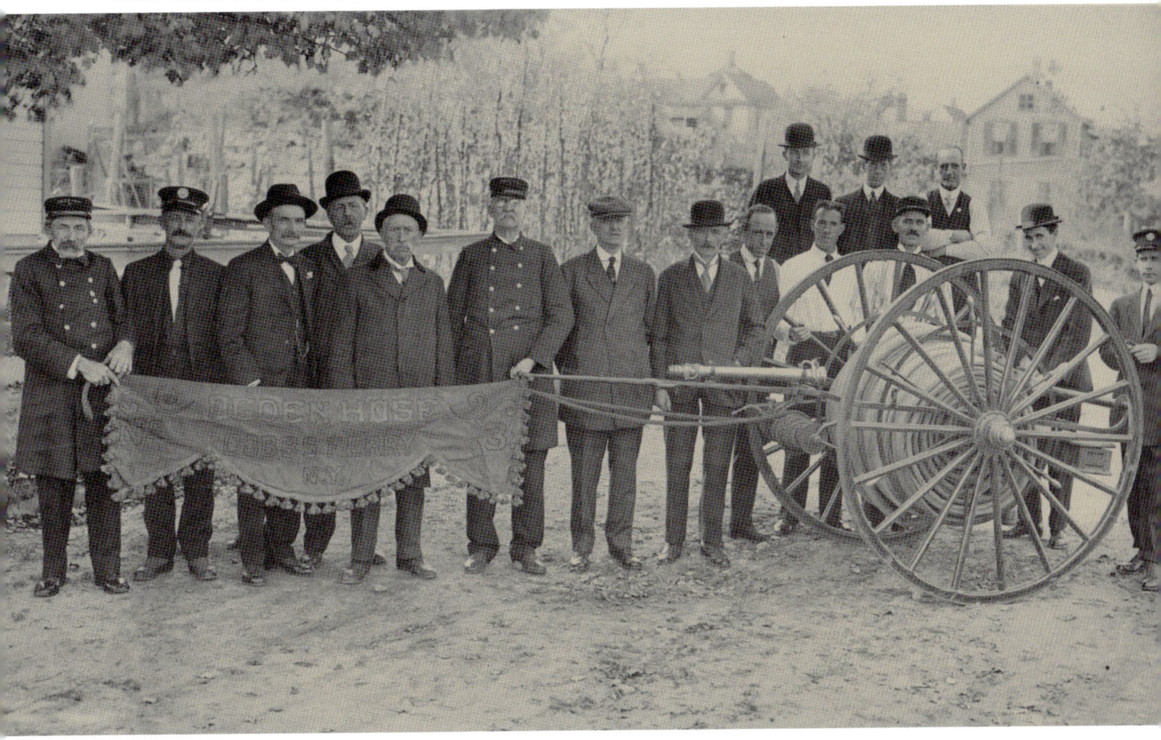

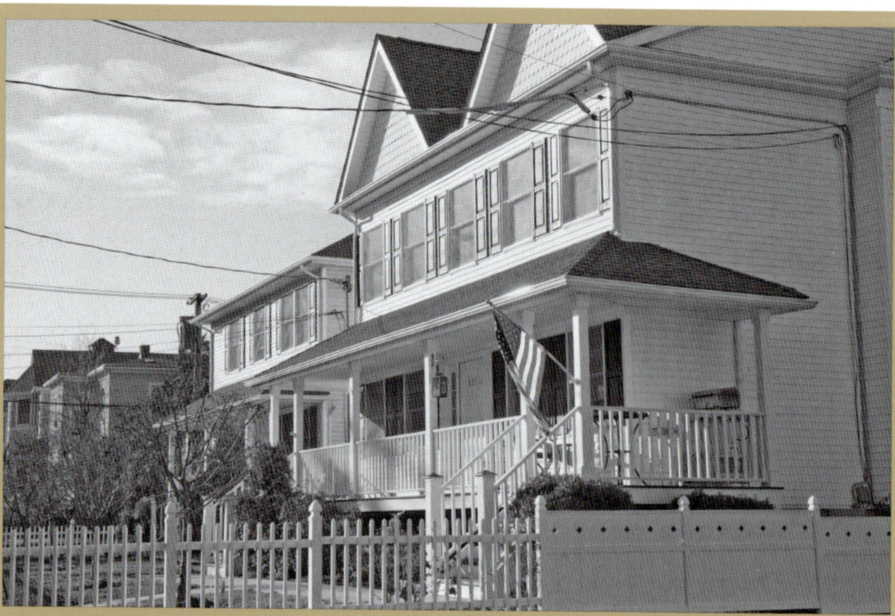

Young relatives of Mr. and Mrs. Robert M. Johnston play in front of the family home in 1927. Also on the Johnstons' eight-lot property was the Johnston Garden Center and greenhouses—originally owned by Alexander McClelland. The business moved, and the property was sold around 1987 with the home relocated to 30 Highland Avenue. Duplex townhouses at 215 Ashford Avenue now occupy the original site and additional residences have replaced the greenhouses.

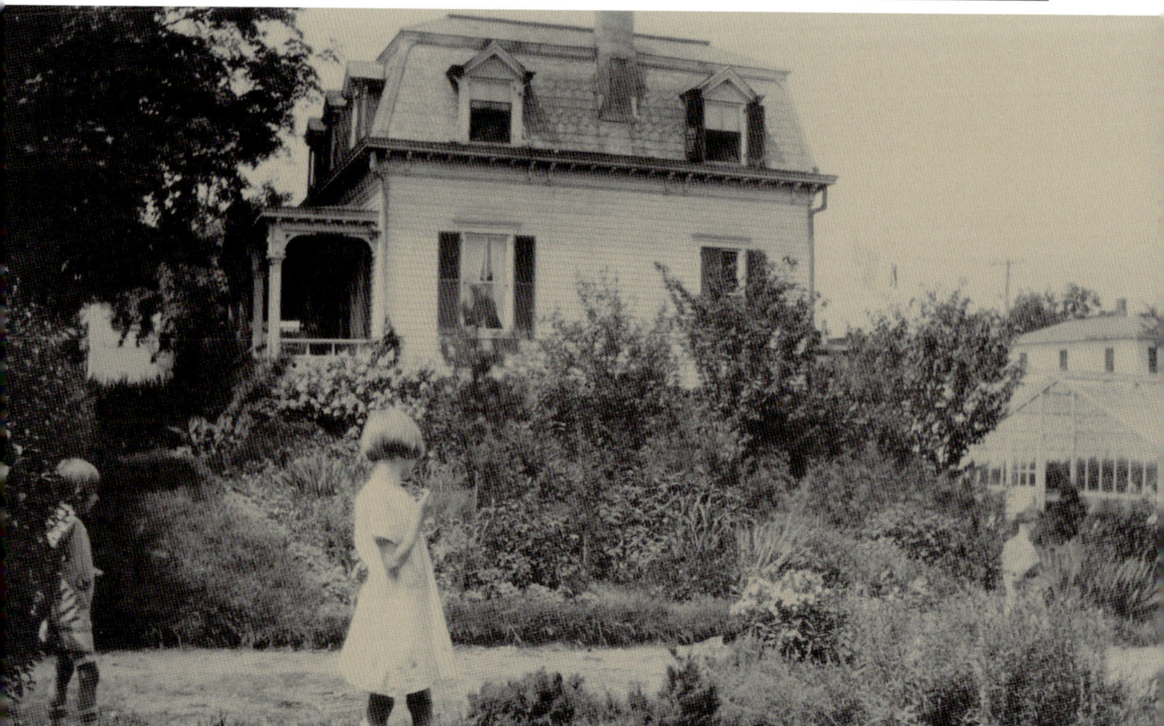

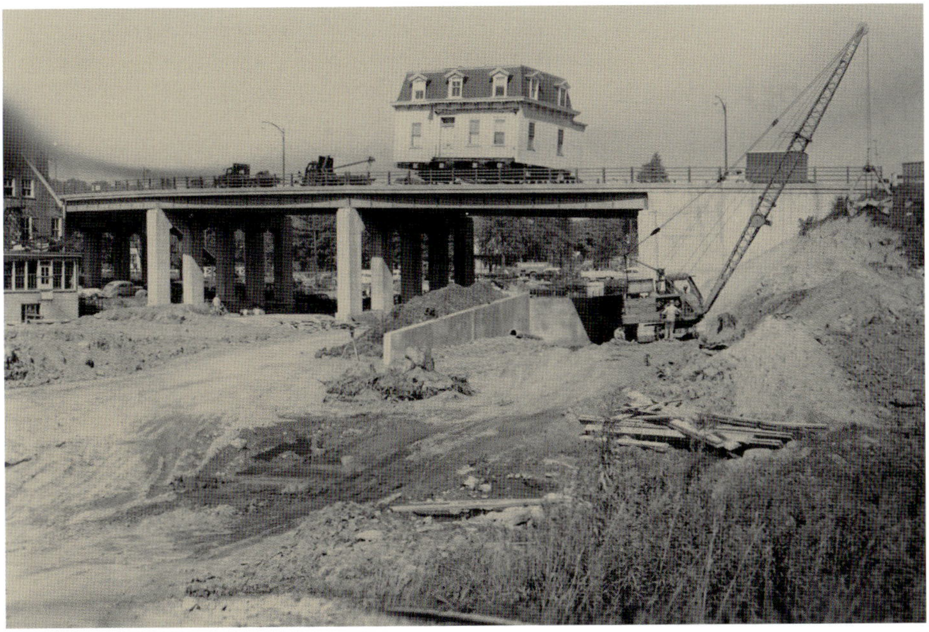

In 1955, the home of Paulo and Maria Fraietta was moved from Nepperhan Street in Ardsley over the new Ashford Avenue Bridge to make way for the New York State Thruway. The six-lane superhighway destroyed or relocated 40 buildings, changed the course of the Saw Mill River, and eliminated major streets. The Fraietta house now stands at 34 Southfield Avenue in Dobbs Ferry. (Then image courtesy of the Ardsley Historical Society.)

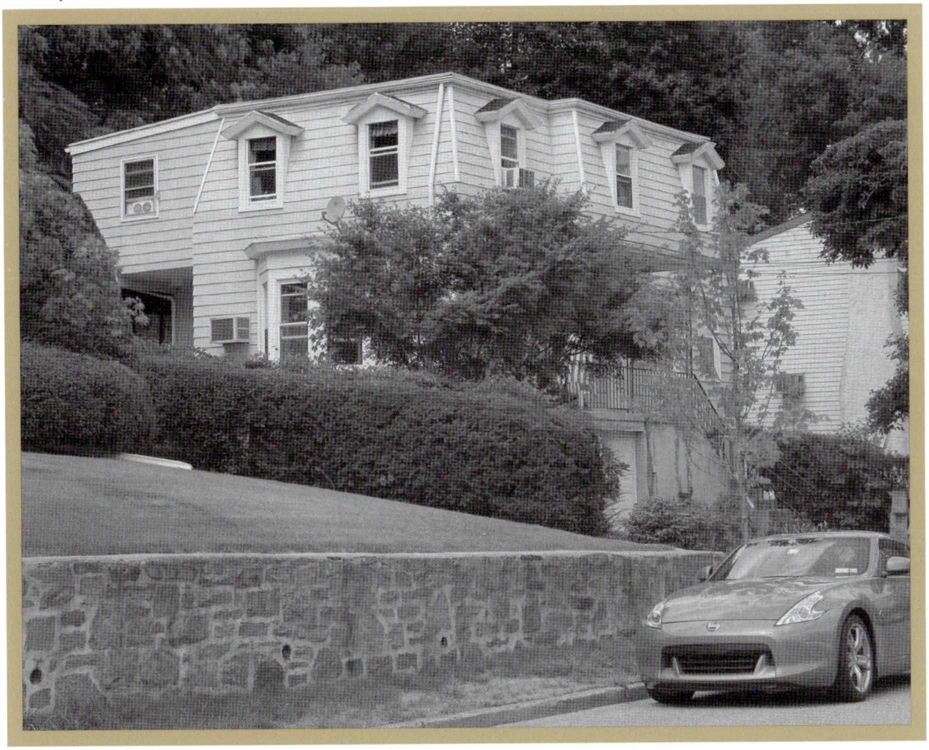

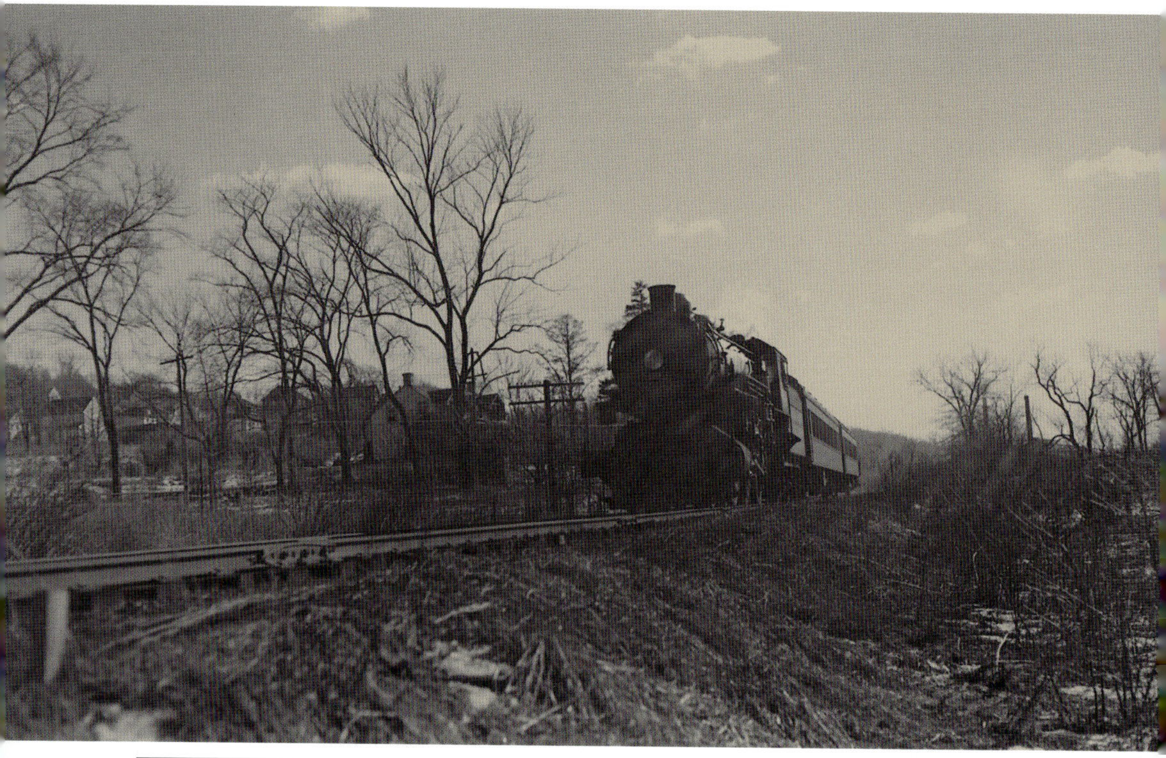

Henry Chauncey Jr., the grandson of a railroad and steamship tycoon, bought department store entrepreneur John A. Stewart's 277-acre estate along the Saw Mill River in 1862. Factories and worker housing came a decade later. The Putnam Division of the New York Central Railroad arrived in 1880, and the depot and post office were named Chauncey. The station stood west of the tracks—now the South County Trailway—south of Lawrence Street. Engine 823 approaches the station headed north in 1939. (Then image courtesy of Joe Schiavone.)

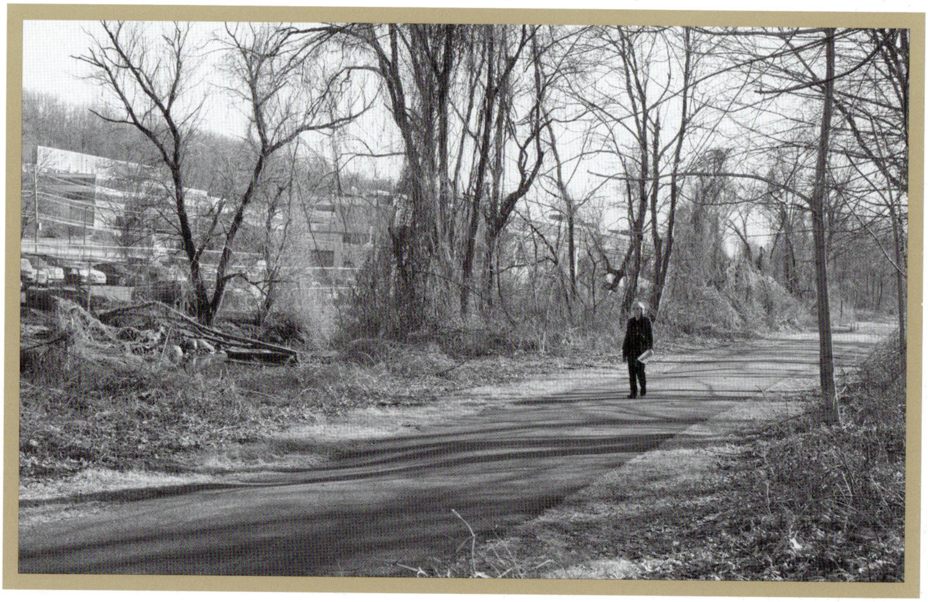

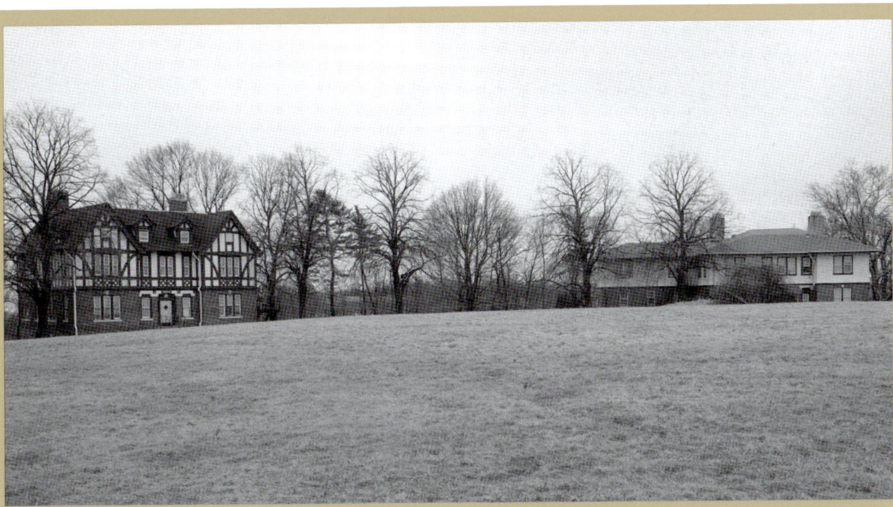

Begun as a shelter for homeless boys in New York City in 1851, the New York Juvenile Asylum moved to the Chauncey estate in 1901. The name was changed to Children's Village in 1920. According to its website, it serves youngsters in New York's child welfare and juvenile justice systems. The residential school occupies 180 acres off the Saw Mill River Parkway. Seen here are two of the eight cottage residences circling the former sheep meadow.

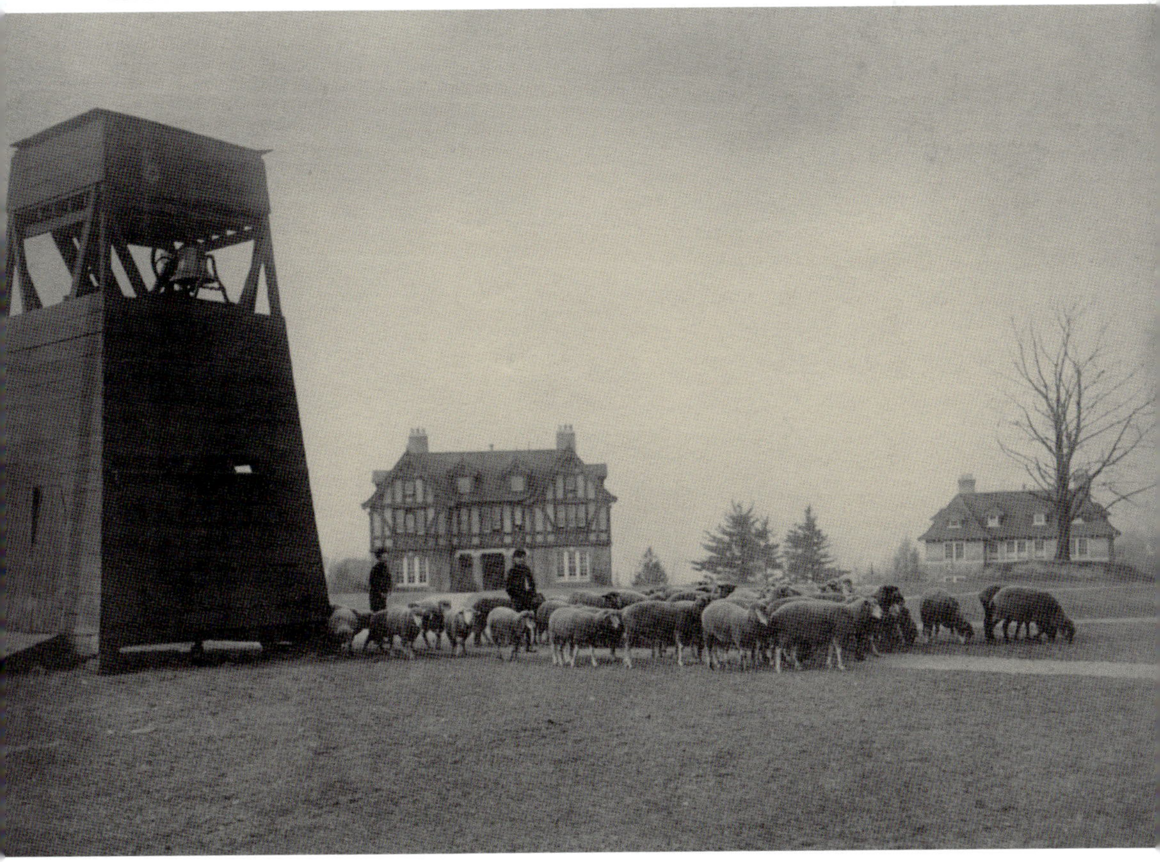

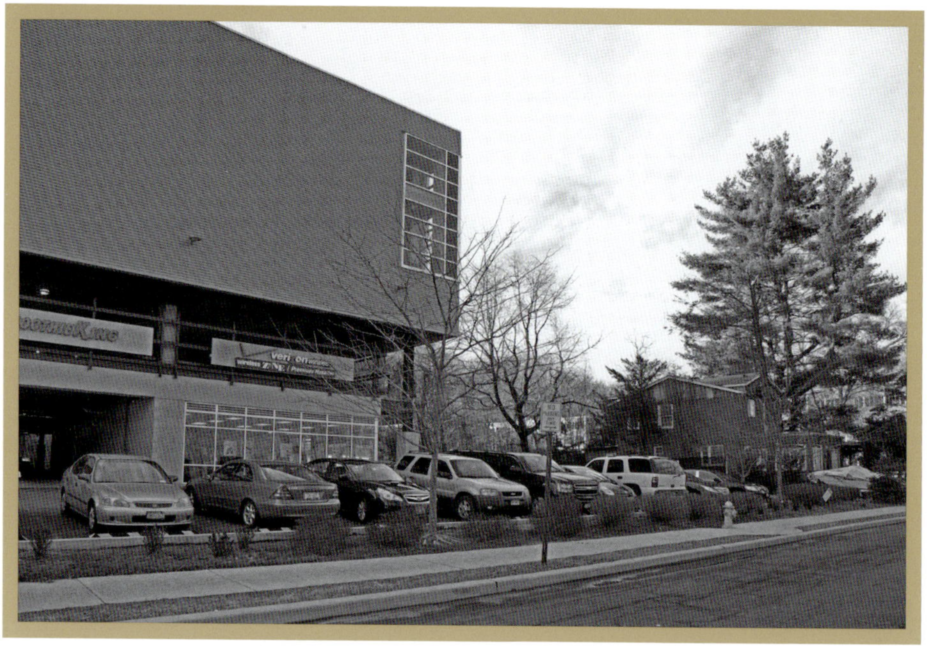

The Saw Mill River Parkway, completed in 1929, obliterated most of Chauncey's streets and buildings. The commuter train was discontinued in 1958 and the postal district in 1963. Akzo Nobel's pharmaceuticals campus closed. A strip mall was built in 2007 and intensive mixed-use development has been proposed. The lone survivor of this row of houses overlooking the Saw Mill River Parkway at Lawrence Street is at 63 Stanley Avenue (right). (Then image courtesy of Patricia Arone.)

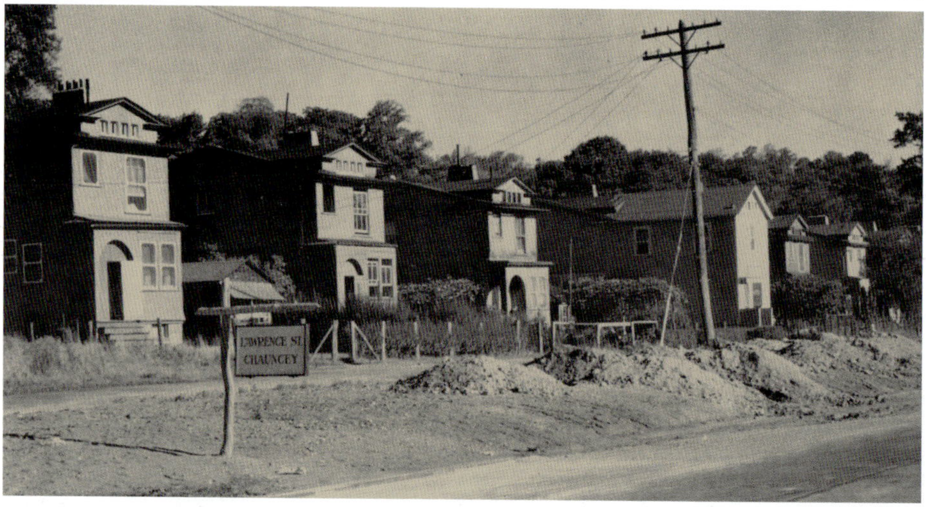

CHAPTER 4

The Hilltop
Villard Hill and Riverview Manor

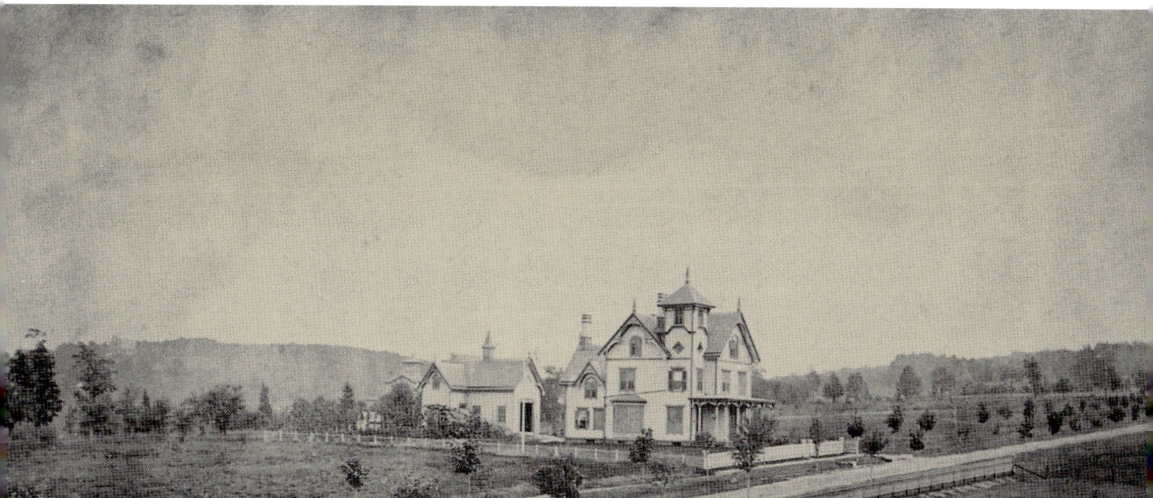

Looking up Clinton Avenue from Broadway in the early 1870s, the only residence in view belonged to Dr. Champion H. Judson, founder of the Dobbs Ferry Hospital; the beginning of the meandering driveway leading to 12 Clinton Avenue is on the right. Around 1881, John Jennings McComb acquired this land for his estate, Estherwood. Dr. Judson's house remains at 23 Clinton Avenue as Cochran Cottage of the Masters School.

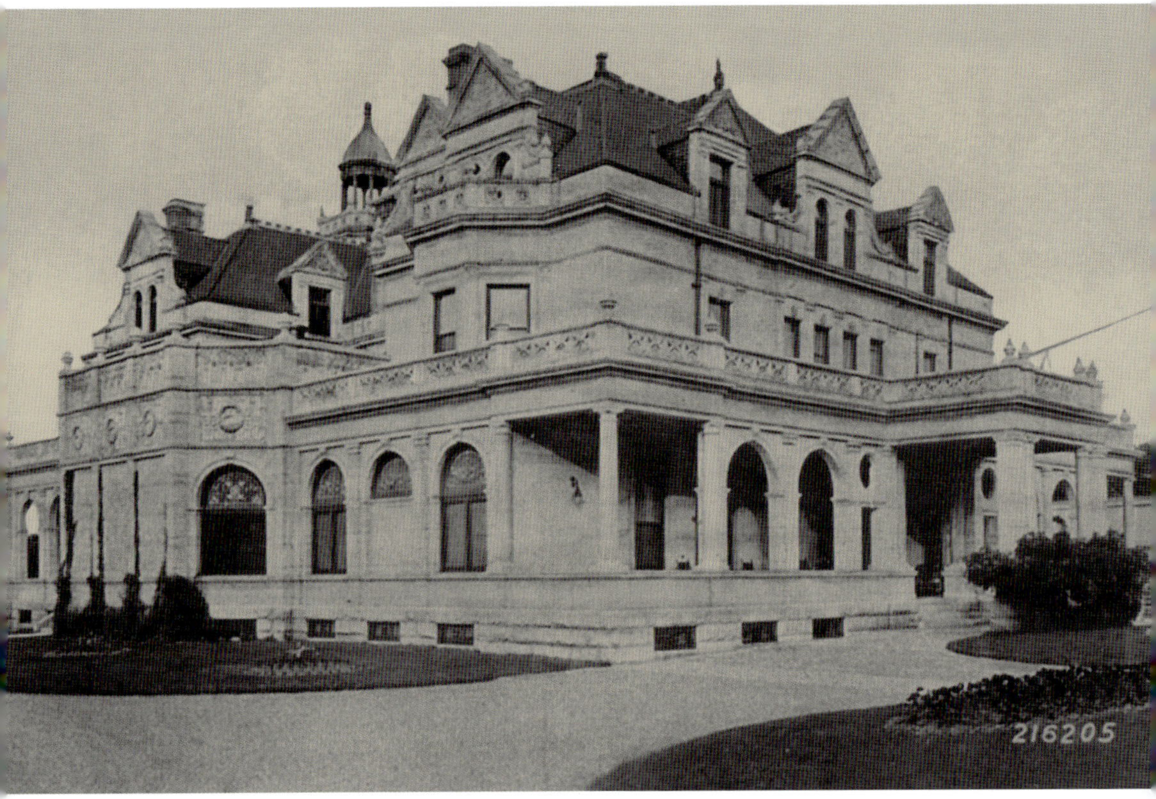

Among the palatial estates that spread over the Westchester Hills following the Civil War, John Jennings McComb's was the grandest. Of humble birth, McComb made a fortune from his cotton-baling machine. After moving to Dobbs Ferry in 1877, he acquired contiguous estates owned by William Barbour, Philip J. Armour, and others, building his own chateau, Estherwood, in 1894. It is listed in the National Register of Historic Places. (Then image courtesy of Jane Faber.)

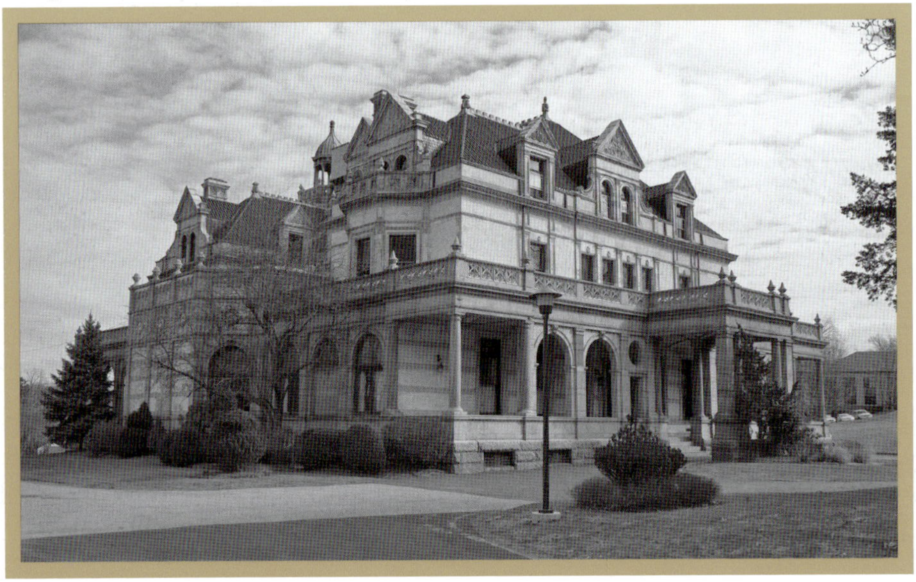

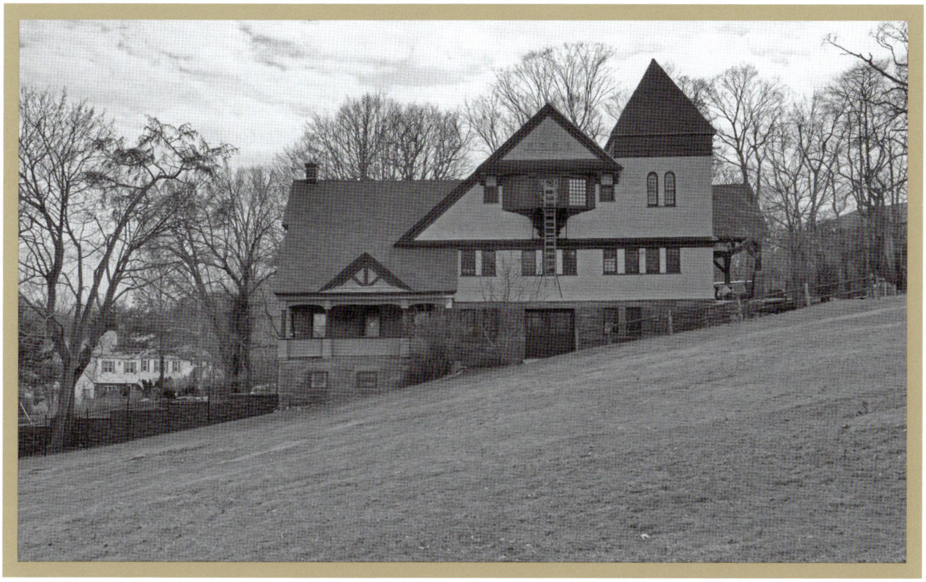

Estherwood Avenue originally led to the carriage house, built in 1880 under the ownership of Philip J. Armour, of the McComb estate. The McCombs were close friends of Fanny Howell Masters and her daughters, Sarah and Eliza, who founded the Masters School in 1877. When the McCombs died in 1901, the school had long occupied many structures on their property, and it retains 96 acres as its campus today. (Then image courtesy of Larry Blizard.)

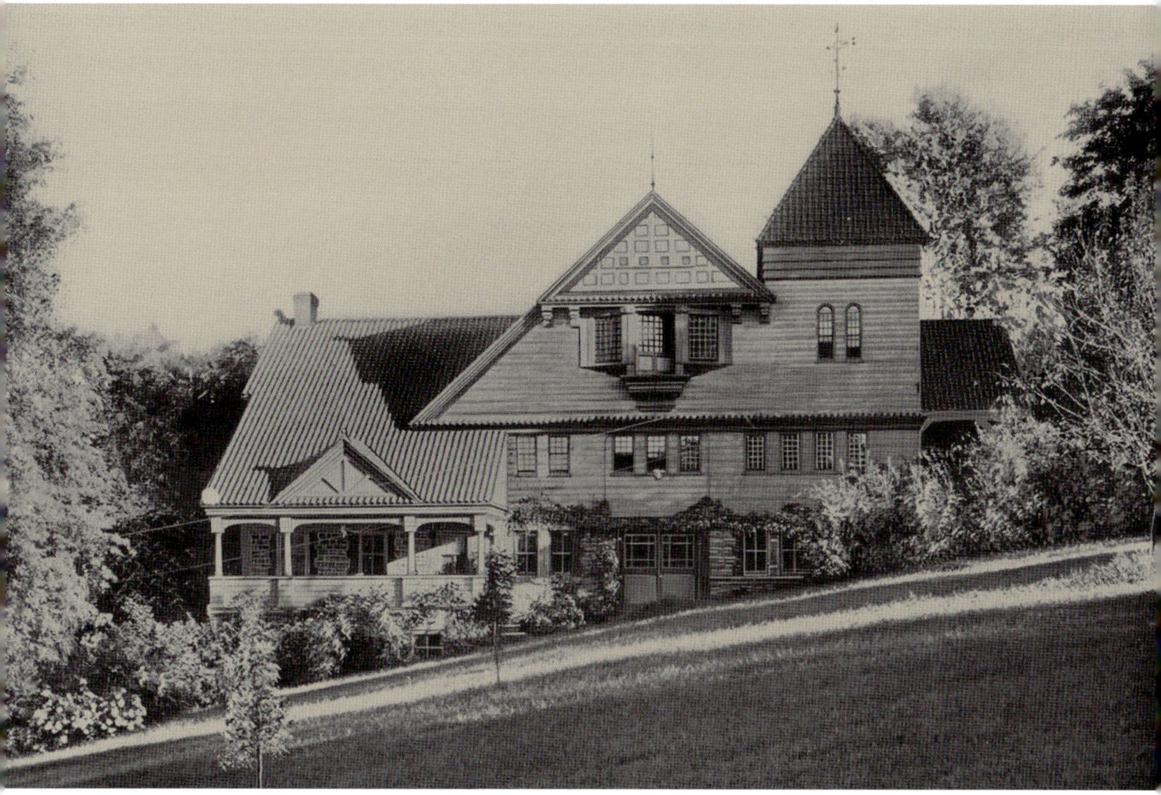

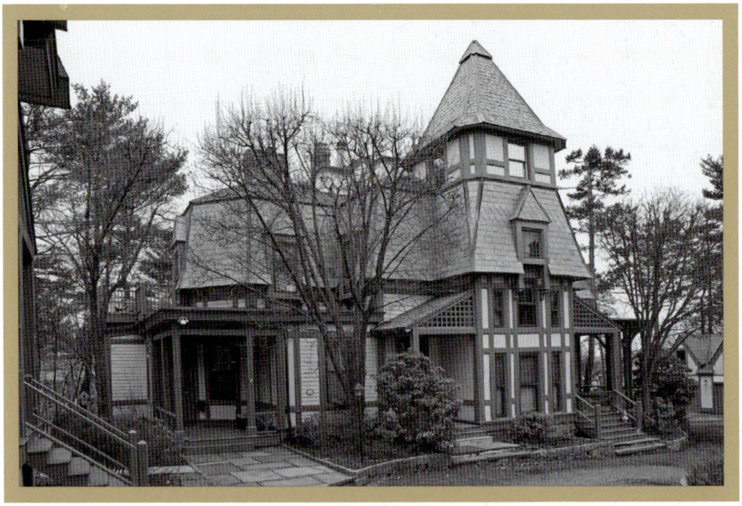

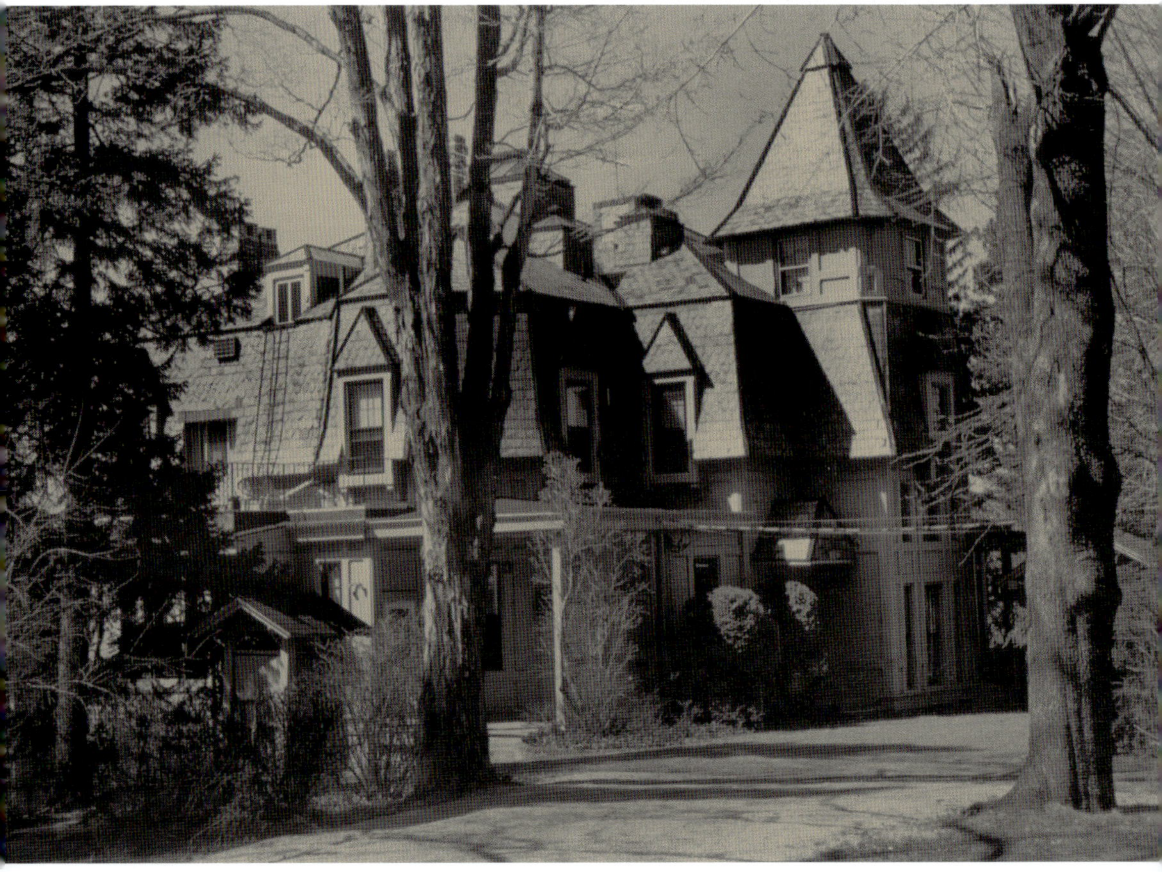

Wit's End, the Second Empire–style residence of Maj. David B. Williamson, is the middle building as viewed from 12 Clinton Avenue today. It was built in 1880 on land formerly belonging to P.J. Armour. It remained a single-family residence until 1968, when it passed to the Masters School for faculty housing. The mansion was sold 20 years later and renovated into three condominium units accompanied by two compatibly styled new buildings.

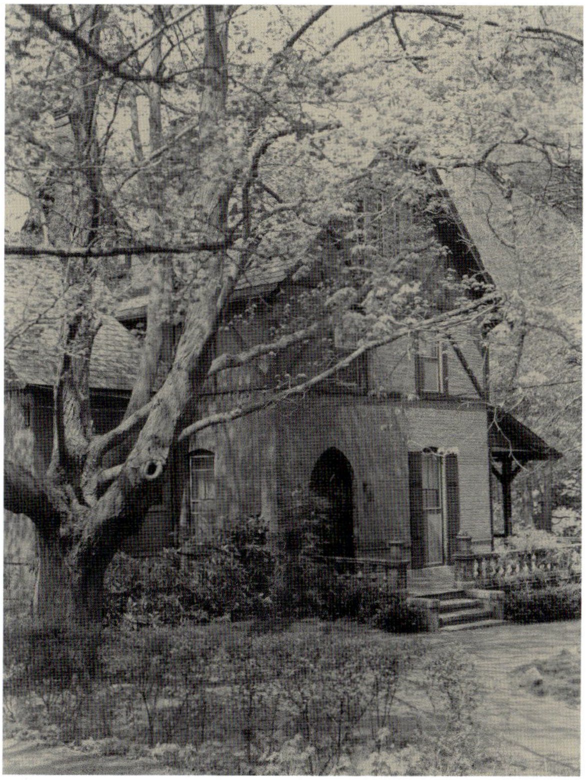

This 17-room home at 34 Clinton Avenue was built in 1878 for Edward Satterlee on a lot purchased from P.J. Armour. From 1894 to 1915, it was the property of state senator Charles P. McClelland, who named it Glenluce, after his birthplace in Scotland. He held many public offices, including time as a law officer and as first deputy collector of the New York Custom House. He was also a member of the board of general appraisers in New York City, and in Dobbs Ferry, he was village president, school board president, and a popular citizen.

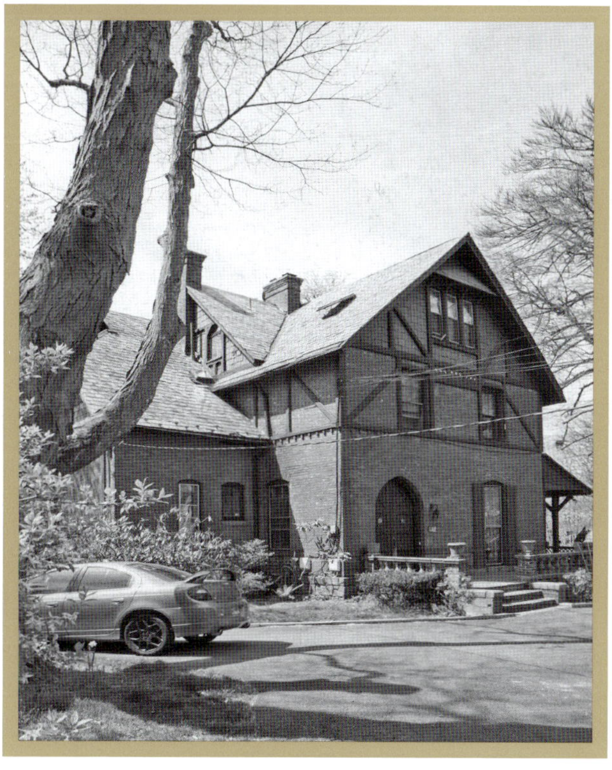

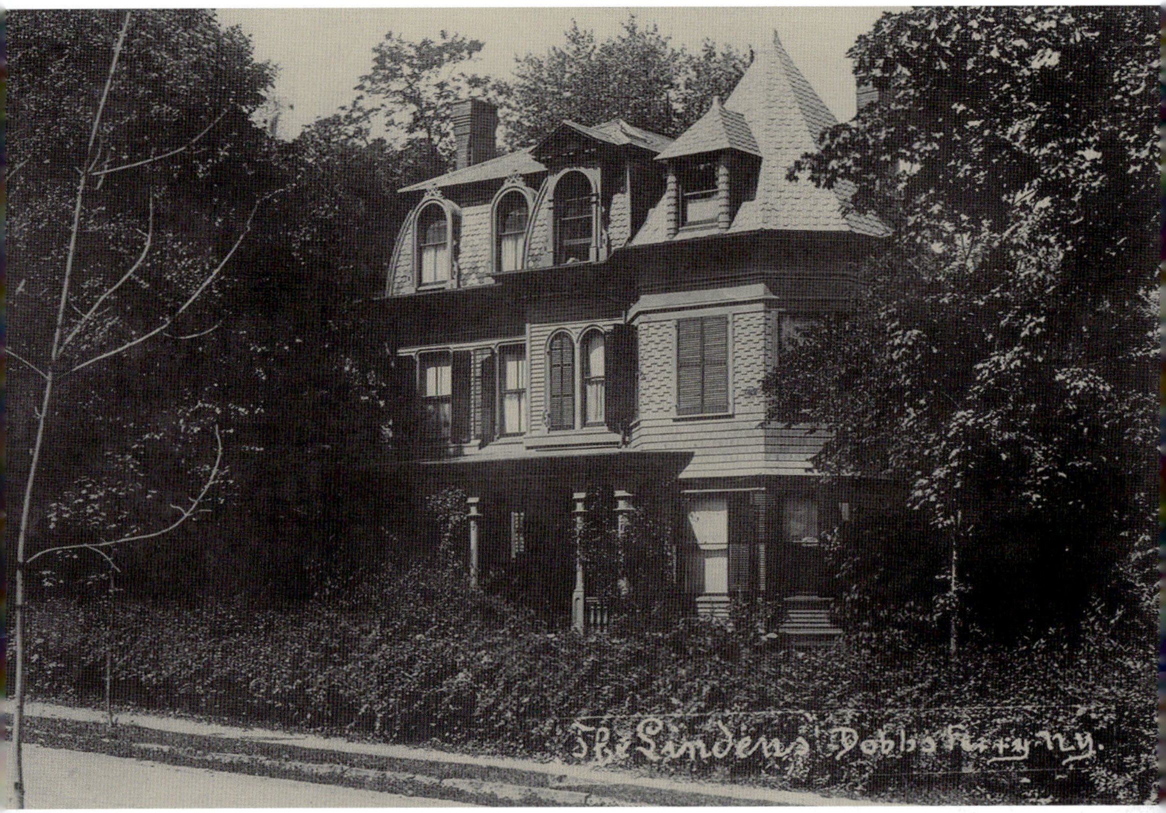

Built before 1870 and owned in 1885 by Mrs. A.E. Ross, the original section of this awe-inspiring structure at 70 Clinton Avenue is in the French Second Empire style. The conical tower was added in 1890, as was the Queen Anne–style carriage house. Known as The Lindens, it was a Masters School dormitory for many years and is now a private home. (Then image courtesy of Patricia Arone.)

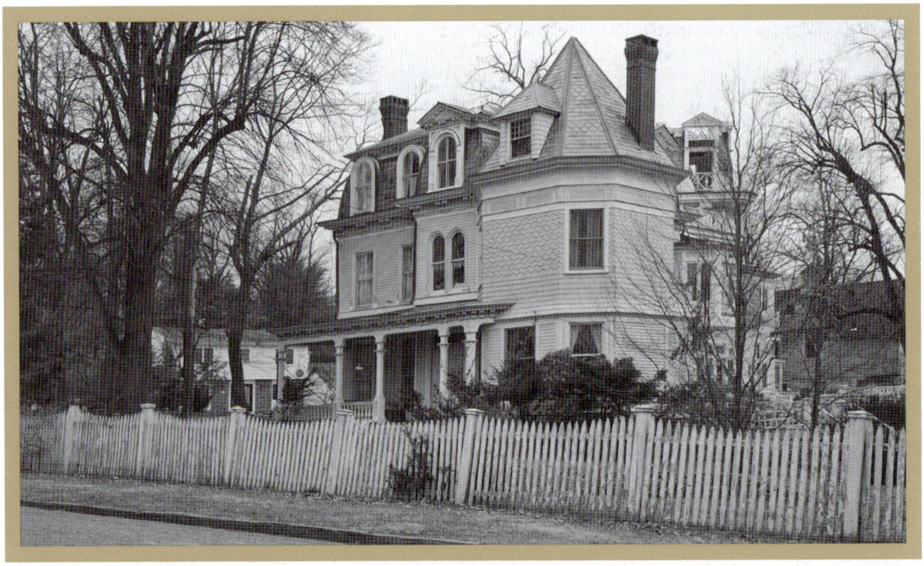

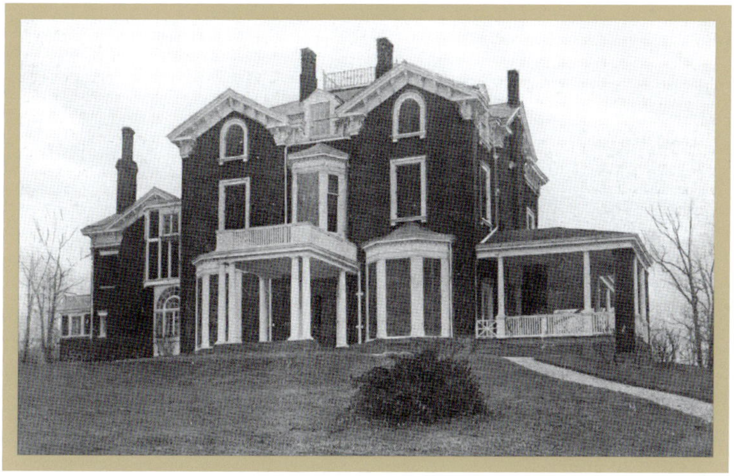

About 1855, Thomas and Samuel Cochran built identical mansions on 100 hilltop acres laid out by Frederick Law Olmsted. Henry Villard purchased Samuel's Thorwood in 1879 and added two wings. Arriving from Germany in 1853, Villard gained fame as a Civil War correspondent and the owner of the *New York Post* before acquiring great wealth as president of the Northern Pacific Railroad and Edison General Electric. Thorwood, which stood on the same site as this current house at 21 Clinton Avenue, was razed in 1935.

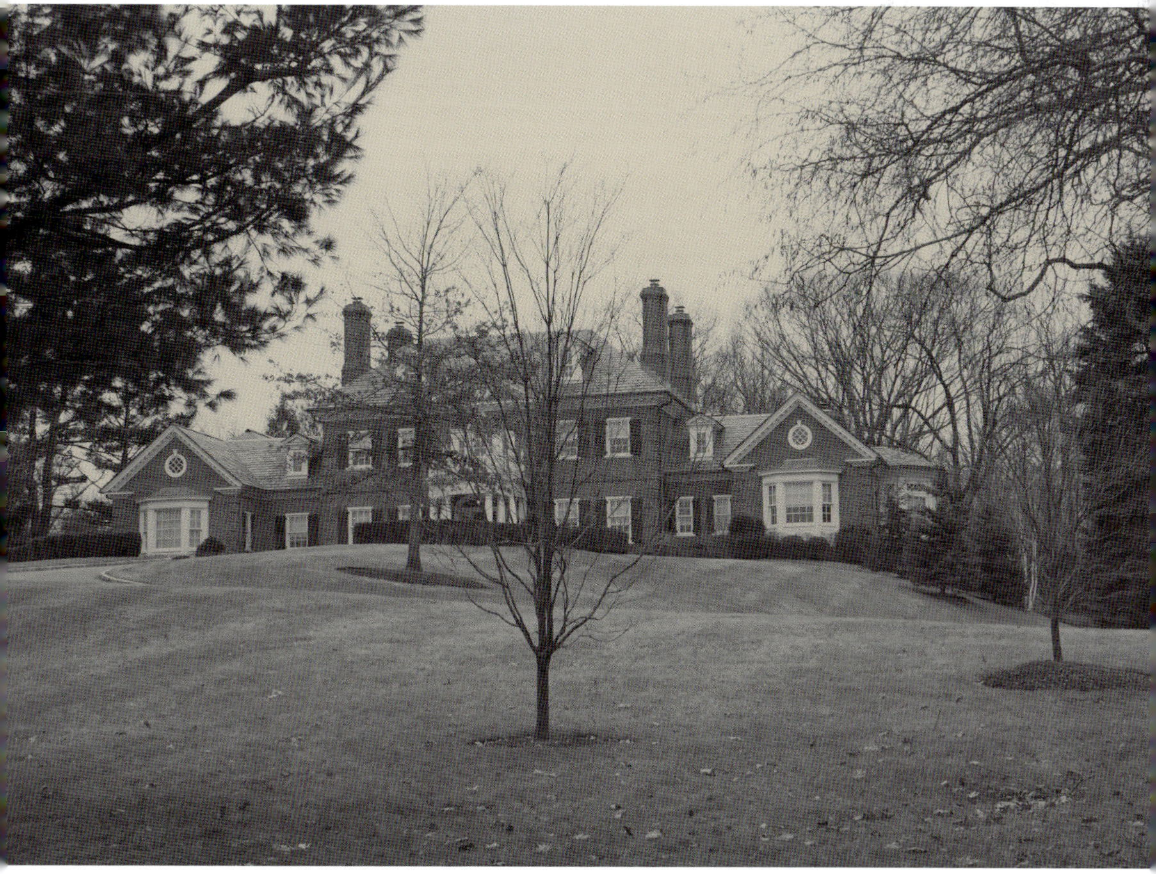

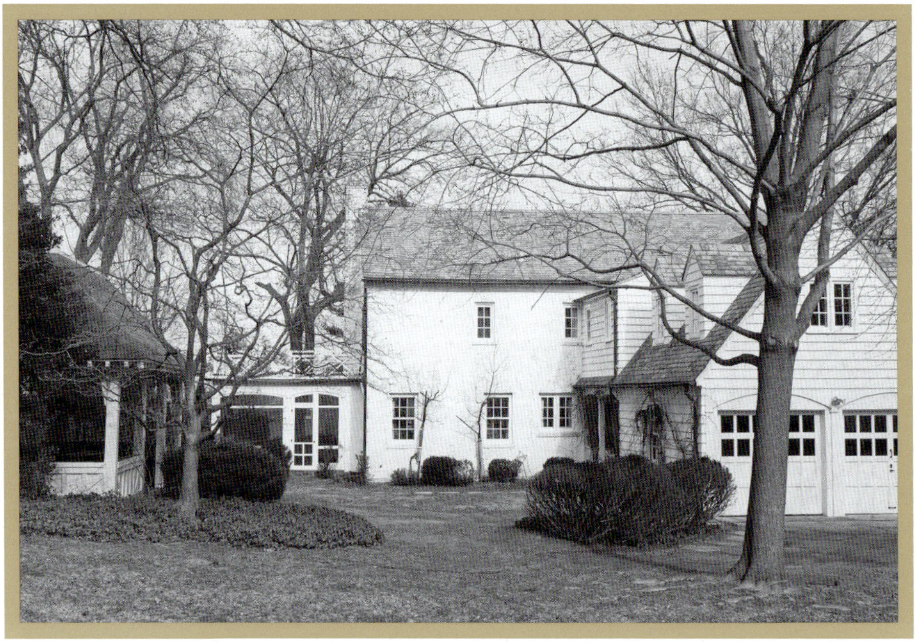

Upon Henry Villard's death in 1900, his estate passed to his son, publisher Oswald Garrison Villard, who was named for his mother, Fanny Garrison, the famed pacifist and suffragist. Oswald sold the 100-acre estate in 1932 to Joseph Meddill Patterson, the publisher of the *Daily News*. In 1935, Patterson subdivided the land into 275 lots and razed all the structures except the tea pavilion that stands at the far left in the rear of 26 Judson Avenue, one of the first residences in the Villard Hill development. (Then image courtesy of Mildred Persinger.)

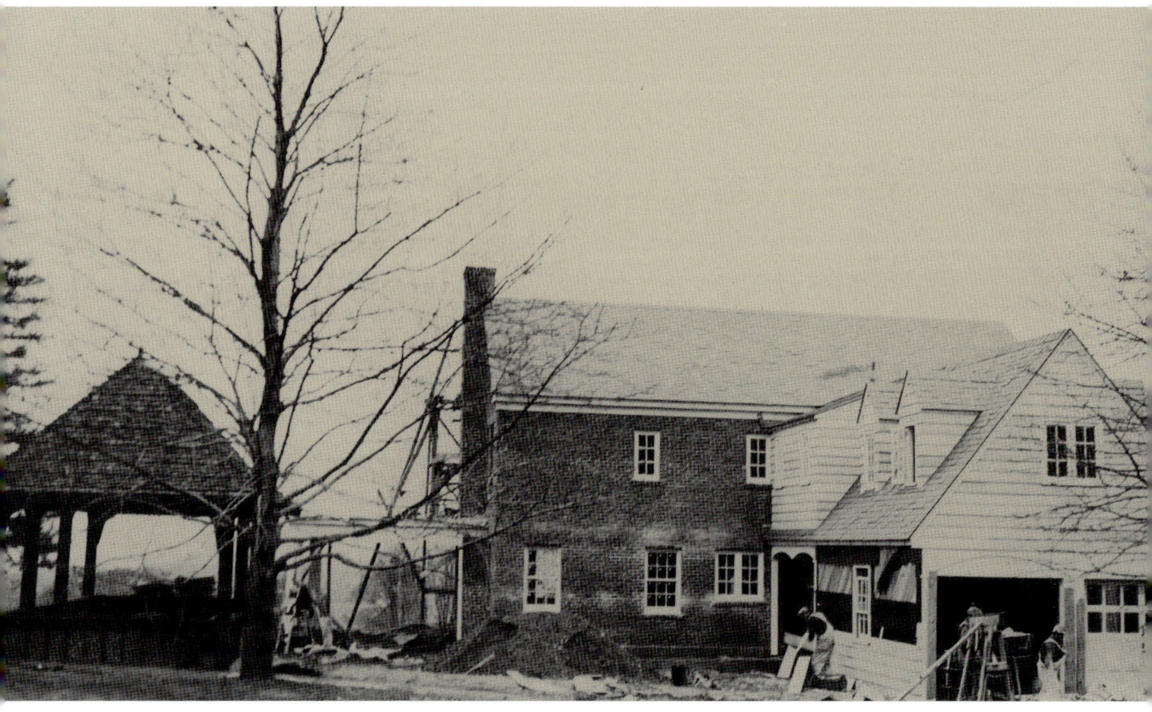

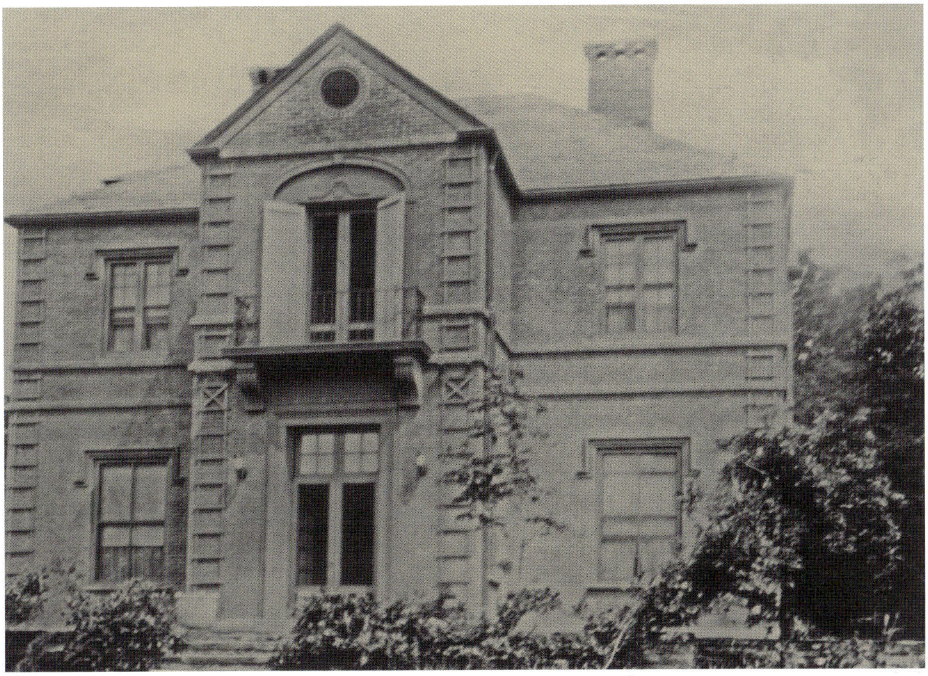

Originally extending to the Hastings-on-Hudson border, Southlawn, at 106 Magnolia Avenue, had four owners before John D. Flower, the financier brother of New York governor Roswell P. Flower, took possession in 1898. The residence may have been built for the Paulding family around 1855, or in 1863 for Robert M. Olyphant, a president of the Delaware and Hudson Railroad. The wide verandas and mansard-roofed third floor were removed in 1927. Most of the land was subdivided as part of the 1908 Riverview Manor development. (Then image courtesy of Jacque Jennett.)

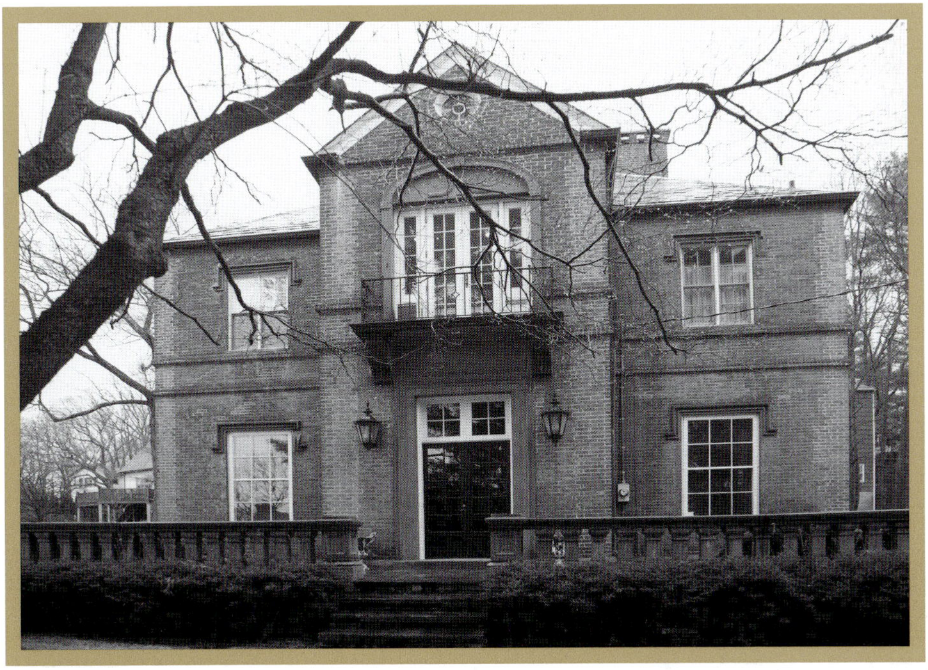

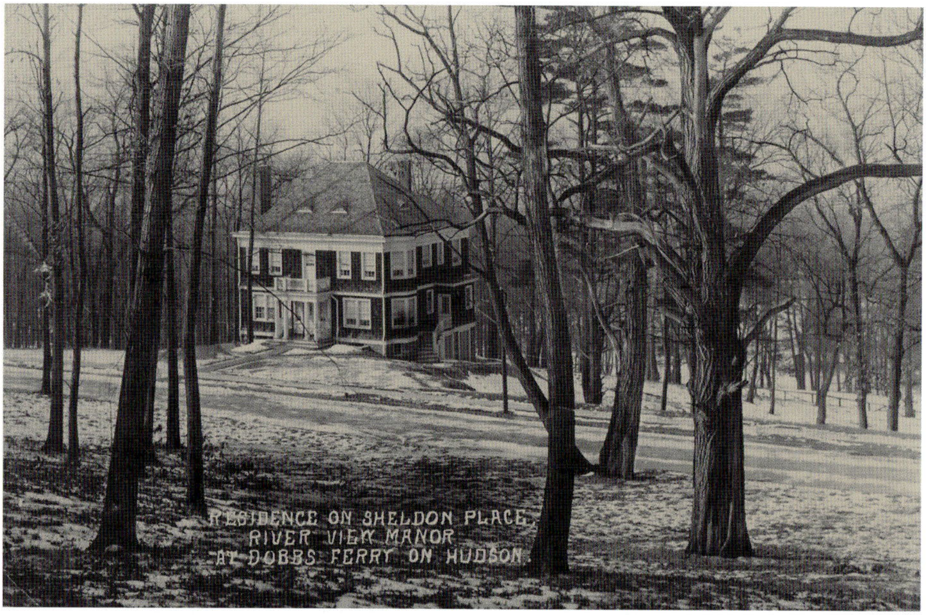

In the early 1850s, Robert Bowne Minturn of the shipping firm Grinnell, Minturn, and Company bought the 200-acre Anthony Constant estate overlapping the Dobbs Ferry/Hastings-on-Hudson border. Frederick Law Olmsted landscaped the estate in 1865. Southlawn, solely on the Dobbs Ferry side, was also landscaped by Olmsted and was joined with Minturn's estate in the 1908 development of Riverview Manor by the National Conduit and Cable Company. Shown here is one of the first Riverview Manor residences, now addressed as 41 Southlawn Avenue.

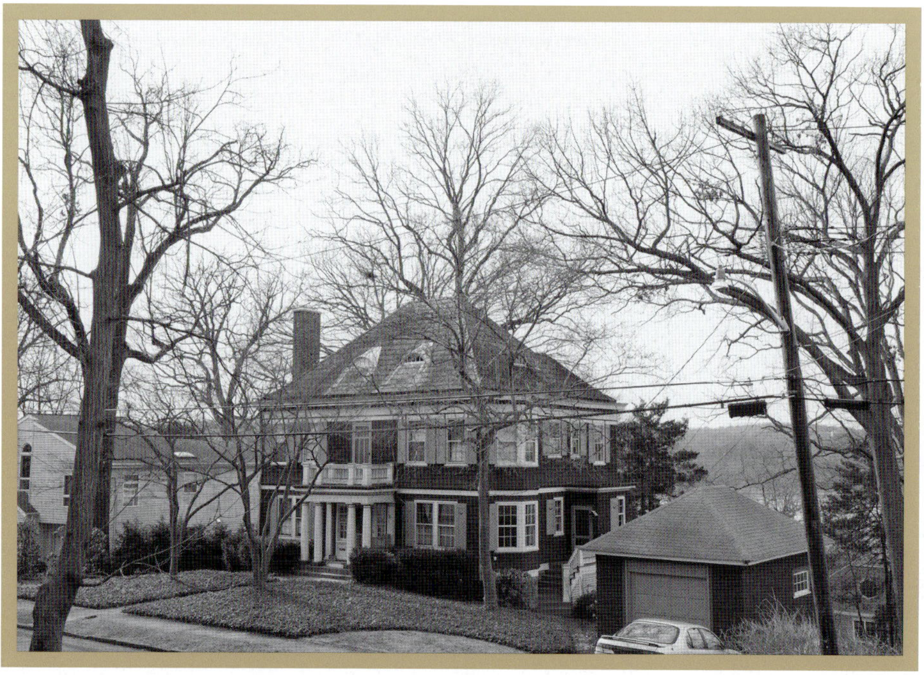

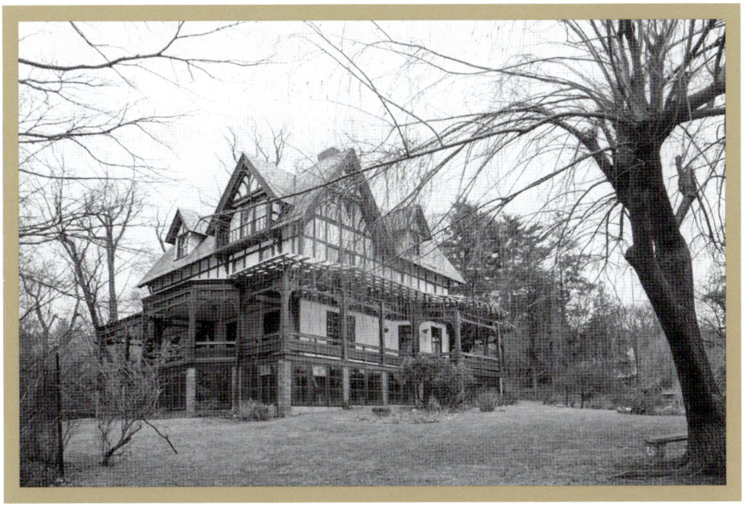

Ches-Knoll, the 1876 estate of Charles Loring Brace, who died in 1890, at 67 Olyphant Avenue, adjoined the Villard, Fraser, and Southlawn estates. Brace, a philanthropist, founded the Children's Aid Society in 1854 and devoted his life to child welfare. His son of the same name resided there until 1910, succeeding him as secretary of the Children's Aid Society and assisting him in founding Children's Village. He died in 1938. (Then image courtesy of Walter Gotshalk.)

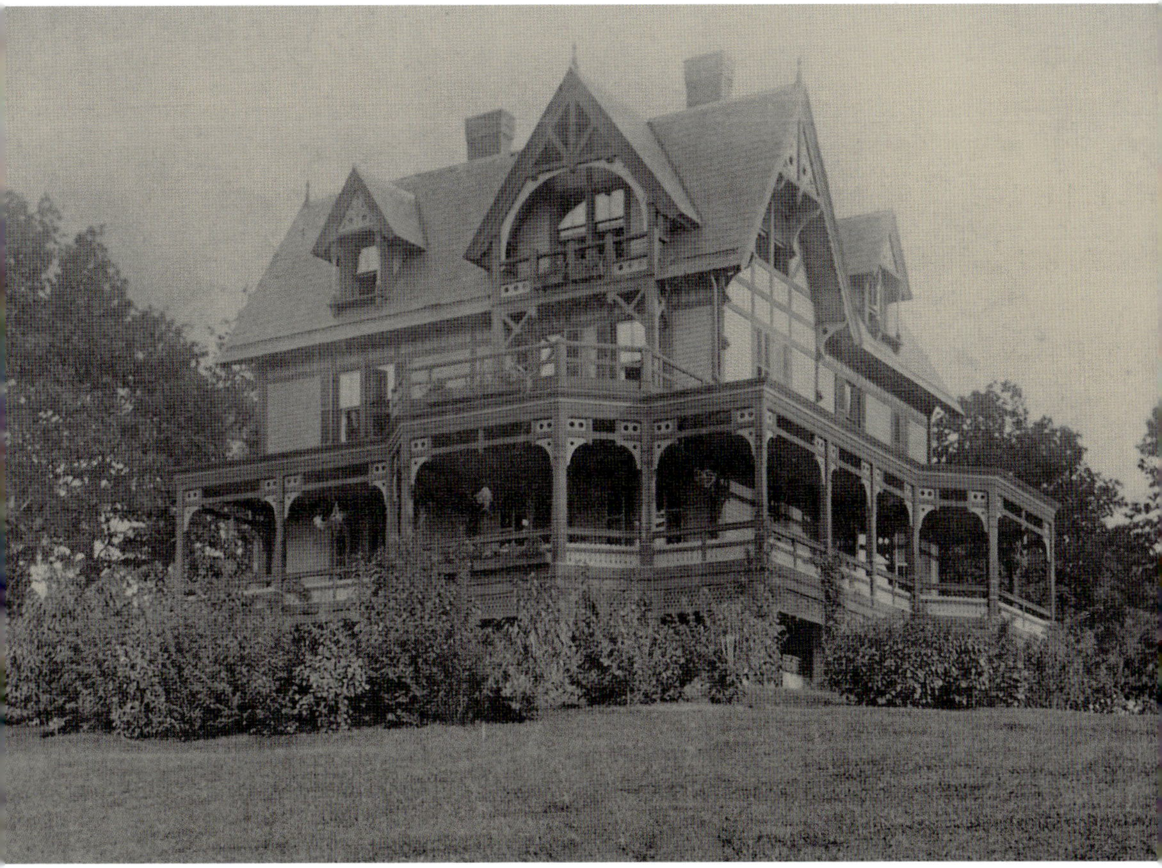

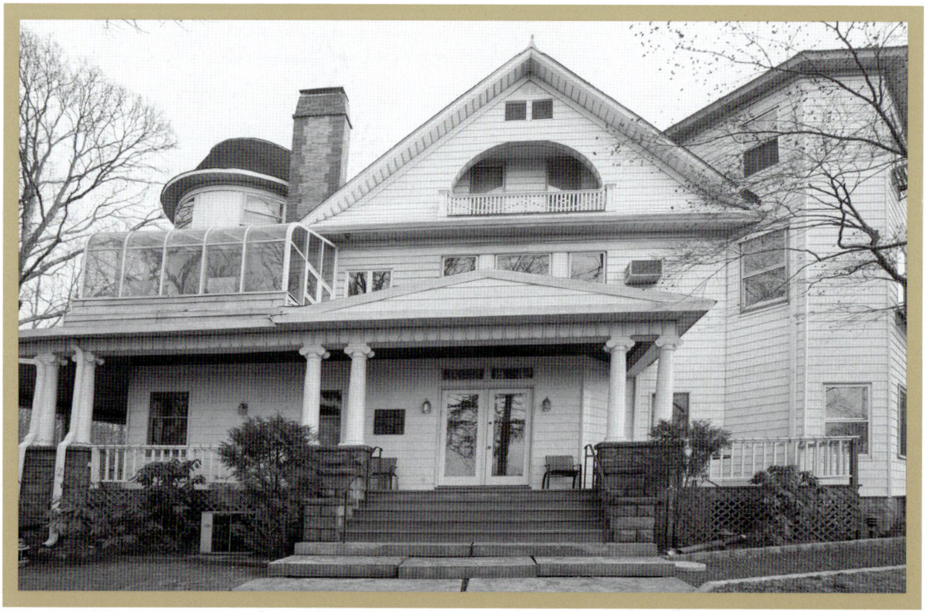

Genehurst, at 38 Olyphant Avenue, was built in 1878 for insurance executive Andrew C. Fields, the son of the pastor of Summerfield Methodist Church. Fields was the president of the village from 1882 to 1893, the director of the Dobbs Ferry Bank, a delegate to the state constitutional convention, and a lobbyist for the insurance industry. The family remained on the four-acre estate into the 1920s. In 1929, the mansion was converted into a nine-family dwelling and in 1988 into seven condominium units. (Then image courtesy of Robert Casino.)

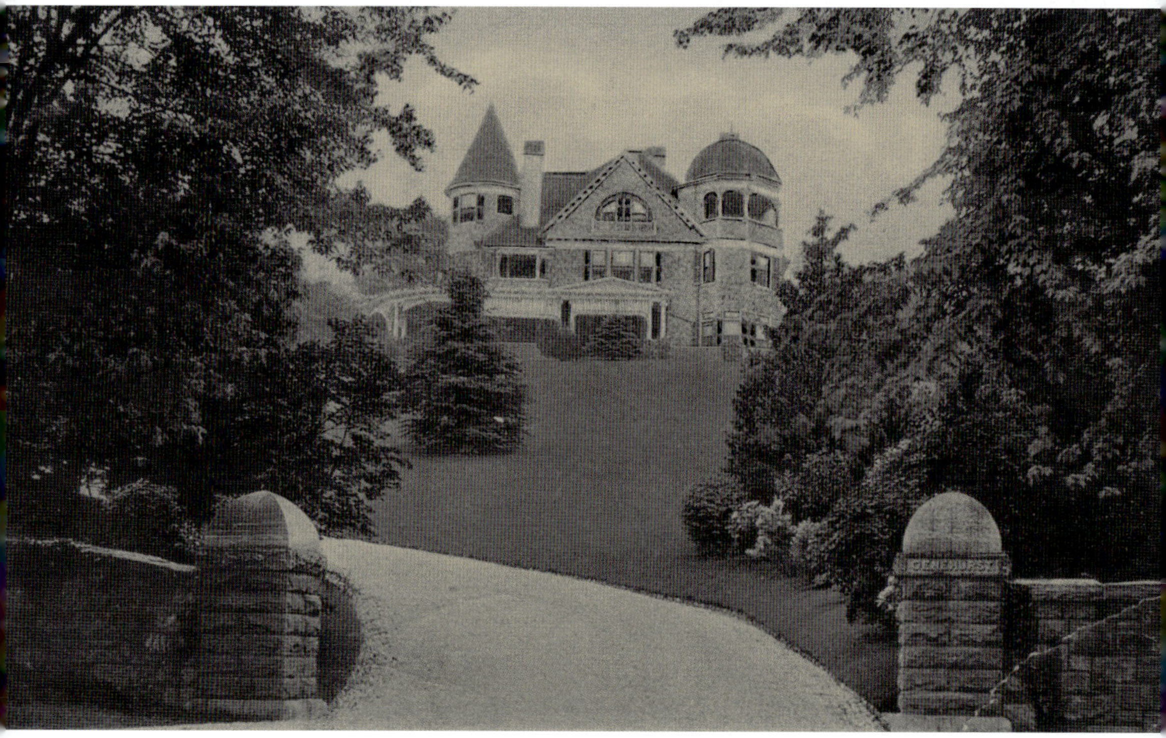

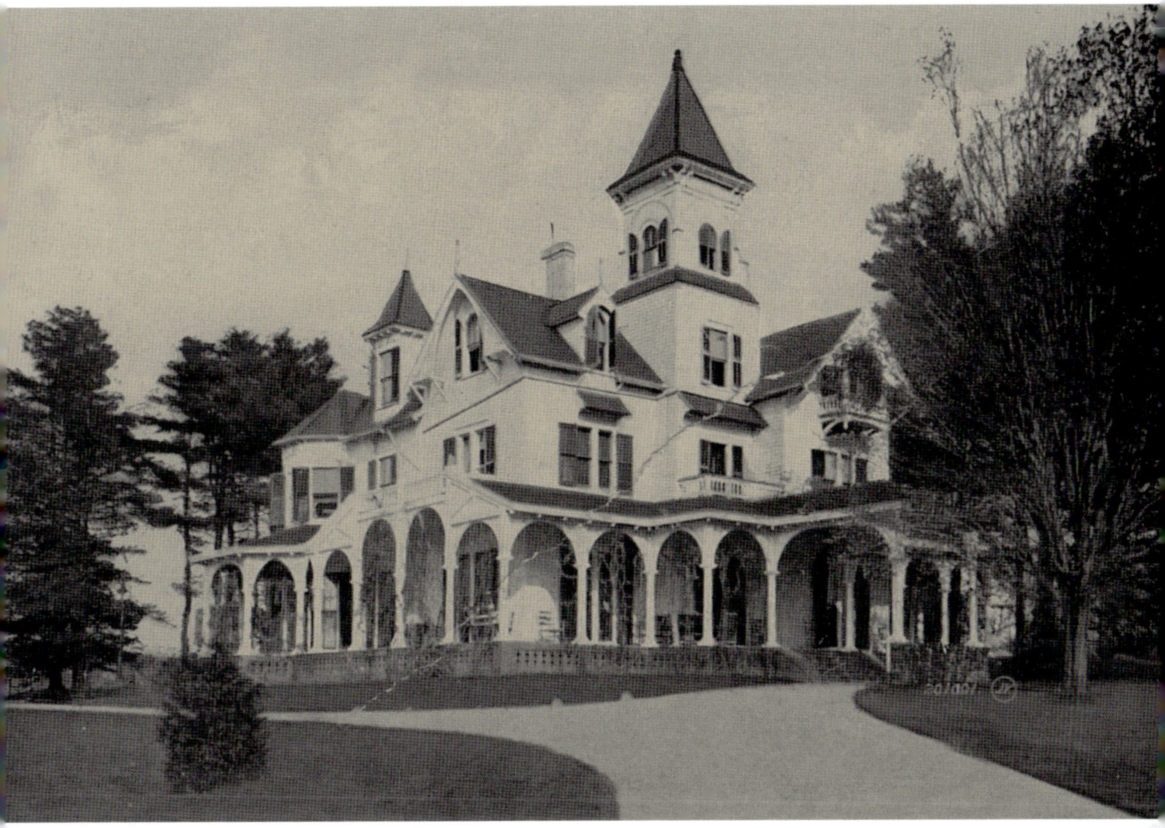

Village benefactors Franklin Quimby Brown and his wife, Ida Eldridge Brown, built Springhurst on 15 acres at the end of Walgrove Avenue in 1896. He was president of the Florida Southern Railroad, a senior officer of the Redmond & Company banking firm, and president of the village from 1912 to 1919. Ida was active in social work. The mansion was razed in 1955, and the Springhurst Elementary School was built on its site and dedicated in 1960. The eagle monument, a relic of the estate, was recovered during excavation of the site.

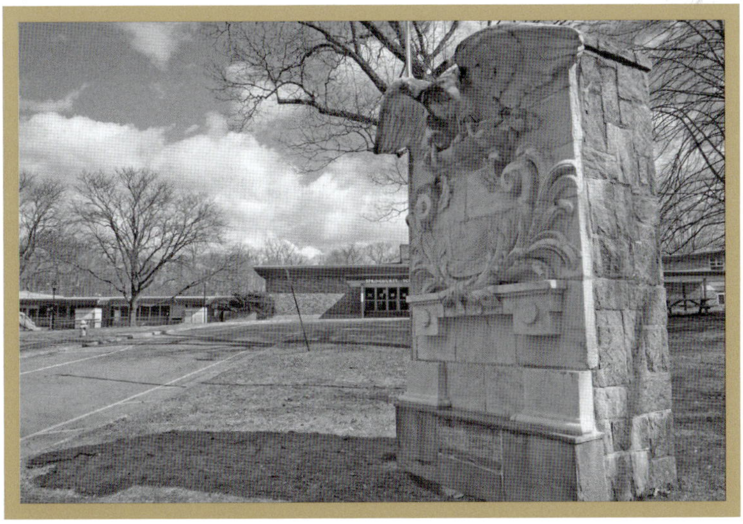

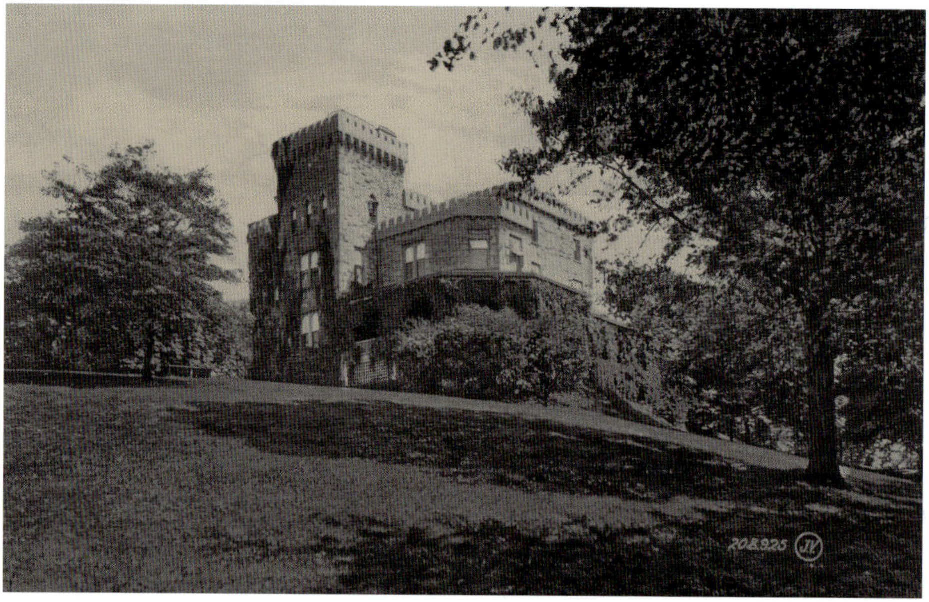

In 1879, Beacon Hill Drive led to Stone Cliff, the 100-acre estate of lawyer Frederick J. Stone, a nephew of Cyrus Field. In 1889, Walston Hill Brown purchased the crenelated mansion and 25 acres for his bride, Eva Ingersoll, who renamed it Walston. The daughter of famed lawyer, orator, and agnostic Robert G. Ingersoll, she was a prominent suffragist. By 1929, the mansion was converted into the 11-family dwelling Castle Apartments, at 155 Beacon Hill Drive. In 1949, it was surrounded by apartment buildings. (Then image courtesy of Robert Casino.)

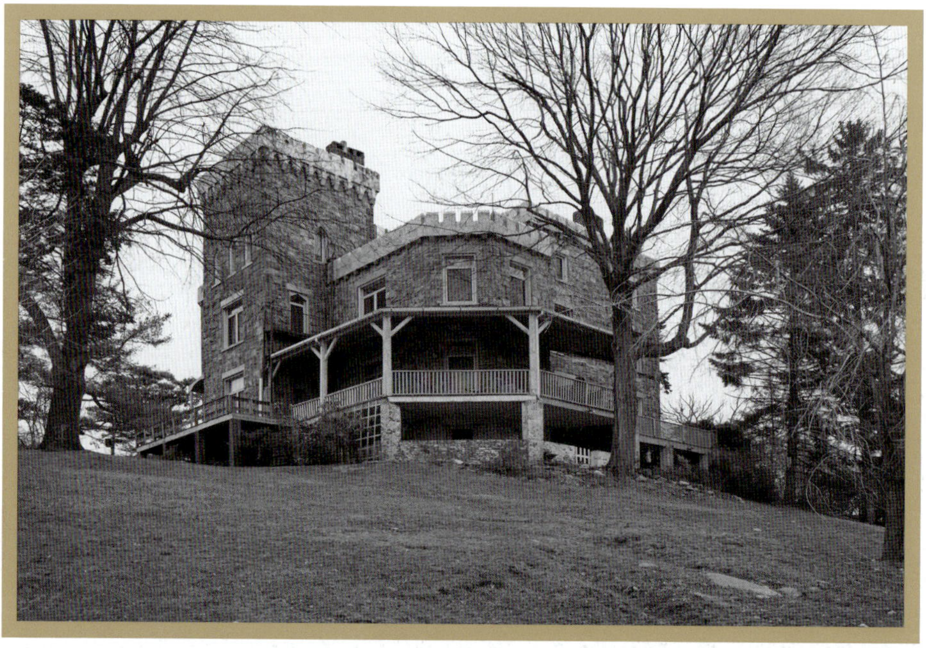

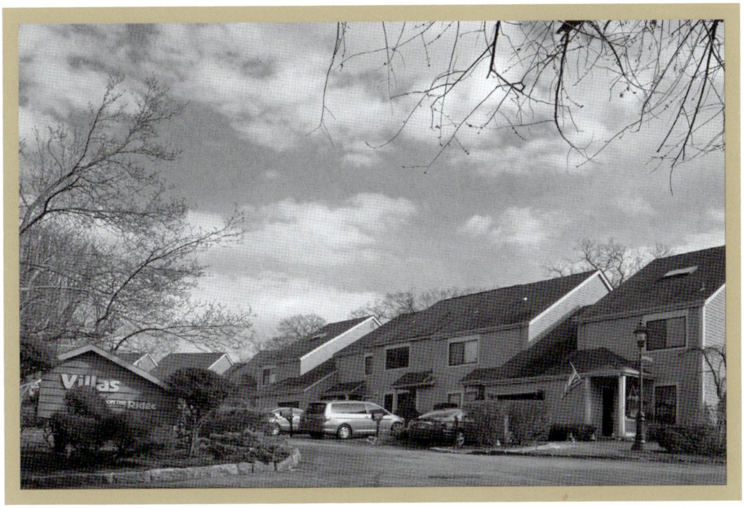

In 1926, Irma and Louis Samter Levy bought 15 acres of the original Stone estate, including the 30-room Tudor mansion, Beacon Hill, at the end of Manor House Drive. Society columns highlighted Irma's interest in rock gardening and in breeding "police dogs." Her kennel master lived with the dogs on two acres at 17 Forkland Lane. Much of the estate was subdivided for the Beacon Hill cooperative apartments from 1953 to 1958. The mansion was converted to a clubhouse before it burned in 1973. (Then image courtesy of the Dobbs Ferry Building Department.)

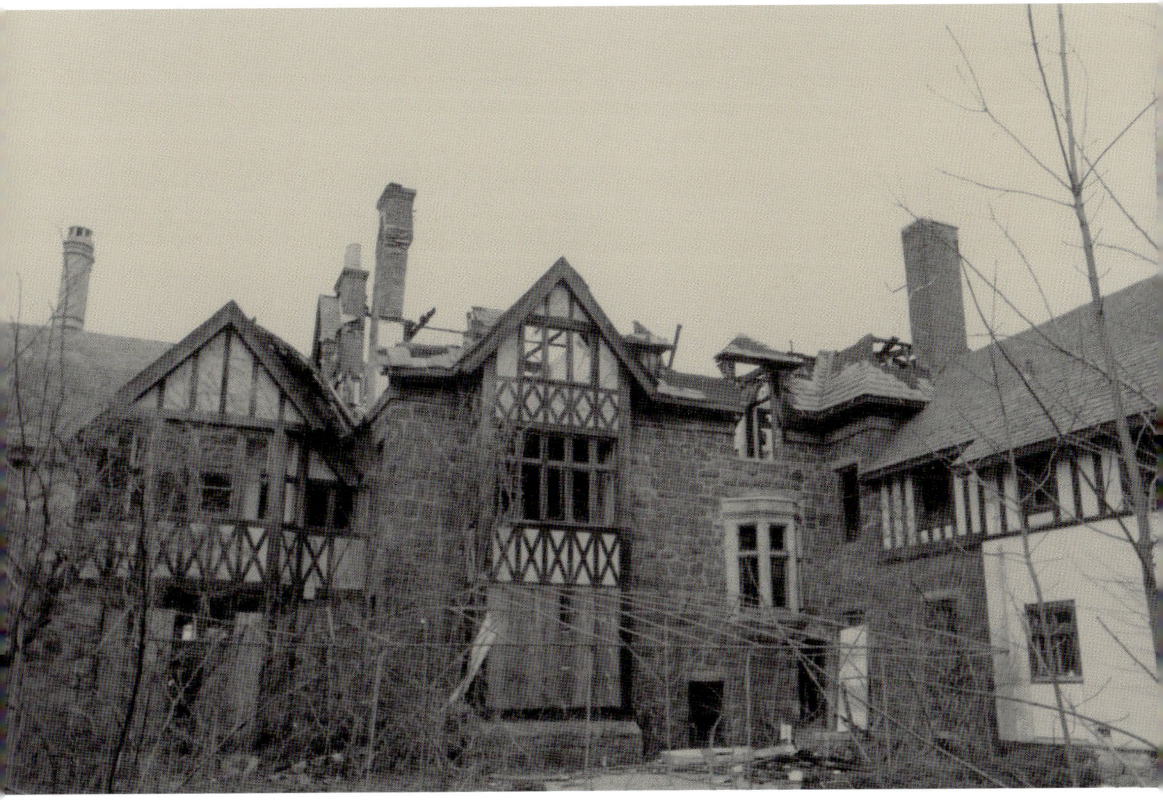